THE FAKE

Forgery and Its Place in Art

Sándor Radnóti

TRANSLATED BY ERVIN DUNAI

ROWMAN & LITTLEFIELD PUBLISHERS, INC.
Lanham • Boulder • New York • Oxford

ROWMAN & LITTLEFIELD PUBLISHERS, INC.

Published in the United States of America
by Rowman & Littlefield Publishers, Inc.
4720 Boston Way, Lanham, Maryland 20706

12 Hid's Copse Road
Cumnor Hill, Oxford OX2 9JJ, England

British Library Cataloguing in Publication Information Available

Library of Congress Cataloging-in-Publication Data

Radnóti, Sándor.
    The fake : forgery and its place in art / Sándor Radnóti.
        p.   cm.
    Includes bibliographical references and index.
    ISBN 0-8476-9205-1 (cloth : alk. paper). — ISBN 0-8476-9206-X
(pbk. : alk. paper)
    1. Art—Forgeries. 2. Art forgers—Psychology. I. Title.
N8790.R34   1999
702' .8'74—dc21   98-46565
                                                                CIP

Printed in the United States of America

♾" The paper used in this publication meets the minimum requirements
    of American National Standard for Information Sciences—Permanence
of Paper for Printed Library Materials, ANSI Z39.48–1984.

CONTENTS

PREFACE

"This is a medusa," said a friend of mine after reading this book. I assume he was referring to the free-floating, soft, and indeterminate materials that compose my subject matter. This is a book about forgeries in art, but even a brief glance at the table of contents reveals that it is not limited to giving yet another account of the most famous cases in the strange history of fraud and deception. Rather, it focuses on a range of artistic reproductions, replicas, variations, and pastiches, some of which are forgeries. In addition, the book deals with the dilemma of artistic illusion and "poetic license," or this probing of the conceptual definition of forgery. As some of the great masters of modern art have shown us, even when two works of art are indistinguishable, one is not necessarily the original and the other a fake. This problem of indiscernibility is addressed in what follows. In fact, while antonyms of the word "forgery"—original, autonomous, authentic, genuine, real, true, and so on—are as numerous as its synonyms, the notion of forgery itself is perpetually changing. Sometimes it has a concrete meaning, at other times it becomes an inflated and self-defeating metaphor.

The original idea for the book, one that has intrigued me for over a decade, is quite simple: those who make forgeries are bound to know a great deal about what art *really* is since it is their job to keep a watchful eye on the art world. Like originals, forgeries inhabit two worlds— the art tradition and their own tradition. Yet since theirs is not a free art, forgeries belong more to the esoteric history of art than to its exoteric history. There may be a large number of artists who, like the Hungarian poet Attila József, think, that "a poet—why should I care about poetry itself?"; but the forger cannot afford to think about anything but art. The forger is constantly meddling in the fundamental issues of art, whether forging a style or the works of a particular artist (in some cases predisposed by his own skills and temperament, in other cases driven by market forces), or when unintentionally "sharing his hand," or even when seeking self-justification.

A selection from the history of *forgeries proper* is provided in chapter 1 along with an attempt to define the *genre*. Chapter 2 highlights the original, one antonym of the forgery. In chapter 3, forgery is placed within the continuum of pattern maintenance, with the variety of copies forming the basis of conventions. In chapter 4 copies and forgeries are discussed in the extreme, though hypothetical, situation of their indiscernibility from the original. Since this is not just a theoretical problem, but one that is closely related to the latest experiments in modern art, it solicits the question: does the distinction between the original and the copy still make sense in discussions of modern art? (It does.) Chapter 5 extends the scope of this examination from the field of visual arts into the area of literary forgery, where I conclude that the roots of forgery in literature are not the same as those in the fine arts. Nevertheless, my consideration of the deceptive nature of artistic fiction paves the way for the polemical discussion in chapter 6 of the attempt to make the theory of forgery comprehensive by way of the simulacrum theory, according to which it is impossible to distinguish between true and fake on any level. Chapter 6 also argues against the idea of forgery as *the* paradigm of modern art.

Unlike its literary analogue, forgery in art is a *modern* problem. Its regular practice began during the Renaissance, but the theoretical frames that were needed for deeper insight developed only in the eighteenth century. In short, the forgery of art is a phenomenon that belongs to modern art and aesthetics. The reader might notice a return to an older use here of the word "modern." Such a choice of terminology is, of course, tantamount to a statement. The crucial moment in the philosophy of art was the emergence of the modern system of art: the interrelatedness of artistic autonomy and heteronomy. And although I am aware of the current crisis of art, it is within this framework that I envisage its renewal in the most general form. This amounts to another statement, namely, that it is probably impossible, and definitely unwise, to abandon the concept of modernity. To use Odo Marquard's expression, I regard myself a *modernity-traditionalist*. In this spirit I see vigor and merit in the pluralistic and open traditions of modernity. These stand in contrast to both a radical experimentation with the future and a homogenization of the traditions of the past. In other words, I am opposed to radical antimodernism, both conservative and futurist.

As I said, when I write about forgery I am thinking of the visual arts. I wrote only one chapter about forgery in literature, and that only to establish a contrast. Naturally, this is highly selective. I do not mention the analogous examples in music (composition and performance), cinema, etc., nor do I cover the broad hunting ground for forgeries outside art (money, commercial and luxury products, valuable consumer goods, such as video recorders, watches, perfumes, clothing, wine, or cigars, nonartistic memorabilia, and scientific research). These would have been distractions from the use of forgery as an aesthetic concept.

In his book, the famous art historian Sir John Pope-Hennessy talks about someone "who has the morbid taste for reading books on forgery."[1] Well, I have read a good many books on forgery, and even written one.

────────────────── **Note** ──────────────────

1. John Pope-Hennessy, *The Study and Criticism of Italian Sculpture* (New York: Metropolitan Museum of Art/Princeton, NJ: Princeton University Press, 1980), 241.

ACKNOWLEDGMENTS

The following is a list of friends and colleagues to whom I owe grateful thanks. Some of them discussed my work with me chapter by chapter, some improved my style, and some advised me on specialized topics by contributing ideas or calling my attention to pertinent articles and books: Miklós Almási, Béla Bacsó, Zoltán András Bán, László Baránszky, László Beke, Marinella D'Alessandro, Péter Dávidházi, Anna Eörsi, John Fekete, Géza Fodor, Lisa Gabor, György Geréby, Péter György, Ágnes Heller, Miklós Kállay, Júlia Kállay Muskát, the late Gitta Kardos, Éva Kocziszky, András Lakatos, Gwyneth Lewis, Mária Ludassy, György Márkus, Ernö Marosi, István F. Mészáros, Péter Pór, András Rényi, Pál Réz, Kornél Steiger, Laurent Stern, János György Szilágyi, Katalin Szöke, Gáspár Miklós Tamás, Zádor Tordai, Mihály Vajda, Anna Wessely, and Victoria de Zwaan.

I must say a few words here about the late Ferenc Fehér, who has always had an enormous influence on both my career and character. Over the course of a friendship that lasted more than 30 years, he read and criticized my work with unceasing interest. Although more an intellectual brother than "a master and a fatherly friend," and although I do not wish to slavishly follow his relationship with György Lukács, I nevertheless cannot find words more appropriate than those with which he dedicated his book on Dostoyevsky to Lukács in dedicating this book to him, "as a late and inequitable reciprocation of his long-lasting faith in me."

IX

Finally, I would like to acknowledge the following institutions: the Aesthetics Department of the School of Arts at the Eötvös Loránd University (Budapest); The Getty Grant Program (Santa Monica, California); MTA-Soros Foundation (Budapest); and Österreichische Literaturgesellschaft (Vienna). Their support in 1993 and 1994 enabled me to work on this book in Budapest, Vienna, Rome, and New York.

1

PICARESQUE AESTHETICS

One Story, Four Interpretations

Every book about art forgery mentions the classic case of the young Michelangelo's "dio d'amore dormente," a sleeping Cupid, which was fraudulently sold as an antique piece. Vasari provides the classical source: in the second edition (1568) of his work he gave a detailed account of the incident, borrowing extensively from Condivi's biography of Michelangelo (1553), so as to repay him in kind for lifting material from the first edition of his own book (1550).[1] Michelangelo

> immediately began to carve a life-size figure of a sleeping Cupid. When this was completed, Baldassare del Milanese showed it as a beautiful piece of work to Pierfrancesco [de' Medici], who agreed with Baldassare's judgement and declared to Michelangelo: "If you buried it, I am convinced it would pass as an ancient work, and if you sent it to Rome treated so that it appeared old, you would earn much more than by selling it here." It is said that Michelangelo treated it in such a way that it appeared to be ancient, nor is this astonishing, since he had the genius to do this and more. Others maintain that Milanese took it to Rome and buried it in a vineyard he owned and then sold it as an antique statue to Cardinal San Giorgio for two hundred ducats. Still others say that Milanese sold a copy Michelangelo made for him to the cardinal, then wrote to Pierfrancesco, telling him to give Michelangelo thirty *scudi*, declaring he received no more than that from the cupid, thus deceiving the cardinal, Pierfrancesco, and Michelangelo; but later the cardinal heard from someone who had seen the cupid being carved in Florence, and, using every means to discover the truth through one of

1

his messengers, he then forced Milanese's agent to return his money and take back the cupid, which then fell into the hand of Duke Valentino, who gave it to the Marchioness of Mantua, and she took it to her own city where it can still be seen today. This affair did not come about without damage to Cardinal San Giorgio, who did not recognize the value of the work, which consists in its perfection, for modern works are just as good as ancient ones when they are excellent, and it is greater vanity to pursue things more for their reputation than for what they really are, but these kinds of men can be found in any age, men who pay more attention to appearances than to realities. Nevertheless, this affair gave Michelangelo such a reputation that he was immediately brought to Rome . . .[2]

At the end of the last century several attempts were made to identify the sculpture. Several suggestions were put forward as to where it might be found, all to no avail. Today, following Charles de Tolnay, art historians generally regard it as a lost work.[3] From Vasari's account (and Condivi's as well), it is not entirely clear whether Michelangelo was accomplice to or victim of the fraud. According to another story by Vasari, which is confirmed by Condivi but with slight modifications to emphasize the humorous side of it, Michelangelo had indeed been in the habit of copying the old masters' works he had borrowed. He apparently treated *his* copies to make them appear old, and returned these copies to their owners in place of the originals. "He did this for no other reason than to have the originals, giving away his copies, because he admired the originals for the excellence of their skill, which he sought to surpass in his copies."[4] Nor can it be taken for granted that the victim of this fraud was Cardinal Raffaele Riario, one of the greatest collectors of antique pieces in that period. In any case, it is not the historical truth that I am interested in but the story itself, and that in no less than four forms: first, according to Vasari's intentions; then, looking behind these and discovering his motives; third, in the interpretation of the author (Hebbel) of a lesser-known work (*Michel Angelo*) from the nineteenth century; and finally, in my own reading.

As Svetlana Alpers suggests,[5] "probably the most significant feature about Vasari's attitude in writing the *Lives* is his belief that he has witnessed the perfection of the arts in his own time." This perfection is manifest in the copying of nature, of classical antiquity, and of the old masters' works, reaching its height in the chronicler's own age, which followed both the age of antiquity, which had set the model, and the medieval age, which had provided the countermodel. It is a conclusion that he *canonized* in the *Lives,* and *institutionalized* in the first art academy founded by himself. The process of the perfection of artistic progress[6] had completed its course when Leonardo, Raphael, but above all Michelangelo, "transcended" their predecessors. "Michelangelo 'surpassed' even those—the masters of antiquity— who themselves had already 'surpassed' nature."[7]

This is a distinctly normative conception and, from the viewpoint of the *future* of art, a conservative one. It looks upon progress or "history" as something that has already run its full course and therefore has no room for future development. (Although Vasari's views are somewhat modulated by the mannerism[8] of his own artistic practice and critical attitude, which originated in the story detailed above and served as a basis for his theories.) Such a conception leaves room only for thematic variations on the artistic achievements of the previous generation of artists and completely rules out any further artistic progress. At the same time, by conceiving of stylistic development as a normative process, Vasari effectively lessens the importance of individuality, which is an interesting point to have come from an author of biographies. The significance of an artist's personality (which can be entirely independent of the significance of his art) is lessened, not only by regarding him as a modest disciple in the line of tradition— a subordinate to the norm, more a copier, less a modifier—but also by presenting him as the personification of the norm, someone who has left everyone far behind in the *great race* called art. This is why there is no contradiction between Vasari's depreciation of artistic individuality on the one hand and the deification of his main protagonist, Michelangelo, on the other.

The story of the *Sleeping Cupid* provides the earliest evidence of Michelangelo's triumph over antiquity. It is not Michelangelo's originality that puts him ahead in the game against the classical artists, but his ability to mimic, to make a perfect imitation. It is proof that the young artist can do as well as the old masters. It is also a declaration of Michelangelo's willingness to abide by the norms of artistic effect and imitation. The Cardinal's fury is unwarranted because it goes against the natural norms of perfection, which a contemporary work of art might realize just as well as the antique masterpieces. Anyone impressed only by the works of antiquity proves his own vanity. The context in which Vasari presents his story sheds light on one of the important aspects of cultural life in the late Cinquecento. As is well known, the systematic search for antique relics began in the Renaissance, with several of the important works of classical art being uncovered in the fifteenth and sixteenth centuries. Michelangelo's

Cupid is not the only example of forged provenance, the burying and uncovering of "antique" objects. An artist by the name of Pier Maria Serbaldini della Pescia is also known to have uncovered and sold his own works.[9]

While these instances might provide some rather bizarre examples of the admiration held for antiquity, deliberate imitation was nevertheless considered to be a perfectly natural means of competing with classical art. Johannes Wilde even suggested that Michelangelo's *Cupid* might actually be the copy of an existing antique work.[10] The situation is somewhat reversed in the case of another "Cupid," previously attributed to Michelangelo, which John Pope-Hennessy showed to be a genuine antique work, with its torso restored in the Renaissance and reset with a Michelangelesque head.[11] Finally, Panofsky mentions a pseudoantique relief owned by the Kunsthistorisches Museum of Vienna, which was made by a Venetian forger sometime between 1525 and 1535. This relief features, in addition to two figures copied from an Attic stele, two variants of Michelangelo's sculptures, one modeled on *David* and the other on the figure of *Christ* in the S. Maria sopra Minerva. Panofsky describes the situation this way:

> The works of a great Cinquecento sculptor appeared to his contemporaries as no less classical, if not more classical, than Greek and Roman originals . . .; or, put in the other way, Greek and Roman originals appeared to them as no less modern, if not more modern, than the works of a great Cinquecento sculptor. The Venetian forger relied on the fact that in his age no basic difference was felt between the *buona maniera greca antica* of an Attic relief and Michelangelo's *moderno si glorioso. . . .*[12]

In this particular story, Vasari attaches no significance to originality, either as individual invention or as historical authenticity.[13] Michelangelo's individual invention is simply equated with his ability to produce a free imitation of a classical work, not a straight reproduction that can even pass as an antique piece. Parallel with the artistic qualities required to make a free imitation, the treatment of making the *Cupid* "appear old"—or in the case of the reproductions of the earlier-mentioned drawings, the smoking, staining, and besmearing—demanded the skills of a craftsman. Vasari was a forceful propagator of the Renaissance tendency to separate craftsmanship from art, thus establishing the difference between autonomous and applied, or high and low art. Ironically, even though his view was to exert an influence for centuries to come, Vasari himself cannot avoid combining invention and craftsmanship, when he suggests that Michelangelo "had the genius to do this and more." That is, on the one hand, Vasari describes Michelangelo's remarkable ability to conform, in a craftsmanlike manner, to traditional conventions of antiquity; and on the other, he shows that Michelangelo's work itself becomes an original creation, which then becomes the norm for others.

By presenting Michelangelo as a champion who scored a victory over classical art, Vasari completely overlooks the issue of forgery. Still, several important aspects emerge of the problems and perspective of forgery from Vasari's account. I will discuss some other aspects of this story later, in another context. Nevertheless, the possible lessons of all three interpretations share an important distinction, one that I make use of only for the time being: they apply to deliberate forgeries and falsifications, that is, works originally intended to be counterfeits and were fraudulently manipulated later.[14] This is regardless of the fact that a large portion of fakes cannot be interpreted on the basis of this distinction; that is, most fakes result neither from forgery nor falsification.

Vasari's rhetoric aside, we can say that there are two strong inducements to deliberate forgery: money and competition. Both can be derived from normative value judgments. The reason why something sells better than one's own work is that, according to the prevailing norms, it is highly valuable. In other words, one competes with something that is, according to the norms, worth competing with.

For reasons mentioned above, it is not immediately apparent from Vasari's narrative whether forging presupposes the notion of originality as historically authentic and/or individually characteristic. In fact, this is illustrated in the logical (and moral) contradiction in the story of the forged drawings. That is, if Michelangelo returned the counterfeit copies and retained the originals, then these originals must have possessed, at least in Michelangelo's eyes, a certain "ontological" surplus value. Vasari cannot deny this, even when his main point is to prove that the original and the copy were indiscernible. After all, Vasari's criticism of the Cardinal is precisely for discerning this difference.

There is, of course, an important difference—an embryo of a distinction—between the two cases of forgery. In the case of the drawings, the word *original* refers to a known work of which indiscernible copies were made. In the case of the *Cupid*, however, there is no such concretely identified model (unless one accepts Wilde's hypothesis, but there is no mention of that in the story). Rather, what is considered original here is the appearance of the historically authentic spirit of antiquity. One is associated with the cult of the normative personality of an artist, the other with the cult of a normative style.

This notion of *indistinguishability* will eventually develop a destructive tendency, in so far as it undermines the aesthetic appeal of works of art, precisely as a consequence of the damage it does to the surplus value of the original as well as to other values associated with it, either individual or stylistic. Vasari, however, uses the notion of indistinguishability on both occasions only in the sense that it was used in classical anecdotes about antique artists. That is, as a positive value, referring to the indistinguishability between a work of art and reality, a work of art and nature.[15]

In Vasari's story, Michelangelo's collecting of the works of the old masters points toward the inextricable connection between the collection and the forgery of art, though it is usually the other way around: collecting increases demand, which in turn encourages forging. Thus forgeries find their way into collections. The collection of the first modern art collector, Jean Duc de Berry (1340–1416), already included some of the earliest modern forgeries. Two beautiful coins from this collection, one of Constantine the Great and the other of Heraclius, are known to us in reproduction.[16] This is rather reminiscent of the case of Michelangelo's modern-age *Cupid* finding its way into the antique collection of the Cardinal of San Giorgio.

Although forging presupposes the association of positive values with the notion of "originality"—and this is a relatively late development in aesthetics—from a conceptional point of view forgeries lend significance to originals by virtue of negating them. While forgery is a steady companion of art, it can never share in art's autonomy. And as long as the difference between autonomy and heteronomy, high and low art, free and applied art, is not relativized, an element of adaptation—its epiphytic existence as a form of adherent and applied art—must be present in forgery. After all, Michelangelo added something to his imitations in order to turn them into forgeries: he manufactured the appearance of antiquity. The close relationship between craftsmanship and forgery can be traced in several languages. For instance, the etymological origins of both the French *forger* and the English *forge* point back to such Latin words as *faber* (craftsman), *fabrica* (workshop, craft primarily working with hard material, but also trick, ruse, artifice), and *fabricare* (to fabricate).

Finally, the faithful copying of drawings together with the creative imitation of a style form the two basic models of forging. Neither of them automatically qualifies as forgery since without the intention of creating a false illusion the first might form part of an artist's training, and the second might take the form of quotation, pastiche, historicizing, or retrospective revival.

To the best of my knowledge, in the entire literature discussing the Michelangelo forgeries there is no mention of an adaptation of the Vasari anecdote in a relatively unknown "satirical drama" entitled *Michel Angelo,* written in 1850 by Friedrich Hebbel.[17] Hebbel's is a free adaptation in which the story is moved to Rome and Michelangelo is depicted as a mature artist. He happens to be working on a sculpture of Jupiter when he discovers that the Prince has people digging up the Capitol in search of antique works of art. This gives him an idea: "Verfluchtes, windiges Geschmeiß, / Das uns mit der Antike quält . . . / Du sollst heut Nacht zu Grabe gehn / Und morgen wieder auferstehn! / Doch richten wir dich erst würdig zu, / Bevor du eingehst in die Ruh'! / Wir bräunen dir zunächst die Haut, / Weil's Archäologen vorm Weißen graut! / Die Kunst ist Gott sei dank nicht schwer, / Die Farbe gibt der Schornstein her. / Dann schlagen wir noch den Arm dir ab, / Denn einen Torso will das Grab. . . ."[18] (You damned and lazy scum who torture us with the antique. [to the sculpture] Tonight you sink into your grave, so that tomorrow you will be resurrected! But before you are buried I must prepare you properly! Since the archaeologists loath the color of white, first we give you a good tan. Thank God, this is not such a difficult art, since I can recover the paint from the chimney. Your arm still needs to be cut off, as a grave calls for a torso. . . .)

The next day this torso is indeed dug up. The rapture of the archaeologist, the art collector, and the minor artists (Bramante, Sangallo) is surpassed only by their glee at the idea that Michelangelo will arrive as the master only to become a student. Only Raphael, who arrives at the same time as Michelangelo (each accompanied by twelve pupils), states that whoever made this statue must have been the forerunner of Michelangelo. The Prince offers to pay Michelangelo the price of the entire sculpture for completing only its missing arm. At this point, Michelangelo pulls out the arm of the sculpture from underneath his cape, thereby causing the utter embarrassment of the art world: "Glaubt nicht, daß ich, weil euer Verstand / Mein armes Werk für antik erkannt, / Es selbst so hoch halte, o nein, ich weiß, / Wie viel ihm noch mangelt zum höchsten Preis! / Doch weiß ich auch, mehr fehlt mir nicht / Zum Phidias, als euch gebricht, / Um mir zu gleichen, und wie ich ihn, / So habt ihr mich zu ehren!"[19] (Do not believe that just because you mistook my worthless work for an antique piece, I, too, think of it so highly! Oh, no, I am aware of all that it lacks to fetch that highest prize. But I also know that what I lack in comparison with Phidias is no less than what you fall short of in reference to me. The way I admire him, so you must admire me!)

In talking about Michelangelo, Hebbel is referring to himself. It was precisely while writing *Michel Angelo* that he wrote words of praise in his diary about Aeschylus and Sophocles.[20] They are to Hebbel what Phidias was to Michelangelo. Hebbel humbly bows to them, so that the disdain he felt for contemporary dramatists, theatre directors, and critics was better founded. It must be added that the final justice in this little drama, rather than being expressed in this crude though justified feeling of superiority, belongs to the Pope, who enjoined Raphael and Michelangelo, two truly equal masters, in a brotherly embrace.

The tone of Hebbel's drama is one that glorifies the artist, aesthetic and intellectual values, the awareness of hierarchy, and the religious faith in art. The same spirit is to be found in Delacroix's painting, *Michelangelo in his Studio,* also done in 1850. In the drama, forging is presented as a Romantic gesture, which presents a sharp contrast to the farce. The artist is a demigod, whose artistry is to be distinguished from his mischievous acts. The satisfaction of paying back past injuries is irreconcilable with the power attributed to the genius in the play. Similarly, the metrical form of the drama—the *doggerel*: "the almost sacred tradition of these plays ever since Goethe's farces written in Frankfurt about the human and artistic existence"[21]—contradicts the theology of art that is openly professed by Michelangelo in his great monologues and demonstrated by the twelve students.

Apparently, forgery in the visual arts—unlike literary forgery, literary mystification—contains something that rejects the romantic paradigm.

A fourth reconstruction of the story[22] returns us to Vasari's original version, but it draws a different conclusion: the entire story is really a *farce.* Everyone is unmasked and everyone is deceived. The Cardinal, a respected judge and collector of art, becomes a laughing stock when he fails to spot the fake. Once his suspicions are raised, not as the result of closer examination but on receiving certain confidential information (in other words, through spies), he makes some inquiries and annuls the transaction. By doing this, he starts an avalanche of disturbing revelations. Now it turns out that besides Michelangelo, Pierfrancesco, Baldassare del Milanese, and possibly the agent of the latter are also implicated in the fraud. They have even deceived each other. Of the 200 ducats paid for the statue, Michelangelo receives only 30 scudos. Frustrated by living at the mercy of his patrons, clients, and masters, the artist deceives the unknown buyer, and in turn is himself deceived by the dealers. Everyone in this story looks foolish: the Cardinal, the dealers, and Michelangelo himself. Popular interpretations of this story usually emphasize another aspect of the farce—namely, that the fake eventually becomes considerably more valuable than the nonexistent original. In the end, the Cardinal deprived himself of an *original* work by Michelangelo.

All the essential ingredients of forgery-as-prank are present in this story. The first of these ingredients is *demand,* in both the cultural and commercial senses of the word: the age is marked by a frantic search for antique works; and Rome is the center of the greatest demand. The second ingredient is *ability,* that particular combination of imitative artistic ability and actual manual dexterity. The third is the institution of *mediators* (in this case the art dealers). The fourth is the *art expert* (still an individual rather than an institution), who is to be deceived. Fifth is the *legend* surrounding the forgery, the invented provenance that supports the scheme of deception. In the case of the *Cupid* the legend is simple: the object is buried and then uncovered. Later on, the need to sustain the legend will generate an entire supporting industry, such as the production of forged documents about ancient treasures, etc. But simpler forms of mystification also work well: the pattern of an impoverished aristocrat not wishing to disclose his identity "for obvious reasons" is one popular favorite. Furthermore, in one of the most successful legends in the history of forgery, the piece of art is (known to be) stolen, (and this may be) enough reason for the buyer to refrain from searching for its origin and publicizing the sale.[23]

Once it has acquired a clear definition, deliberate forgery comes to constitute a moral sin—unless it is a harmless joke that the prankster himself reveals after a while—because of its association with fraud, lies, deception, stealing, reception of stolen goods, false testimony, and the like. Even the divine Michelangelo cannot escape this verdict (provided the story holds true). As a youngster he deliberately deceived those who had lent him the master drawings by stealing them; later, at age twenty, he followed the advice, nay order, of his respected counselors to give his imitation the appearance of a genuine antique, precisely with the aim of deceiving the prospective buyer. At this point the offense had not yet been criminalized. We can see this, in fact, from the Cardinal's response, which is to get his money back. Far from pressing charges,[24] he invites the clever forger to his home.

This fourth interpretation clarifies the fact that forging art works is wrong and that the forger commits a crime; but the point of it is surely not a moral lesson of this kind. It is more a prank than a crime, and the laugh at the expense of the deceived and the double-deceived deceiver usually negates the moral message, not only in Michelangelo's story, the first recorded incident of art fraud, but also the stories of each of the countless art forgeries that followed. Hans Tietze is right in maintaining that there is something puckish about forging, and that deception is an act of justice that the deceived brings upon himself either for pretending to be an art expert or for adulating the old masters at the expense of the living.[25] And while forgers should not be seen as gentlemen of impeccable reputation, they are not necessarily criminals. Rather, they are rogues, rascals, impostors.

─────── The Genre of the Forgery Anecdote ───────

Over the last four or five centuries anecdotes about forgery in the visual arts have frequently demonstrated the characteristics of picaresque prose, or at least they allow picaresque interpretation, stylization, or completion. In every forger we tend to see the picaresque hero, whose unmasking, voluntary or involuntary, always reveals something about art and the art world. The popular forgery stories that have sprung up in this century constitute modern-day picaresque tales. Newspaper articles usually focus on the mischief and satire of forgery cases as well as on the embarrassment of the experts and snobs. And although the audience has also been deceived in most of the cases, it usually sides with the forger against the art world.

Before setting out to qualify the above statements, it is important to note that it is not the strict philological definition of the *novela picaresca* (a form of prose fiction that was first developed in Spain in 1554 with the publication of *The Life of Lazarillo de Tormes,* to be followed, after a strange hiatus of almost 50 years, by Mateo Alemán's *Guzman de Alfarache* and eventually spreading to the whole of Europe, where for almost two centuries it remained one of the most successful forms of popular prose and occasionally of drama) that I wish to apply to forgery anecdotes. At the same time, it seems that the extension of the category is not entirely alien to the casual nature of the origin of this late-Renaissance genre. This is evident in the inflated usage of the word *picaresque* itself, as well as in the history of the reception, which has a tendency to extend in time—in both directions—of the validity of the term on the basis of certain physiognomic resemblances—from Petronius's *Satyricon* right up to the latest developments in literature.[26] A brief list of writers whose works have been associated with the picaresque tradition, despite the fact that they were active after the genre had formally ceased to exist, must include Dickens, Thackeray, Gogol, Mark Twain, Kafka, Hašek, Ehrenburg, Silone, Faulkner, Steinbeck, and Thomas Mann. Wolfgang Hildesheimer's picaresque satire *Paradies der falschen Vögel* (1953) itself touches on the subject of forgeries in art. And we have still not mentioned the attempts to present the rascal as a general type, or even an archetype, in intellectual history, in psychology, or in mythology. In his wonderful essay, André Jolles describes the three basic directions of *cultural criticism,* of the escape from culture: *upward* (the heroic), *outward* (the bucolic), and *downward* (the picaresque).[27]

The literary genre-type of the *picaro* (the rascal, the rogue, the impostor) has become an established entry in our cultural catalogue, so much so that it serves as a poetic role-model in everyday life and is used as a poetic standard in the interpretation of characters. The notion of the "confidence man" has no such general cultural relevance, yet the confessions of con men are picaresque stories, because the form of the narrative itself adds to the story an entertaining and critical element, which lends the swindler's often banal and dull figure a poetic significance. The situation is somewhat similar with forgers.

Indeed, the heroes of picaresque anecdotes view society and culture from below. Motivated by meagre circumstances, they typically get the better of their powerful antagonists by resorting to mischief. Checked neither by law nor by morality, they nevertheless always stop short of that other barrier that marks the territory of the true villains and criminals. Frank W. Chandler, the monographer of picaresque literature, puts it this way: "As the typical crime of the villain is murder, so the typical crime of the rogue is theft. To obliterate distinctions of *meum* and *tuum* is the rogue's main business. He aspires to win by wit or dexterity what others have wrought by labor or received of fortune. He may cheat at cards or snatch purses. He may forge a check or a will. He may beg with a painted ulcer, or float a commercial bubble. He may scheme for title and fortune by means of a worldly marriage, or pocket his hostess's spoons. He may prey on the government as smuggler, illicit distiller, or counterfeit utterer. He may play the quack, levy blackmail, crack a safe, or even rob on the highway. But the use of personal violence usually ends his career as rogue and stamps him the villain."[28]

These examples help reveal the social conditions of the picaresque scenario: urban life, a slackening social hierarchy accompanied by growing social mobility, and a broad range of opportunities for pretension, illusion, and disguise.

It has often been pointed out that the picaro is an antihero, and that the origin of the genre is closely related to the waning of the heroic myths of chivalric romance. In contrast with heroic idealism, here we have carnivalesque realism; instead of the viewpoint of the master, here we see life through the eyes of the servant. A rascal often enters service and his frequent change of masters is one of the standard devices of picaresque novels. As a result of the episodic structure, a short anecdote can qualify as being picaresque, as can *Gil Blas* with its endless supply of episodes.

Well before Bakhtin, José Ortega y Gasset distinguished between the two medieval trends, tracing the contrasting literatures of chivalry and of roguery—the respective viewpoints of master and servant—back to the categories of noble and plebeian. He described the latter form of prose as literature that does not create a world of its own, but rather produces a cutting and accurate copy of reality, a copy that is full of angry criticism.[29] And while it is quite obvious that picaresque literature, in the extended and generalized sense of the term, cannot be presented as the permanent antithesis of chivalrous romance, the servant's anger vented through laughter, along with (both positively and negatively) the destructive and hero-demolishing criticism, form an essential part of it. The realism resulting from seeing the world through scornful eyes or through a veil of the passion raised by envy, jealousy, anger, or revenge exposes the higher ranks with an ever-present moral message that ranges from the merely hypocritical or banal (designed so as to pass censorship), right up to the outline of a new order of entirely different moral values. Picaresque literature has a range of aims running from pure entertainment to moral didacticism, and the history of the reception of the genre shows that the same work is often known to have attracted both interpretations. The picaresque hero's moral character also has a relatively broad spectrum: having accepted Chandler's distinction between roguery and villainy, we must also see that no such definite boundary exists in the other direction. The range of picaresque characters varies from the morally infantile to the singularly immoral, with the story line alternating between frolic, prank, harmless joke, and cordial mischief. The aim of any one of these can be either didactic or entertaining.

The earliest forgery anecdotes often show a striking resemblance to the classic picaresque novel. In Cellini's story, for example, the forger (mediator) is a paramedic, a distant cousin of the charlatans who are the favorite minor characters of picaresque novels. Like so many of his peers in the roguery novels, he is on the run—his patients are dying on him. But before he sets off, while still in Rome, he takes a fancy to one of Cellini's sketches, orders a few silver vases, pays for them, and leaves. Once in Ferrara, he presents these vases in a mist of legends that is designed to increase both his medical reputation and the value of his treasures:

> [A]nd [he] told them that they were presents from a great nobleman at Rome, of whom he had demanded them upon undertaking to cure him of a disorder; that the nobleman had told him they were antiques, and begged he would rather ask anything else, which he would freely part with, and leave him those; but he refused to cure him on any other terms, and thus got them into his possession.

The story would not, of course, be complete without an art expert making a fool of himself: "there has not been a man these thousand years able to make such figures."[30]

Also present in the story is the familiar parodic element, one with considerable resonance in our century, of the forger having to confess to *prove* that he is the author of the work in question. Cellini thought that this story—the Renaissance idea of triumphing over antiquity—so important that later on in his *Autobiography,* in his usual vainglorious manner, he repeated it in an essentially identical form, only this time at the expense of a different art expert.[31]

Although still in an embryonic form, the destruction of heroes is directed, both in the Michelangelo story and in the Cellini anecdote, against antiquity. Neither Vasari nor Cellini was aware of this. Neither of the works was intended to be a fake; in the first case the artist took the advice of mediators to make the sculpture look antique, while in the second case it was the mediator who fabricated the legend of antique origin. Yet the great Renaissance *agon* conceals the question of whether the veneration felt for antiquity is actually lessened by the realization of the duplicability of its masterpieces.

This is the dilemma that will constitute the invisible nucleus of late forgery stories, especially after the eighteenth century. It is an intriguing paradox of cultural history that two of the outstanding heroes of Renaissance culture (one in his own right, the other partly on account of his vainglorious boasting, so typical of the spirit of the time and partly as a result of Goethe's stylization) should start the ball rolling in a story, the story of art forgeries, in which every episode is about the destruction, deglorification, and mockery of everything that the Renaissance stands for—the autonomous work of art requiring the heroism of inimitability, uniqueness, and originality.

This is how forgery stories should be translated into the language of picaresque: the forger is the servant of the original. But if there is any truth in the saying that no one is a hero in the eyes of his own servant, then this is precisely the kind of servant a forger makes. He knows everything about the technical process and is able to repeat it at will, but he knows nothing about the creation or the fate of works of art. Forgery is the democratic satire and parody of the aristocracy of art; in the carnivalesque horseplay of parody and miming, forgery annihilates the uniqueness of a work of art by way of the implicit criticism of copying. In the debate between imitation and creation, forgery plays the role of the former, imitating, and by annihilating and destroying thereby creates. This is the criticism of the artist as craftsman winning out over the artist as creator.

The glorification of art as creation on the one hand and its degradation as a craft on the other are part and parcel of the changes that the Renaissance introduced into the rules of art. These changes are characterized by Ernst H. Gombrich, in connection with an early example, as follows: Ghiberti's second door made of bronze "really stands on the watershed of the two worlds. It is the last goldsmith's work to be quite in the vanguard of artistic progress. Henceforward there will be a growing gulf between the intellectual pursuits of Art and the 'applied art' of the craftsman. A new hierarchy is created by which true nobility in art has no need to 'flatter the eye' or to rely on surface attractions."[32]

Forgery is an applied art that relies for effect on the surface attractions of *another* work, or another style, flattering the eye by pretending to be exactly *that*. Of course, the history of forgeries is largely about fake designer objects or works of applied art; although they offer a less lucrative business, the risks involved are incomparably smaller. Museums all over the world are full of works with dubious pedigrees on the one hand, and of undetected forgeries on the other, not so much because of deliberate deceit, but largely because of dealers' errors or from false attribution. It was mainly *after* the Renaissance (due to the fact that during the Renaissance the new hierarchy of artists was still not firmly established, as we can see from Cellini's permanent inability to decide between goldsmithery and sculpting) that to make a complete story or a full picaresque tale, the forger had to be a craftsman; it had to be a story in which the craftsman's approach either struck at the intellectual conception of art or questioned the "surplus value" of antique art. In either case, the point of the story is that the forgery undermines the entire system. In most cases this sabotage is not deliberate and the forger is only aware of his paradoxical self-justification in trying to prove that he too belongs to the higher order of the hierarchy; that he too can compete with the old masters. However, whenever the artist stays outside the new hierarchy of art and displays the calm self-esteem of a craftsman who produces historicizing, and occasionally virtuoso, pastiches (which are turned into forgeries by the dealer, as was perhaps the case after the World War I with Alceo Dossena [1878–1937],[33] and probably also with the Odessa goldsmith Israel Rouchomovsky, whose *Saitaphernes Tiara* was bought by the Louvre at the end of the nineteenth century, to be revealed as a fake soon afterwards), then either the story is not a picaresque one or it is not the artist who plays the impostor.

In the rest of this chapter I would like to recount, or reconstruct, a few typical anecdotes from the history of art forgery. It should be clear from the above that it is not my intention to give a historical overview of forgeries, but rather to provide only a selection of forgery stories. Since we are dealing here with an artificially constructed territory, defined strictly from a theoretical point of view, topics such as forgery workshops and the forgery industry, obviously vitally relevant in a historical analysis, will not be addressed here. Moreover, for the purposes of this discussion I will regard the retrospective and, even from a theoretical point of view, fundamental issues of the increased demand for antique art and the cult of artistic individuality only as boundary conditions, since they open up for artistic practice the vast areas of studies, replicas, reproductions, and restorations. These form a continuum with forgeries, with their products often *becoming* fakes over the course of time. I want to discuss here, however, some anecdotes detailing the mischievous practices of willful and deliberate forgery. The first clear examples of which are encountered in the Renaissance, but were typically discovered only in the nineteenth century—that golden age of forgeries—as well as in the twentieth century. In Panofsky's words, it takes a long time before the forger's pursuit is emancipated from that of a copier.[34] Although after the Renaissance the retrospective and decorative schools produced masses of fakes, the borderline between forgery and imitation is a difficult one to draw. And while we know the names of several disreputable imitators with malicious intent and are conscious of the immense problems that the large number of replicas caused to successful artists from Dürer to Claude Lorrain and are even aware of the existence of the legal statutes against forgery,[35] to catch a glimpse of the inner workings of a forger we often have no more evidence than that of a joke or prank. And even then we cannot be sure that we are not actually projecting back in time our notion of forgery as established in the nineteenth century.

Gustav Glück, for example, captured an instance of satirical self-reflection in an important episode in the history of forgery, one that had already begun in the lifetime of the master and reached well into the seventeenth century, namely, the industry of Dürer imitations. "In this case the forger took the liberty of making an extremely characteristic joke: he placed Dürer's monogram and the date 1514 in the direction one of the little angels' fingers was pointing. Hans von Kulmbach's true monogram can be found underneath Mary's cape, and it was revealed by a nineteenth-century restorer."[36] Kulmbach (c.1480–1522) was Dürer's student and imitator. His works were often antedated and subsequently provided with false signatures by others. Apparently, the *reverse* is suggested by Otto Kurz: he thinks that the false monogram and date in *The Assumption of the Virgin Mary* were arranged at the above-mentioned place, *because* the angel was pointing there.[37]

An Excursion: A Collection of Anecdotes

The main talent of Mignard (the principal painter of Louis XIV; most of the exaggerated reputation he enjoyed in his life dwindled away with the passing of time) was his ability to capture the manners of certain Italian painters so well that it was almost impossible to distinguish his copies from the originals. Once he painted a Mary Magdalene in the manner of Guido Reni, which he then sold as Guido's original work straight in from Italy to a so-called amateur for 2,000 livres. Soon afterwards Mignard had the suspicion planted in the buyer's ears that he had been cheated: he bought a Mignard, not a Guido. Not knowing what else to do, the amateur turned to Mignard himself, who assured him that the Magdalene had not been his work and referred the case to Le Brun, then the principal court painter and regarded as an oracle in his art. The amateur invited both painters to his table and presented his problem, asking Le Brun to deliver his verdict. After long and careful deliberation, Le Brun declared the painting to be Guido's work. This was the moment Mignard was waiting for. "Now I admit that I painted it myself," he said; and in order not to leave any doubt, he revealed that underneath the locks of the beautiful repentant woman they would find a cardinal's hat. And since this could only be proven by demonstration, he had conveniently brought along all the necessary tools; he cleansed the appropriate part and the cardinal's biretta appeared. "I will return your money," he said to the buyer, "and the painting returns to me; the person who painted it will also be able to restore it." Then he left, thinking to himself what a great man he was and how well and truly he had hoodwinked the good old Le Brun.[38]

The above anecdote was written by Christoph Martin Wieland at the end of the eighteenth century; he published it in his magazine, the *Teutscher Merkur,* as a witty sketch. And although the narration of - the mischief begins and ends on a note of reproval so as to maintain the semblance of a moral lesson, the entrapment and derision both of the amateur and, even more importantly, of the respected rival, along with the underlying motive, are all in evidence.

The following story was recorded by Goethe on November 18, 1786:

> Some years ago a Frenchman lived here, who was a well-known lover and collector of art. In one way or another, this Frenchman acquires an *antique* work painted on limestone. He has it restored by Mengs, and then adds it to his collection as one of its more valuable pieces. Even Winckelmann mentions it somewhere in highly laudatory tones. It shows Ganymede handing a goblet of wine to Zeus, who kisses him in return. The Frenchman dies, leaving the painting to his housekeeper in the belief that it is an *antique.* Mengs dies, too, and on his dying bed he announces that *it is not an antique painting, he painted it.* And now everyone starts disputing the case with everyone else. Some people say Mengs was only fooling with the painting, meaning it to be a joke; others say that Mengs did not have it in him to paint such a work, and that it is too beautiful even for a Raphael. I saw it yesterday and I must confess: I, too, have never seen anything more beautiful than Ganymede's figure, head and back; the other figure has been restored too heavily. In any case, the painting has lost its pedigree, and nobody is willing to relieve this poor woman of her treasure.[39]

The story turns out to be even more perplexing, as a reconstruction published in a remarkably entertaining art historical study has revealed.[40] According to this, there was a conspiracy, with Mengs, his friend Giovanni Casanova (painter, copier, and adventurer, the younger brother of the famous lover), and the Frenchman Chevalier Diel de Marsilly all taking part—unless the latter was also deceived. But the chosen victim was no other than their good friend, Winckelmann. First, the picture's legend of provenience was invented (it was claimed to have been removed from the wall at an excavation in Herculaneum with the help of a mason, and to have been smuggled into Rome piece by piece), which Winckelmann took at face value, so much so that he even wrote an article about the incident. The theme of a famous homoerotic scene was chosen, albeit in an unusually intimate rendering for an antique work of art. Ganymede is depicted as an androgynous beauty. "The painting corresponds so exactly both in theme and in the physical attributes of Ganymede, to Winckelmann's own taste and persuasion, that the virtually inescapable conclusion presents itself that the forgery was deliberately conceived with these factors in mind."[41] It was a complete success, with Winckelmann enthusing over the picture in his letters, declaring it to be the most beautiful of all antique paintings, a verdict he reconfirmed in his *Geschichte der Kunst des Althertums*, dedicated, incidentally, to Art, the Age, and Mengs.[42]

Still not content, the culprits continued the joke. Other paintings were being "uncovered" at the same excavation, although these were said to have already been sold by Casanova, but not before he made copies of them. Two of these copies even made it into the great *Geschichte*. Then in 1766, some six or seven years following the incident and two years after the publication of the history of Greek art, Winckelmann learned about the fraudulent origin of these *copies* (he never discovers the truth about the *Ganymede* painting). Being notoriously proud of his ability to recognize forgeries, he was greatly upset by the news. He publicly reproached Casanova, who issued a reply. The reaction of the latter is a familiar one in the history of forgery: he claims that although he never sold any pictures, he did produce some drawings, but only to show Winckelmann's arrogance and incompetence. Mengs made no attempt to interfere in this little exchange (both he and Casanova had left Rome by then), but his early biographer d'Asara revealed that in 1779, on his dying bed, Mengs admitted to the mischief, and even disclosed that he had left a mark in the picture, which he now wished to make public.[43]

No other painter's works have been forged as frequently as Corot's. One day a gentleman shows up in the master's studio, who, having bought a painting signed "Corot" in a small art shop, wants to know whether it has really been painted by Corot. After one brief look at the canvas Corot shakes his head. Transported by rage, the buyer declares that he will report the art dealer to the police. "Report to the police?," the painter vents his annoyance. "Nonsense, that man has a wife and a child. Do you want to ruin the life of that fellow?" "What do I care about wife and child? A fraud is a fraud and the law. . . ." "The law? Bah, it won't take much to turn this little painting into an original Corot." With that, the master puts the canvas on the easel and adds a few brush strokes, thus turning the fake Corot into a genuine one. "There," he murmurs in a satisfied voice, returning the painting to the buyer, "now you won't be able to say anymore that this is forgery and fraud. You could see it with your own eyes how I painted it."[44]

Camille Corot was indeed one of the most frequently forged painters. Popular forgery stories usually include a joke that starts out by giving the number of works Corot painted in his lifetime, of which a certain number (and here comes a figure several times higher than the first number) can presently be found in the United States. The follow-up to this joke is the story of a certain Dr. Jousseaume, who, by the time of his death in 1924, had managed to collect, one by one, 2,414 paintings by Corot—nearly all of them fakes. Besides several formal factors (Corot's easily forgable tones and signature, etc.) as well as his lasting popularity, it must have been the master's naive and roguish nonchalance in relation to artistic originality that lay at the root of the phenomenon; he carelessly allowed his works to be copied, often adding his own corrections and signature to the resulting reproductions.[45]

In his book published in 1933 and entitled *Geschichten neben der Kunst,* Julius Meier-Graefe provided a fine portrayal of a Dane by the name of Gretor. A person of dubious existence who commanded an impressive knowledge of art, Gretor lived in Paris in the 1890s, keeping a low profile of his dealings, which were sometimes benign and at others quite malevolent. His Paris acquaintances included Albert Langen, a wealthy young German who later became a famous publisher. At Langen's request, Gretor put together, in less than a year, a large and stylistically representative collection of art works—forgeries from first to last. He probably had them painted by Parisian masters, with himself making quite a bit on the side, too. When Langen became suspicious and questioned him about the matter, Gretor displayed an unruffled suavity in admitting that all the works, and not just some as Langen had thought, were forgeries. And when the conversation turned to the subject of fraud and damages, he pointed out that there were certain benefits as well. He inquired about Langen's intentions regarding the collection. Langen, himself a gentleman, would have been embarrassed to mention speculation and profits, while Gretor considered any suggestion of financial gains to be an outright insult. He emphasized the educational value of the pictures and contrasted them with gambling (Langen suffered even greater financial losses through gambling at the time), entering these offerings to the Muses on the credit side of the balance. And the validity of such reasoning could not be made dependent on the authenticity of the pictures. "Perhaps you were a fool when you thought they were genuine, but this is why they should be all the more valuable to you now."

Langen, who appreciated the humorous side of this reasoning and had no hopes for any compensation, besides being averse to the prospect of becoming a laughing stock, refrained from filing a lawsuit. As a prospective publisher, he hit on the idea of Gretor *writing* the story in the then-fashionable form of a one-act drama which he, Langen, would publish. The figure of the art collector would make an excellent character for a satire. With an air of dignity, Gretor rejected the idea that he use his private experience for financial gain. (Later, Langen also suggested the theme to Wedekind, who was unable to make any progress with the idea, although in another work of his he did portray Gretor's figure.) Unexpectedly, however, Gretor found a splendid way (and a rather ironic one, if we may add) of satisfying the publisher, Meier-Graefe relates. He set out the detailed plan of a modern satirical weekly magazine, which was to scourge the ignorance of the bourgeoisie. Langen moved to Munich and founded *Simplicissimus*, while Gretor continued in his old ways. In Berlin he frequented high society, with Wilhelm von Bode, the director of the museums of Berlin, making use of his services. He allegedly played a part in the acquisition of *Flora*, a bust thought to have been made by Leonardo (in connection with which Meier-Graefe sarcastically commented that once a piece of nineteenth-century cartoon was recovered from its inside; in fact, the bust's provenance is still being debated). In Rome he established contacts with Dossena, who "enriched the trecento with sought-after sculptures." Gretor took part in expeditions, at one time excavating the graves of the pharaohs in Giza and at another rescuing the mosaic work of a Byzantine church near Athens. Due to his blundering in Palermo, however, he was thrown into prison, and that was where he died.

> His life—there is no use denying it—was full of contradictions and was not without blemishes; but regarding the fundaments of his deportment, it was not without the perspective of reconciliation. Even if he did deceive people, he only gave them what they needed. A true *Kenner*.[46]

A man called Louis Marcy, of whose background nothing is known, appeared in London in 1894. With excellent timing and the backing of a first-class forgery workshop, he offered interesting and exquisite Renaissance and medieval objects for sale: statues, drinking horns, pyxes, goblets, rosaries, and chess sets. These were not mere copies; rather, they appeared to be inspired historicizing and eclectic works combining clearly identifiable styles. The expression "Marcy forgery" has become a standard term in the history of styles. After the sensational reception of ecclesiastical treasures exhibited at the historical fair in Madrid, any Spanish provenance in this category of objects came to be considered an excellent reference. Over a decade, Marcy concluded extensive business dealings with the British Museum, the Victoria and Albert Museum, and also with several private collectors.

An atmosphere of suspicion began to surround these art objects, precisely for the reason that their characteristic and unprecedented styles were irreconcilable with their sudden appearance on the market in such quantity. In 1903 Marcy left London and moved to Paris, where he was arrested for being an anarchist in that same year. A large quantity of art treasures was found in the ensuing search of his house. According to von Falke: "In 1907, when his forgeries were no longer successful, he founded the journal *Le Connaisseur* in Paris; in this he unmasked and chastised, with a great deal of wit and even more vitriol, others' forgeries in art dealership."[47] This anticapitalistic *Revue critique des arts et curiosités*, which continued being published until 1914, was "extremely entertaining although libelous."[48] In 1918, Marcy left Paris and moved back to Reggio Emilia, his home town. Nothing more is known of his further escapades, except that in 1932 he donated his collection to found a museum. Galleria Parmeggiani (the museum bears our hero's original name) stands on the main square of the town, with a plaque commemorating the man. It makes a very strange collection, with a Jan van Eyck, which has not been mentioned anywhere in the literature, and a Greco, which has. Then there are, of course, the characteristic Marcy items: architectural pix, drinking horn, chess set, all falsely attributed. The latest travelers' guidebook by Michelin recommends the gallery with a one-star rating, and without mentioning a word about forgeries.[49]

The story of Han van Meegeren (1889–1947), the most famous figure in the history of art forgeries, is a well-known one. Still, his case cannot be omitted from the present account, since it is rightfully regarded as the most analyzed, referenced, paradigmatic case in the entire philosophical discourse on forgery. I shall present the most important elements of his story under separate items[50]:

1. The initially successful (strongly conservative, historical, and symbolist) painter is deserted by his good fortune; with his art scorned by critics and his paintings selling poorly, he is obliged to take on second-rate artistic tasks for which he places the blame

entirely on the art world's parasitic and hypocritical institutions—critics, art dealers, and experts.

2. Beginning in 1923, he engages in the forging of works from the Golden Age of Dutch painting. He establishes a working relationship with the restorer and art dealer Theo van Wijngaarden. When one of Meegeren's forgeries, a "Frans Hals" restored by Wijngaarden, is accepted as original by one famous art expert (Hofstede de Groot) and rejected as fake by another (Abraham Bredius), Wijngaarden decides to take revenge. (We only mention it in passing that de Groot, in defense of his expertise and reputation, feels obliged to buy the painting.) Using synthetic paint, Wijngaarden paints a Rembrandt and shows it to Bredius. "A great expert works largely from the splendid intuition of his; he likes to give from time to time a virtuoso performance by instantly recognizing the 'unmistakable' work of a master. That is precisely what happened as Bredius saw the joke picture painted by Wijngaarden. The latter, since it was a joke, had given Bredius an invented account of the picture's provenance such as, if it had been true, would have gone far towards proving its authenticity, and this Bredius would have had no reason to doubt. As far as he could have known, it would be perfectly simple to check it before his judgement became public (and since van Wijngaarden would have been aware of this, it would never have occurred to Bredius that the whole thing might have been invented). Thus he fell fair and square into the trap. After one superficial glance he pronounced the work a Rembrandt, adding with a smile that it would make up to van Wijngaarden for the Hals. This it certainly did, though not at all as Bredius expected: the artist approached with his palette knife and ripped the canvas to pieces before the doctor's eyes."[51]

3. After careful preparation that lasts several years, van Meegeren is ready to start his great ploy. He embarks on a series of complicated technical experiments, studies the history of styles and selects the precise target. The master is Vermeer van Delft, the artist in whose town he had lived for a long period, in whose supposed lack of due recognition he saw an analogy with his own fate and whose star was beginning to rise again at the time. The victim is, once again, the aging Bredius.

4. As has frequently been the case in the history of forgery, the ploy is based on the "missing link," or more precisely, the heightened state of expectation associated with it. There is a known hiatus between Vermeer's early and mature works. It was generally assumed that in his younger years Vermeer had been influenced by the Utrecht Caravaggisti. Bredius, who had previously identified *Christ in the Home of Mary and Martha*, an important early work of Veermer's, and

who was convinced that in his younger years the painter had traveled in Italy, had predicted the discovery of further Vermeer paintings on Biblical themes. It was on this prophecy that van Meegeren based his ploy. In 1937 he painted *Christ at Emmaus,* a work of large format (as were all the early Vermeers) that was stylistically related both to *Christ in the Home of Mary and Martha* and to Vermeer's bourgeois period, besides having a magnificent signature.

5. The next thing to do was to find a reputable mediator who would believe the invented legend (van Meegeren's lover, a descendant of an old Dutch family now living in Italy, wanted to sell the family's art collection; however, because of the Fascist government's ban on exporting art treasures, the painting had to be smuggled out of the country). He and the dealer agreed on a second legend (the painting was discovered in a chateau in the south of France and was covered with a second coat of paint), this one for the art expert, Bredius.

6. Complete success: Bredius writes an elated article in the *Burlington Magazine.*[52] With decreasing fastidiousness, which probably reflected his growing contempt for art experts, van Meegeren continued his scheme, producing an additional six "Vermeers" on biblical themes by the time of his apprehension in 1945. He procured a great fortune.

7. During World War II one of the forgeries was purchased by Hermann Göring.[53] He paid with paintings, returning to the Netherlands over 200 works of art earlier seized by the invaders. After the forger's apprehension, this little side-story was reported in the newspapers and was received by the public as if van Meegeren had cleverly pulled one over Göring. Such a suggestion is completely unfounded: all the evidence confirms that van Meegeren's mediators acted against his directives when they entered into negotiations with Göring.

8. Finale: as a result of this last transaction he is charged with collaboration and arrested immediately after the war. He confesses his forgeries, but no one wants to believe him. In order to verify his story, he paints his last "Vermeer." In court, he denies that he was motivated by material gain. On the one hand, he presents himself to the jury as a dedicated scholar who has been carried away by his interest in developing technical methods; and on the other, he revives his old resentments toward the critics for having wrecked his art career. Although he receives the minimum sentence, van Meegeren dies in prison.

In the past few decades there have been a number of autobiographies by forgers. In 1970 Tom Keating, who forged Samuel Palmer's works, published *The Fake's Progress,* with the title fashioned after Hogarth's series *The Rake's Progress*; this was followed in 1991 by Eric Hebborn's book. "There is nothing criminal in making a drawing in any style one wishes, nor is there any criminal about asking an expert what he thinks of it."[54] Keating, who wrote his autobiography after being exposed, was made into a national hero of sorts. After receiving a minor punishment he went on to become a television celebrity. His story must have provided Ken Follett with some ideas for his excellent picaresque novel on art forgery, published in 1976 under the title, *The Modigliani Scandal.*

The book is about two great swindles, in which the joys of taking revenge on others and making fools of them are the main motives, more than the actual pecuniary gain. Artists, art historians, and art dealers act out the story, which is arranged around some of the more commonplace facts of modern culture. One of the most romantic, but also the most superficial, commonplaces is the apparent contrast between the art business and the artists who are trying to make a living (wealthy art dealer versus starving artist). Modigliani's figure, whose unknown painting forms the object of a wild pursuit in one of the two story lines, could have been the best example of this contrast, with his brief life spent in poverty and with the spectacular rise of his works after his death. The other story line is about an artist who, regardless of his slightly more secure existence, essentially faces the same fate: he wants to demonstrate that the London art world, which focuses on masterpieces and dead artists, is insincere to the core and that the art dealers know nothing about art. The guarantee of authenticity has become more important than aesthetic enjoyment, to the point that the former is now considered the precondition of the latter: "They've proved that the high prices paid for great works of art reflect snobbery rather than artistic appreciation. We all knew that already. They've proved that a real Pissarro is worth no more than an expert copy."[55]

The book focuses on two forgery cases corresponding to the two basic types of forgeries I mentioned earlier: One is the perfect *copy* of a newly discovered authentic Modigliani, discernible from the original neither by the naked eye nor by artistic sensibility, nor by anything short of chemical analysis. The other is a *variation,* the result of profound familiarity with a style or drawing technique. The hero of the story is a likable impostor who teaches the art world a lesson—and makes a fortune in the process.

Over the centuries the same schemes keep reappearing in forgery stories. This might not be true in the case of the Renaissance—it was with the hindsight of later developments that we gave a new reading to Vasari's story, one which is in disagreement with the author's own interpretation. Nevertheless, ever since the end of the eighteenth century, by which time the modern framework of art emerging from its Renaissance beginnings had consolidated and become universal, we have been thinking along similar (similarly simple, comic, and often unjust) lines on the subject. Despite the two unfortunate deaths in Goethe's anecdote, the rowdy atmosphere of the commedia dell' arte pervades it. The popular-entertainment character of the story always requires a full acknowledgment of the fraudulent element of a deceit or trap. This, in turn, presupposes the awareness of the artistic binaries of imitation *or* creation, conventionality *or* originality. On the theoretical level this was borne out by the great debates of aesthetics in the eighteenth century; this became the form in which art was eventually interpreted, and this turned out to be the consensus of culture, of educated people.

This is so much the case, that when Goethe attended the academic session of the "Olympians" of Vicenza, he encountered the same problem: "The Chairman proposed the following problem for today's session: what is more advantageous for art, originality or imitation? It was a rather opportune idea; if we start analyzing the alternative concealed in it, we might go on debating for a good hundred years even."[56] And although the emerging new system of art was presented in the form of mutually exclusive alternatives only in such provincial feasts of the intellect, it was at that moment in history that the relativized, subordinate, and applied role of copying in the *self-consciousness* of art—not in its day-to-day practice, needless to say—was decided, with lasting effects right up to the current crisis of art.

To describe this turning point with an aphorism, one might say that until the turn of the eighteenth century, the forgers were copiers, and afterwards that the copiers became forgers. An extreme case of copying is *plagiarism*. The difference between *plagiarism* and *forgery* was defined by Monroe C. Beardsley, who suggested that one amounted to "passing off another's work as one's own," while the other meant "passing off one's own work as another's."[57]

In artistic practice, such a fine logical distinction is irretrievably lost. As long as the retrospective protection of originality did not place the complementary function of creative restoration out of bounds; as long as imitation patina, manufactured damages, and concocted torso did not fulfill their intellectual task; as long as replicas remained an integral part of artistic practice; in other words, as long as the emerging new system of art did not relegate copying to an inferior position, referring it either to the realm of the learning process or to that of decorative, applied, and utilitarian art, merely liberating it—in the Renaissance—from the strict observation of the traditional standards of the immediately preceding age; well, as long as all those conditions applied, the use of the word *forger* in connection with this practice is problematic. This is in spite of the fact that a large number of the works of art produced in the era beginning with the Renaissance and ending with the late Baroque of the eighteenth century eventually became forgeries, and that an artist in Rome might have had little difficulty in misleading the culturally starved British, French, or German travelers with his *free* restorations and replicas. Still, it would be wrong to call Piranesi or Bartolomeo Cavaceppi a forger, regardless of the several forgeries that can be traced back to their workshops.[58] What they lack is the self-identification of the forger, which is masked by the *mixtum compositum* of their artist–archaeologist–plagiarist–restorer–collector–dealer identity.

The self-identification of a forger makes its first appearance, at least in the sphere of literary legend, with the confession of Mengs, and it does so in a manner very appropriate to the momentousness of the situation: on his dying bed, in the form of his guilty conscience.

What are those standard schemes that we encounter over and over again in forgery stories? One is the ridiculousness of amateurs *and* experts. The joke always has a double-edged effect: on the one hand, it unveils the snobbery and conceit of art lovers and collectors motivated externally, and on the other, it relativizes the expertise of the professionals. The motif we already saw in Cellini's case is repeated again and again, almost in the fashion of fables. There is no other way for the forger to break the disbelief of the art world and to prevent his own incrimination than to make another forgery. This is what happened to such forgers as Giovanni Bastianini, Rouchomovsky, Dossena, van Meegeren, as well as to Beppi Rifesser, a woodcarver from Tyrol whose work was auctioned by an art dealer as a fourteenth-century piece from Burgundy, and a Mexican sculptor who was arrested for allegedly stealing a pre-Columbian clay figure from an excavation, and who was able to prove his innocence only by making another copy in his prison cell.[59] The figure of the forger, quite often wholly independently from the true character of the actual person, is endowed with the image of the great joker, the impostor par excellence. And the joke invariably serves to undermine the notion of originality.

─────────────────────────── **Notes** ───────────────────────────

1. Cf. Julius Schlosser, *Die Kunstliteratur* (Vienna: Schroll, 1924), 240.

2. Giorgio Vasari, *The Lives of the Artists* (New York: Oxford University Press, 1991), 423.

3. Cf. Charles de Tolnay, *The Youth of Michelangelo* (Princeton, NJ: Princeton University Press, 1947), 24ff. and 201ff. Cf. Paul F. Norton, "The Lost *Sleeping Cupid* of Michelangelo," *The Art Bulletin* 39, no. 1 (1957): 251ff.

4. Vasari, op. cit., 478.

5. Svetlana [Leontief] Alpers, "*Ekphrasis* and Aesthetic Attitudes in Vasari's *Lives*," *Journal of the Warburg and Courtauld Institutes* 23 (1960): 204.

6. Cf. Ernst H. Gombrich, "The Renaissance Conception of Artistic Progress and Its Consequences." In *Norm and Form. Studies in the Art of the Renaissance.* (London: Phaidon, 1971).

7. Hans Belting, "Vasari und die Folgen. Die Geschichte als Prozeß?" In *Das Ende der Kunstgeschichte?* (Munich: Deutscher Kunstverlag, 1983), 71.

8. This is emphasized in Schlosser's *Die Kunstliteratur* analyzing Vasari's work, and also in Anthony Blunt's study, *Artistic Theory in Italy 1450–1600* (New York: Oxford University Press, 1978), chapter 7.

9. Cf. Ernst Kris, *Meister und Meisterwerke der Steinschneidekunst in der italienischen Renaissance* (Vienna: Schroll, 1929), vol. I: 39 and 97. In this case, forgeries in applied art are discussed, including a cup made of porphyry. Annius Viterbensis, a famous forger of historical works, resorted to a similar method, when he buried a stone with inscriptions, making sure that it would be found soon. His aim was to prove that Viterbo had been founded before Rome.

10. Cf. Johannes Wilde, "Eine Studie Michelangelos nach der Antike," *Mitteilungen des kunsthistorischen Institutes in Florenz,* vol. IV, brochure 1, June 1932. Paul F. Norton (op. cit., 251) suggests the same.

11. John Pope-Hennessy, "Michelangelo's *Cupid*: The End of a Chapter." In *Essays on Italian Sculpture* (London: Phaidon, 1968), 111ff.

12. Erwin Panofsky, *Renaissance and Renascences in Western Art* (New York: Harper & Row/Icon Editions, 1975), 41.

13. This indeed does not hold true elsewhere. We only have to turn a couple of pages forward in the Michelangelo biography to discover among the several typical anecdotes one in which the author emphasizes the importance of protecting personal intellectual property, precisely by way of adding signatures; it is revealed that, in addition to artistic value, Michelangelo also carefully guarded his own artistic reputation. After being told by visitors that his *Pieta* was attributed to Cristoforo Solari, "one night he locked himself inside the church with a little light, and, having brought his chisels, he carved his name upon the statue." Vasari, op. cit., 425.

14. For the distinction between originally intended fakes and works of art fraudulently manipulated afterwards ("Fälschung" and "Verfälschung"), see Hans Tietze, "Zur Psychologie und Ästhetik der Kunstfälschung," *Zeitschrift für Ästhetik und allgemeine Kunstwissenschaft* 27 (1933): 209ff.; Peter Bloch, "Fälschung," in *Reallexikon zur deutschen Kunstgeschichte,* ed. Otto Schmitt

(Munich: Alfred Druckenmüller Verlag, 1973), vol. 6: 1407ff.; Peter Bloch: "Gefälschte Kunst," *Zeitschrift für Ästhetik und allgemeine Kunstwissenschaft* 23, no. 1 (1978): 52ff.

15. What I have in mind are the model stories of Zeuxis, Parrhasios, and Apelles, which were followed by several similar episodes related later by authors of short stories and anecdotes about art—including Vasari. Cf. Ernst Kris and Otto Kurz, *Die Legende vom Künstler* (Vienna: Kristall, 1934), 69ff. The problem of indistinguishability will be discussed in more details in Chapter 4.

16. Cf. Julius von Schlosser, *Die Kunst- und Wunderkammern der Spätrenaissance. Ein Beitrag zur Geschichte des Sammelwesens* (Braunschweig: Klinkhardt & Biermann, 1978), 34 and 35 (plate 12); see also *Fake? The Art of Deception,* ed. Mark Jones (Berkeley: University of California Press, 1990), 135, exhibition item no. 137. Millard Meiss at the same time assumes that, contrary to general opinion in the sixteenth century, Jean de Berry and the Limbourgs knew that these were in fact modern works made in antique style. Cf. Meiss, *The Limbourgs and their Contemporaries* (New York: Braziller/ Pierpont Morgan Library, 1974), 130f. This view is not shared by Andrew Burnett in "Coin faking in the Renaissance," in *Why Fakes Matter. Essays on Problems of Authenticity,* ed. Mark Jones (London: British Museum Press, 1992), 15ff. The Limbourg brothers are also known to have presented an ornamented wooden "book" to the prince, as a practical joke, on New Year's Day in the year of 1411. Cf. Meiss, op. cit., 69 and 76.

17. Friedrich Hebbel, *Tagebücher* Bd. III. *Sämtliche Werke* 2. Abt. Historischkritische Ausgabe (Berlin: Behr, 1905), 371. The entry is dated December 31, 1850.

18. Friedrich Hebbel, "Michel Angelo." In *Werke,* Bd. III (Berlin: Weichert), 185f.

19. Ibid., 198.

20. Cf. *Tagebücher* (Hebbel, op. cit., 361). The entry is dated October 21, 1850.

21. Oskar Walzel, *Friedrich Hebbel und seine Dramen* (Leipzig: Teubner, 1913), 94.

22. A fifth possibility was suggested by Peter Bloch, who gave a political–historical interpretation to the anecdote; he started out from the assumption that Michelangelo's instigator, a Medici, wanted to ruin Cardinal Riario's reputation—first of all as a fine appreciator of art, but consequently also as a statesman. The Cardinal's participation in the Pazzi conspiracy more than two decades earlier could have served as motive. (When Giuliano Medici was murdered in the Cathedral of Florence, the Cardinal celebrated Mass.) I have chosen to reject this possibility for the simple reason that Bloch—similarly to many others in the literature—mistakenly identified the instigator, Lorenzo di Pierfrancesco de' Medici (1465–1507, according to Chastel's commentary on Vasari; 1463–1503 according to Panofsky [*Renaissance and Renascences in Western Art,* chapter 4, note 101]) with his second cousin and Giuliano's brother, Lorenzo il Magnifico (1449–1492), who had passed away before

PICARESQUE AESTHETICS 29

1495, the approximate origin of *Amorino dormente*. Cf. "Gefälschte Kunst" (Bloch, op. cit.), 67.

23. Cf., for example, Frank Arnau, *Kunst der Fälscher, Fälscher der Kunst* (Düsseldorf: Econ, 1960).

24. The early development in legal doctrine of the notion of *falsum* is outlined in Thomas Würtenberger, *Das Kunstfälschertum. Entstehung und Bekämpfung eines Verbrechens vom Anfang des 15. bis zum Ende des 18. Jahrhunderts* (Weimar: Böhlaus Nachf., 1940. Reprinted Leipzig: Zentralantiquariat der DDR, 1970), 205–21. Elsewhere in the book he brings several Renaissance examples of similar informal procedures following the unveiling of forgeries (the case of Tommaso della Porta and others), 145f.

25. Cf. Tietze, op. cit., 213f.

26. The most important studies on the subject can be found in *Pikarische Welt. Schriften zum europäischen Schelmenroman*, ed. Helmut Heidenreich (Darmstadt: Wissenschaftliche Buchgesellschaft, Wege der Forschung, CLXIII, 1969).

27. Cf. André Jolles, "Die literarische Travestien. Ritter–Hirt–Schelm" [1931]. In *Pikarische Welt* (Heidenreich, op. cit.), 101ff.; also cf. Carl Gustav Jung, "Zur Psychologie der Schelmenfigur." In Paul Radin, Karl Kerényi, and C. G. Jung, *Der göttliche Schelm: Ein indianischer Mythenzyklus* (Zurich: Rhein Verlag, 1954), 191ff. Reprinted in *Pikarische Welt* (Heidenreich, op. cit.), 245ff.; Walter Muschg, *Tragische Literaturgeschichte* (Bern: Francke Verlag, 1957), 245ff.

28. Frank W. Chandler, *The Literature of Roguery* (London: Burt Franklin, 1907), vol. 1: 5.

29. José Ortega y Gasset, "Die originelle Schelmerei des Schelmenromans" [1910]. In *Pikarische Welt* (Heidenreich, op. cit.), 11.

30. *Memoirs of Benvenuto Cellini, a Florentine Artist: Written by Himself*, trans. Thomas Roscoe (London: Henry Colburn, 1823), vol. I: 93f.

31. Ibid., vol. II, 93. The earliest work known to make a systematic distinction between forgeries, copies, and originals is Enea Vico's book entitled *Discorsi di M. Enea Vico sopra le medaglie degli antichi* (1555); it lists Cellini among the forgers of antique coins. Cf. AB [Andrew Burnett], "Renaissance forgeries of ancient coins." In *Fake?* (Jones, op. cit.), 136.; also cf. Jeffrey M. Muller, "Measures of Authenticity: The Detection of Copies in the Early Literature on Connoisseurship." In *Retaining the Original: Multiple Originals, Copies and Reproductions: Studies in the History of Art*, vol. 20 (Washington, DC: National Gallery of Art, 1989), 141ff. It should be noted that the origins of the Renaissance sensitivity towards the issue of forgery is closely related to the counterfeiting of coins. Enea Vico's example was soon followed by a Spaniard, Antonio Augustin, whose dialogues on coins, inscriptions, and other antiquities were published first in Spanish in 1587, then in Italian in 1592. His refined instinct to unmask forgeries never prevented Augustin from admiring well-executed fakes or respecting the great antiquer in Pirro Ligorio, "the blackest name of the calendar of Renaissance forgers." Charles Mitchell, "Archaeology and Romance in Renaissance Italy," in *Italian Renaissance*

Studies. A Tribute to the Late Cecilia M. Ady, ed. E. F. Jacob (London: Faber & Faber, 1960), 458.

32. Gombrich, op. cit., 8.

33. Dossena was the most versatile forger of sculptures. "He produced archaic works, enriching the oeuvre of the Pisanos, of Mino da Fiesole, Donatello and Rossellino, of Desiderio Settignano and Verrocchio, and also fashioning Simone Martini's only contribution to the plastic art (based on the *Visitation* held in the Uffizi)," Fritz Baumgart wrote on the occasion of Dossena's unmasking. "Zu den Dossena-Fälschungen," *Kunstchronik und Kunstliteratur. Beilage zur Zeitschrift für bildende Kunst* 1 (April 1929): 3; also cf. David Sox, *Unmasking the Forger: The Dossena Deception* (New York: Universe, 1987).

34. Cf. Erwin Panofsky, "Kopie oder Fälschung. Ein Beitrag zur Kritik einiger Zeichnungen aus der Werkstatt Michelangelos," *Zeitschrift für bildende Kunst* 61 (1927): 221ff.

35. Take, for example, Felipe de Guevara, who in the mid-sixteenth century censured the Hieronymus Bosch forgeries in his *Comentarios de la pintura.* See Muller, op. cit., 142. See also Rudolf and Margot Wittkower, *Born Under Saturn: The Character and Conduct of Artists. A Documented History from Antiquity to the French Revolution* (New York: Norton, 1969), chapter 8: 9–10.

36. Gustav Glück, "Fälschungen auf Dürers Namen aus der Sammlung Erzherzog Leopold Wilhelms," *Jahrbuch der kunsthistorischen Sammlungen des allerhöchsten Kaiserhauses* 28 (1909–10), 19.

37. Cf. Otto Kurz, *Fakes: A Handbook for Collectors and Students* (New York: Dover, 1967), 35; also cf. Jones, op. cit., 123.

38. C. M. Wieland, *Sämtliche Werke,* vol. 33 (Leipzig: G. J. Göschen'sche Verlagshandlung, 1857), 224f. Pierre Mignard: 1612–1695.

39. Johann Wolfgang Goethe, *Italienische Reise I. Teil.* Goethes sämtliche Werke. Jubiläums–Ausgabe. 26. Bd. (Stuttgart: Cotta, n.d.), 159f.

40. Cf. Thomas Pelzel, "Winckelmann, Mengs and Casanova. A Reappraisal of Famous Eighteenth-Century Forgery," *Art Bulletin* 54, no. 3 (1972): 301ff.

41. Ibid., 308.

42. Cf. Johann Joachim Winckelmann, *Geschichte der Kunst des Altertums* (Vienna: Phaidon, 1934), 262f. and 22.

43. Pelzel thinks that it was Casanova, rather than Mengs, who painted the picture. Without questioning Mengs's involvement in the affair, he regards the dying confession to be a legend, drawing attention to a previously unnoticed German criticism from 1769–1770, which gives direct confirmation of Casanova's acknowledging his authorship of *Jupiter and Ganymede.* What could have formed the basis of such a peculiar legend we do not know. And would it not seem likely that, as they planned the joke together, the two friends executed it together? Nevertheless, a story strikingly similar to Michelangelo's has survived from Mengs's (1728–1779) youthful days. According to this, in Rome he produced such a perfect copy of one of Raphael's paintings—as it should be expected from someone who later came

to be to called "the German Raphael" (Winckelmann)—that it was eventually sold as original (Winckelmann, op. cit., 313). Pelzel's hypothesis was rejected shortly afterwards by Steffi Röttgen in her treatise entitled "Stori di un falso: il Ganimede di Mengs" (*Arte Illustrata* 54 [1973]: 256ff.). In her opinion, Casanova was boasting when he added the *Ganimede* to the list of his own forgeries, feeling certain that Mengs would not contradict him. On the other hand, she accepts Asara's account of Mengs's confession as authentic, because it originated from the painter's sister, Therese Maron-Mengs, and also quotes from a letter written in 1780 by Gian Ludovico Bianconi, who thought that the picture was the work of "an excellent modern painter whose efforts to conceal his wonderful manner were unsuccessful" (Röttgen, op. cit., 268). This could only have been Mengs, not Casanova. He furthermore suggested that the painting was much too momentous, both iconographically and compositionally, to be cast in with Casanova's forgeries and copies, and should definitely be attributed to a more significant artist, who at the time could have been no one but Mengs. Perhaps the reason for the failure to discover Mengs' mark—which plays such a characteristic role in forgery stories—was that the painting was missing during the nineteenth century, then was transferred to canvas, and only reemerged in 1895. In his study entitled "Greek Sculpture and Roman Copies I: Anton Raphael Mengs and the Eighteenth Century," A. D. Potts also supports Mengs's authorship (*Journal of the Warburg and Courtauld Institutes* 43 [1980]: 157). Also cf. Herbert von Einem, "Einleitung." In Anton Raphael Mengs, *Briefe an Raimondo Ghelli und Anton Marcon,* ed. H. von Einem (Göttingen: Vandenhoeck & Ruprecht, 1973), 28.

44. Alfred Georg Hartmann, *Das Künstlerwäldchen. Maler-, Bildhauer- und Architekten-Anekdoten* (Berlin: Bruno Cassirer, 1917), 118f.

45. Cf. Kurz, op. cit., 62ff.

46. Julius Meier-Graefe, "Der Kenner." In *Kunst-Schreiberei* (Leipzig: Gustav Kiepenhauer, 1987), 215ff. In the ending of the story one can recognize the old scheme, familiar from Sebastian Brant's *Fools' Ship* as well as other works: *Mundus vult decipit* ("the world wants to be deceived"). Incidentally, Gretor is referred to in Bode's memoirs by the name of Willy Grétor. Cf. Wilhelm von Bode, *Mein Leben* (Berlin: Hermann Reckendorf, 1930), volume II: 188.

47. Otto von Falke, "Die Marcy Fälschungen," *Belvedere* I (1922): 11.

48. Claude Blair and Marian Campbell, "Le Mystère de Monsieur Marcy." *Connaisance des arts* 375 (1983): 71.

49. Cf. MC [Marian Campbell], "The anarchist and forger Louis Marcy." In *Fake?* (Jones, op. cit.), 185. The article falsely states that the attributions in the museum have been corrected. Also cf. Marian Campbell and Claude Blair, "'Vive le Vol': Louis Marcy, anarchist and faker." In *Why Fakes Matter: Essays on Problems of Authenticity,* ed. Mark Jones (London: British Museum Press, 1992), 134ff.

50. For this purpose I use what I consider the best popular work: Lord Kilbracken's *Van Meegeren (A Case History)* (London: Thomas Nelson, 1967), and Hope B. Werness's essay, "Han van Meegeren *fecit.*" In *The Forgers' Art,* ed. Denis Dutton (Berkeley: University of California Press, 1983).

51. Lord Kilbracken, *Van Meegeren: Master Forger* (New York: Scribner's, 1967), 100.

52. Cf. Abraham Bredius, "A New Vermeer," *Burlington Magazine* 71 (November 1937): 211ff.

53. Cf. Werness, op. cit., 42.

54. The Keating story is told by FC [Frances Carey], "Tom Keating, A Barn at Shoreham." In *Fake?* (Jones, op. cit.), 240ff. Eric Hebborn's autobiography, *Drawn to Trouble: The Forging of an Artist. An Autobiography* (Edinburgh: Mainstream Publishing, 1991). The quotes are taken from page 355. Hebborn regards the criticism of the experts as his main task. See his interview, Georges Waser, "Die Angst vor dem jungfräulichen Blatt. Ein Besuch beim Kunstfälscher Eric Hebborn," *NZZ Folio. Die Zeitschrift der Neuen Zürcher Zeitung. Fälschungen* (October 1993): 10ff.

55. Ken Follett, *The Modigliani Scandal* (New York: Penguin, 1985 [1976]), 230f. An art dealer, forger, and rascal named Lovejoy plays the hero in Jonathan Gash's series, another example of popular literature that later was turned into a television series. On the connections between forgery and detective stories (thrillers), see Walter Grasskamp, *Die unästhetische Demokratie. Kunst in der Marktgesellschaft* (Munich: Beck, 1992); the chapter entitled "Schwarzmarkt der Eitelkeiten. Der Kunstbetrieb im Kriminalroman," 46ff.

56. Goethe, op. cit., 60.

57. Quoted by Michael Wreen, "Is, Madam? Nay, It Seems!" In *The Forger's Art* (Dutton, op. cit.), 199.

58. Cf. Gerard Vaughan, "The restoration of classical sculpture in the eighteenth century and the problem of authenticity"; and also, Seymour Howard, "Fakes, intention, proofs and impulsion to know: The case for Cavaceppi and clones." In *Why Fakes Matter* (Jones, op. cit.), 41ff. and 51ff.

59. Ulrike Henn, "Im Gefängnis bewies Lara sein Fälscher-Genie," *Art* 18 (1987–88). The carnivalesque element of forgeries is revealed by the fact that the Barnum Circus has repeatedly returned to the fakes. They offered to pay the full price for the *Saitaphernes Tiara*. Cf. Sepp Schüller, *Fälscher, Händler und Experten* (Munich: Ehrenwirth, 1959), 71. Several new forgery anecdotes have been collected by Thomas Almerath, *Kunst und Antiquitätenfälschungen* (Munich: Keyser, 1987). For a Hungarian author, it is of special interest that one of the most publicized forgery cases of the second half of the twentieth century involves a Hungarian forger, Elmer (or Elmyr) de Hory, who specialized in the great painters of the twentieth century. A journalist covering forgery cases went even further when he wrote the following: "Bastianini, the first modern forger to appear by name, dominated the latter part of the nineteenth century. Dossena was the next major figure, and was followed by van Meegeren in the 1930s. The fifties' 'star' was Jean Pierre Schecrown; the sixties had Henri Haddad ('David Stein'); the seventies, Elmyr de Hory; and the eighties, Tom Keating." David Sox, *Unmasking the Forger* (op. cit.), 146. It seems, however, that de Hory himself was less of a rascal and more of a victim of clients and mediators. See Clifford Irving, *Fake! The Story of Elmyr de*

Hory, the Greatest Forger of Our Time (New York: McGraw-Hill, 1969). His story, nevertheless, is not short of picaresque elements, beginning with the Texan millionaire whose entire collection consisted of nothing but de Hory works, down to his biographer, Irving, who, having his appetite whetted, himself turned into a forger, attempting to publish the posthumous "diary" of the mysterious millionaire, Howard Hughes.

2

ORIGINALITY

── Uniqueness, Individuality, Novelty, Historicity ──

What is wrong with forgeries? When someone who is part of the art establishment is asked this question and forced to make a theoretical generalization, he often replies by categorically denying the aesthetic value of forgeries. "When real knowledge is missing, then, when a genuine antique piece knock on the door with its magnificent and noble limbs concealed under modest and torn clothing, it is often thrown out as a Cinderella. Instead, her evil sisters, the modern forgeries are chosen, with their faces hidden behind veils and with their bodies patched up," the great classical art historian Adolf Furt-waengler wrote.[1]

This metaphor, put forward by a scholar engaged in a lifetime battle against forgeries (which he evidently held in deep contempt), contains a certain amount of aristocratic, and not entirely unjustified, cultural criticism. In most cases, forgeries are popular variations of a certain theme, adjusted to suit the spirit of the age and designed to be more easily comprehended than the original. The following viewpoint, taken from a study written in 1967 by a noted medievalist, is rather a romantic one, extended to the point of absurdity. "The true work of art is born, forgeries are made. Imitations and forgeries can never have any genuine quality. The so-called 'master forgeries' do not exist."[2] What we have here, therefore, is the purism of the expert; it ascribes the slip-ups committed by *other* experts either to their shortcomings as experts, branding them as banausic craftsmen who have infiltrated the ranks of true experts, or to their insensitivity and lack of Kennerschaft or connoisseurship: that irrational and instinctive talent that "belongs entirely to the realm of the eye."[3]

This is to be contrasted, however, with the purism of the aesthete, which claims that the beauty of artworks is wholly independent of the actual circumstances of their creation, of considerations concerning their originality and authorship. "To those who have and hold a sense of the significance of form, what does it matter whether the forms that move them were created in Paris the day before yesterday or in Babylon fifty centuries ago?" asks Clive Bell.[4] Compared to this absurdly radical opinion, Apollinaire held a rather more moderate view; in his article occasioned by the scandal of the Saitaphernes forgery, he called attention to the fact that the tiara, regardless of the actual date of its origin, was a beautiful work of art, and therefore the immense outrage of the archaeologists was unjustified. He showed common sense in suggesting that a beautiful object should not be removed from sight; at worst, it should be moved from the Louvre to the Luxembourg and exhibited there as an outstanding example of nineteenth-century goldsmithery.[5]

In the intellectual debate over *beauty versus originality,* the art establishment clashed with popular criticism on two fronts. Over the past 150 years there has hardly been a major museum in the world that has not been the object of forgery scandals of considerable publicity. On these occasions, the public has voiced two fundamentally different suspicions, simultaneously expressing their derision of the experts and their sympathy for the forgers: a) they dismiss wholesale the so-called "experts" as incompetent fumblers or charlatans, who have only proven their ignorance by their inability to recognize a fake, a nonoriginal; instead of providing evidence for the progress of science, their judgment only raises suspicion about other works currently still thought to be genuine; and b) they dismiss the "experts" entirely as undiscerning, narrow-minded, bigoted people who study some completely esoteric subject and try to force the public to see things in accordance with their judgment, demanding that it show contempt for objects it had until recently admired so much.

One of the important milestones in the institutionalization of art history was the Dresden conference in 1871, which discussed the authenticity of Holbein's *Dresden Madonna;* the (negative) verdict, generally upheld to this day, stirred among the public emotions such as those outlined above. As a consequence of the historical approach of their discipline, the art historians quite understandably felt no need to respond to the question posed by (among others) the famous psychophysicist Gustav Theodor Fechner. On one of his excursions into cultural history, he used the example of this same Holbein *Madonna* to ask why considerations of originality should be placed before those of beauty.[6]

Jakob Burckhardt, who objected to putting too much emphasis on the importance of attributions in art theory, was also of the opinion that "the hunt for famous names has its own drawbacks, too; in fact it would be better if we appreciated paintings for their beauty only."[7] It was precisely in connection with the Dresden judgment, which he incidentally thought to be unfounded even from an academic point of view, that Burckhardt contrasted the actual verdict with the direct aesthetic experience, suggesting a philosophical explanation for the concern for originality. The Holbein *Madonna* is the only work of art that can bear the "deadly proximity" of the *Sistine Madonna,* he said. How could a genius, able to surpass in sublimity even Holbein himself, suddenly materialize out of the blue and then disappear without a trace in the throng of imitators? In other words, Burckhardt *individualizes* originality, and regards our capacity to penetrate into the spiritual word of a great master, or to "relive" his personal experience, as one of the ultimate gifts of art. But since this spiritual world is susceptible to changes, necessarily accompanied by changes of style, we cannot do without consulting documents. Nevertheless, Burckhardt maintains the Platonic view whereby true beauty, being the symbol of the highest realms, does not belong to the sphere of originality. Burckhardt mentions an old Milanese art collector who proved himself a true philosopher when he dismissed the need to discover the origin of his paintings with the question: "If the merchandise is good, why should I care who painted it?"[8]

This duality of direction, which stands out so well in Burckhardt's lecture, can be called "purely aesthetic" on the one hand, and purely "art-historical" or "art-philosophical" on the other. The *origin* of a work of art, its association with either a definite person or a definite style, plays no part in the aesthetic enjoyment. The validity of this statement presupposes the separation of the aesthetic sphere from the intellectual, something that can never be achieved completely. The intellectual recognition of an illusion might occasionally end our aesthetic pleasure, as in Kant's examples where artificial flowers are planted in the soil or a nightingale's song turns out to be whistled by a boy behind the bushes[9]; similarly, our disinterested pleasure on spotting a well-formed ankle might suddenly diminish if we discover that it actually belongs to the wrong sex. Yet the tendency of pure pleasure obviously exists in which the history of origin need not play a significant part.

By contrast, the history of origin does play a significant part in the aesthetic experience that derives directly from the *historicity,* or historical evidence, of the work of art. This historicity, according to Burckhardt's heroic genius-aestheticism, is supplied by the artist's biography. As with all the other essential features of the modern art establishment, individualizing historicism also originated in the Renaissance, although it was emphasized less in the case of Italian artists, with all their representative objective-aesthetic orientation (realized, of course, by the ideas, inventions, and fantasies of the artists' personalities), than it was in connection with the northern European artists who were more inclined to stress the uniqueness of the artist's life, its irreplaceable and nonrepresentable character. In this respect, special interest should be attached to drawings, which, as Panofsky points out,[10] were first valued in their own right by Dürer. The collection of drawings, as documents of the artist's immanent development, began in the sixteenth century; before that time they were regarded merely as workshop material or were valued for their subject matter only. With drawings, the notion of *original- ity of invention* was complemented by the notion of *originality of autography.*

Individuality forms but one element in the complex notion of origi- nality. The role of historicity in artistic comprehension does not by any means have to be reduced to the cult of historical personality. There is no need to point out the importance attached to the appre- ciation of originality as *novelty* in the modern (i.e., European, begin- ning with the Renaissance) conception of art. This is also the conclu- sion Alfred Lessing draws in regard to the question of what is wrong with a forgery: ". . . the offense felt to be involved in forgery is not so much against the spirit of beauty (aesthetics) or the spirit of law (morality) as against the spirit of art."[11] Vermeer is a great painter not only because he painted beautiful pictures, but also because he is orig- inal: "[H]e painted certain pictures in a certain manner *at a certain time in the history and development of art.*"[12] It is artistic integrity, rather than beauty, that is missing from van Meegeren's *Emmaus.* "Paradoxically . . . [*Emmaus*] is as much a monument to the artistic genius of Vermeer as are Vermeer's own paintings. Even though it was painted by van Meegeren in the twentieth century, it embodies and bears witness to the greatness of the seventeenth-century art of Vermeer."[13]

Such an extension of the concept of originality, or such a re-interpretation of it, has the advantage of diverting attention from the preliminaries of the artwork to the work of art itself; from the artist's biographical details to his solution of artistic problems. Rather than being restricted to the originality of genius, the extended concept covers the originality of movements and styles represented by individual artists, including innovations of lesser importance. Brilliant as it may be, this answer to the proposed problem is not a satisfactory one. Its fallacy derives from the fact that while it universalizes the historicity associated with individual invention in Western art, the art of forgery itself is removed from this context. This is justified insofar as forgery indeed sabotages the new concept of art (while its own concept presupposes its existence), denying the historicity of beauty and the artistic premium of novelty. Nevertheless, Lessing's extended concept of forgery is in many ways self-contradictory. For one thing, despite its denial of historicity, forgery is entirely historical, in the sense that it has to identify to an extraordinary degree with a historical figure or movement from the art of the past (or, more recently, from contemporary art) and, rather than merely aiming for a visual resemblance, it also has to reconstruct, down to the most minute details, a historical painting technique. Its originality dissolves in the technique. This corresponds to Lessing's van Meegeren paradox: in this respect the forger remains a servant, whose mischief enhances the reputation of his master. The question, however, is whether the forger is capable of such identification, and it is immediately followed by another one: whether we should take seriously the criticism of the modern concept of art that he embodies, at least to the point of pausing to consider it even if we cannot accept it?

With regard to the second contradiction, it is one of the recurring claims in the literature on forgery that after a couple of generations, forgeries came to show their true colors as the telltale signs of their *own* period become plainly visible. It has been said about van Meegeren, for example, that the stylistic marks of Symbolism can be detected on his forgeries. It has even been suggested that the facial features of his Christ representations resemble Greta Garbo! One of the important tools in the arsenal of art-historical analysis and the dating of forgeries is the study of the relationship between the period-style (or stylistic trends) and the forger's perception of style. This was how art historians were able to connect a fake Julius Caesar owned by the British Museum with the style of late Classicism, and with Thor-

waldsen in particular; this was also how the head of a colossal Etrus-
can warrior became associated with avant-garde trends, while Dossena's deliberate disfiguration of the faces, unusual in the case of forgeries, was traced back to Post-Impressionistic and late Expressionist
plastic principles concerning the dissolution and reduction of contours.[14] In the forgery industry, the reactivation of a certain entry in
the catalogue of historical styles is obviously related to the reactivation of the original historical style itself, which for some reason or
another seems to strike a chord in the contemporary audience. Also
apparent is the fact that forgeries provide evidence of the forgers'
knowledge (or lack of knowledge) of the historical period in question:
this is how utility objects might be presented as mere ornaments in a
painting, when the forger is not aware of their original functions; this
is also how newly discovered archaic findings might influence forgeries; and finally, this was how the newly gained knowledge about Vermeer came to be incorporated into Meegeren's paintings.

The argument about the necessary perspective of a few generations in the detection of forgeries originates from Max J. Friedländer,
who maintained, in his article entitled *Die Madonna mit der Wickenblüte*, that the painting in question was *not* a fake; rather, it was the
main work of Master William, who was active at the beginning of the
fifteenth century in Cologne. "The story about the one-hundred-
year-old forgery is a childish joke. If the great unknown master could
fool Wallraff and Boisserée, he could not fool the experts in 1900. The
reason is that every generation is under new constraint to see things
differently, and anything that is copied, in this case Veronica's style,
appears differently to every generation. Here is a rule from the development of style: a forger can only deceive his own contemporaries,
every fake has to be served while it is still fresh, straight out of the
oven. The older the copy, the greater and the more apparent becomes
the difference between the original and the copy."[15]

Although it does contain a certain amount of important truth,
this tenet does not hold completely true. Today, with another century
having passed, it is quite obvious that countless forgeries have survived undetected for several generations, while the number of undis-
covered fakes stored in the various collections cannot be estimated.[16]
The marble head of *Julius Caesar* mentioned earlier was bought in
1818, and ever since then, rather than collecting dust in a remote corner of the museum, it has proved to be an extremely popular exhibit.
Still, it was not until 1961 that its antique origin was disproved, and
even that discovery resulted mainly from technical and historical
arguments, to which stylistic reasoning was added only later.[17] It was
purely on technical grounds that the Metropolitan Museum's early

Classical Greek sculpture featuring an equine head was ruled to be a fake in the 1960s, a verdict that was reversed soon afterwards following some more sophisticated technical examinations.[18] One of the possible reasons for the survival of forgeries through generations appears in a subtle way in Friedländer's article: "After all, our *Madonna* was both a starting point and a paradigm."[19] Well, if a forgery is accepted as the paradigm of a genre type, the chances are that it will be used to authenticate further fakes, while remaining itself unsuspected.

"Forgeries may have escaped detection for a long time, and by their long acceptance they may even have influenced the general conception of the period they pretend to represent," Hans Tietze writes.[20] He was also the first to distinguish between two types of forgery: In the division of reproductive versus creative forgery, the latter holds sway in the forging of the works of artists associated with the great individualist schools, which allow more room for the forger's self-expression. However, creativity is secondary to reproduction in the forging of those styles, which themselves are opposed to the individuality of expression—such as medieval art, applied art, folk art, and the primitives. From this distinction follows the two probable fates awaiting forgeries: The first initially generates extraordinary excitement, only to be unmasked shortly thereafter; the second fits-in unnoticed and remains hard to expose.[21] Forgeries of the first type, therefore, receive their stamp of secondary historicity from their own age, as opposed to forgeries of the second type, which shape our historical knowledge of some other age.

The subsequent history of exposed forgeries could be seen as the next dimension of their historicity, since by virtue of their true age forgeries themselves become historical objects—in fact, sometimes quite highly esteemed historical objects. This was the case with the Marcy forgeries at the turn of the century, or with works of the so-called Spanish forger during the late 1930s, of whom nothing is known, although his oeuvre, consisting of fifteenth- and sixteenth-century imitations, numbers over 200 pictures and fetches a very good price on the market.[22] Even the forgeries are forged![23]

There are thus serious arguments in support of the historicity of forgeries, arguments which Alfred Lessing, in his attempt to contrast them with the originals, simply overlooked. But even the historicity of the notion of originality has a circumscriptive interpretation, which broadens the concept of the originality of individuality only insofar as it extends it to include the concept of originality as novelty. Naturally, Lessing was quite aware of the fact that originality as novelty had not been a universal characteristic of art, only of its European branch in modern—i.e., the Renaissance and later—times. I should say it is only *one* of the characteristics, the promotion of which to an exclusive principle is a reduction that impoverishes our concept of artistic culture. All the more so since Lessing commits the mistake, one that is not unusual in our culture, of considering novelty as a value in itself. As one of his critics pointed out, in the notion of originality as historical novelty a distinction should be made between the normative and the nonnormative meaning. According to the latter, any insignificant or worthless work might qualify, while the former requires the existence of valuable components in addition to simply being first and taking the initiative.[24] Nevertheless, the new system of art is not confined to the pursuit of novelty: Foremost among its specifics is the "intellectual pursuit" of art and artistic comprehension, which in turn presupposes a "historical perspective"— the absorption of foreign or indirect traditions.

In discussing *originality* as the physical identity of works of art within themselves, and nonidentity with everything else (a statement too self-evident to be mentioned earlier), we now add to the concepts of individuality and novelty a further, and probably more general, notion: the aspect of *historical authenticity*. This means the assumption that, in a manner that is partly revealed and partly concealed (revealing and concealing different aspects in different periods), the original work of art *contains its own history*, which does not end with the completion of the artist's work but includes its subsequent wear and restoration, as well as any later corrections of restorations, changes in its location or even function, the rises and falls in the interest it generates, and the multitude of its interpretations and traditions. It should be clear from the above that I am not referring here to the strict concept of historical authenticity; that is, to the *record* of origin (which could also be a possible interpretation of originality). The latter is unhistorical in the sense that it focuses on one historical moment and tries to freeze it in time. When considered in a nonpurist sense, historical authenticity is an unbroken and constantly flowing process. However, the ideological trends and reductive practices of purism themselves form part of the story.

Like beauty, this hypothesis has a fundamental significance in the modern reception of art. We judge works of art not only on the basis of their beauty, but also with regard to the *assumed* significance of their history. I must emphasize that in this case, *assumption* is perhaps more important than *knowledge*. The functional history of premodern works—such as their magical effects and religious content, their association with concrete behavioral norms and their regulated role in entertainment, all deriving from immediate traditions—was better understood by the premodern audience than any work of art can be understood in our time. In the new system of art, the functional aura has been replaced by the aura of historicity. A work of art has a history, and it provides historical evidence—that much we know. How much of this history we can actually gather is on the one hand itself part of the work's history, and on the other hand varies on a broad scale between the limits set by that which is historically possible to know at any given moment. If, for some preposterous reason, we could see no more in Leonardo's *Last Supper* than some agitated people at a dinner party (as was the case, for example, with that savage in Panofsky's example[25]) or—what seems to be a more likely assumption—we do not recognize the story of a particular saint, then, in order to prove our membership in modern culture and avoid being stamped as savages, it is enough if we are aware of what we do *not* know: the picture does have a history. And this is not merely the story depicted in the painting, not simply the iconographical program, but also the history of form.

The forger attacks originality from the point of view of historical authenticity, insofar as his work gives the impression that it *contains* the story that conveys the same historical evidence as the original. However, the clock of history is ticking away for the forger's work as well; it too embarks on a life of its own, and it is only a question of quality, good luck, and time that, having survived in historical memory sufficiently long, it becomes authentic: a genuine forgery, in the manner and ways mentioned above. This has, however, the precondition of either remaining undetected and thus continuing to shape the general view about the period of its assumed origin, or just the opposite: being recognized for the recognition of the *difference*. (Between the two stand the forgeries unmasked on historical or scientific grounds: forgeries in which the difference is still not dominant, either as a result of not enough time having passed since their creation or for not possessing independent qualities. Usually, these items become the trash and debris of culture, along with other forgettable objects, or—and this too can happen quite frequently—they revert to being forgeries again, for example in the art business, or alternatively await resurrection in the storerooms of museums.)

In the case of the *Saitaphernes Tiara*, Apollinaire proposed recognizing the difference, which was probably what motivated the Victoria and Albert Museum in its interesting decision in 1869 to buy Giovanni Bastianini's (1830–1868) *exposed* forgery, the bust of *Lucrezia*

Donati, as a significant work of nineteenth-century historicizing sculpture for the price of an original Renaissance statue.[26] The increased interest in differentiation is demonstrated by the fact that over the past few decades museums all over the world have been digging forgeries out of their storerooms, at least for the duration of an exhibition. The two largest exhibitions of forgeries so far were organized by the Folkwang Museum of Essen in 1976–1977 and the British Museum in 1990; they could also be regarded as exhibitions on the history of art collection in Germany and Great Britain, respectively.[27] Finally, the best essay written on the subject of recognizing the difference between the original and the forgery, and on forgery *as* original, is by János György Szilágyi, the Hungarian classical archaeologist.[28]

However, it is the *gesture* of forging that we are interested in: the criticism of the work's historicity. This criticism is related to all four notions of originality: It pretends to be identical with something which it is not; it expropriates the work of another personality; it expropriates the novelty value—or broadly speaking, the problem solution—of another person's work; and finally, it lends historical authenticity to a work that the work (for the time being at least) is still not entitled to, thus claiming a false pedigree and occupying a place in history it does not deserve. The shockingly funny side of the scandalous, roguish, or adventurous nature of forgeries is ultimately rooted in the realization that, with sufficient skills, such stunts can—if only for a brief period—be pulled off, and therefore the modern hierarchy of art can be sabotaged. The apparent willingness of many forgers to confess, which they do despite the dangers of monetary loss and legal liability, testifies to the significance of this gesture—not because the forgers are aware of all this, but because the sensation and fame they strive for are themselves symptoms of it.

But are we right in identifying the essential feature of forgeries' farcical element, or the picaresque gesture, in that it makes a laughing-stock of the historical evidence surrounding a work of art? Might it not be the other way around? What if forgeries actually help expose the lack of historicity—the randomness of the associated traditions—that characterizes the relationship between modernity and art? With our art collections compiling objects from every age and every region, stripped of their historical habitat and functions, is it any wonder that forgeries too have a permanent place in this artificial, ahistorical, and false context? When we consider how much specialized knowledge and how many branches of the historical and natural sciences have to be mobilized in the struggle to screen out forgeries, and all in constant competition with the forgers who, at least in principle, have access to the same knowledge and know-how, can we really be surprised? When discussing the role of art in the premodern era, conservative and romantic critics of the modern art establishment always emphasize its firm and traditional embedding in history, and make a point of contrasting this with its subsequent displacement. The separation of the form and the allocated surface, so to speak, was a direct consequence of the alienation of the aesthetic sphere (to use Hans-Georg Gadamer's expression[29]), together with a shift in character of works of art from functionalism to philosophical and intellectual appeal, and accompanied by a growing significance of individual qualities at the expense of consensual taste.

It is a fact that the rules of art have changed over 500 years of practical and theoretical travail. Nor can it be denied that the historical embedding of art already began declining with the first steps in this process, as evidenced, for example, in art being moved from churches into collections. Nevertheless, this is not in the least in contradiction with the fact that it was precisely this decline that created the conditions for the individual and historical consciousness of creation and reception. On the contrary, the change essentially meant that the traditional functionalism that had earlier accompanied beauty was replaced by *open* historical authenticity. With that, knowledge about the place of art in actual life situations also declined, as did the claim of subsequent works of art to occupy such a place at all; after a time, however, this recognition came to be joined by a certain degree of openness and freedom, which eventually became an integral part of the aesthetic experience: the fact that works of art commemorate different traditions and histories, or to use Novalis's beautiful expression, that art is "the memory of humanity."

I maintain the view that it is this memory that forgeries sabotage in the name of a strong and apparent, although not in the least traditional, functionalism—as a form of applied art paradoxically aiming to liberate artistic creation. The functional concept of art leaves room for the commutability of works of art, of their replaceability. One of the main features of the new conception of art, in addition to its afunctionalism (or in any case decreased functionalism), is the uncommutability and irreplaceability of individual works of art, which, in a sense, decreases their significance as objects—without, of course, completely eliminating their materialness—and increases their signifi-

cance *merely* as works of art. This is the tendency that gradually
becomes the standard of uniqueness at the normative peaks of the art
world's hierarchy, consummating in the dissolution of both the
painters' guilds and the great Baroque workshops, as well as in the
spread of the new and considerably cheaper techniques of reproduction. The latter made it possible for *replicas* (one or more duplicates
either by the artist himself or by his workshop associates; their authenticity raise serious problems, both in practice and theory) to be
replaced by the industry of nonoriginal *reproductions,* along with the
specifically new branches of art producing multiple *originals,* in which
case the uniqueness of works of art is not a precondition of their
aura—their incommutability and irreplaceability. The theoretical dis-
cernibility of originals from nonoriginals is not eliminated by photography either, as shown by the fact that photographs are also forged.[30]

And presuming that we want to consider the problems of originality within the framework of the modern art establishment rather than
from the perspective of its disintegration, the situation has been unaffected by the application of the latest developments in reproduction
technology in the art media, provided that the work of art remains an
object. If I may put forward a hypothesis at this point, I foresee the
most important weapon in the arsenal of forgery, aside from counterfeiting individual authorship or famous names, is the simulation of
technological obsoleteness as a document of the work's historicity.

Forgery is a functional art form, which (in principle) interchanges
the uninterchangeable, substitutes the unsubstitutable. Although pre-
supposing the modern spirit (or to be more precise, the spirit existing
outside post-Renaissance Europe in only a couple of places, such as
ancient Rome, China, and Japan) of uninterchangeability, forgery parodies it with the pre- and/or postmodern spirit of interchangeability.

"The faking of art and antiques occurs only in cultures in which
old objects associated with a famous individual can command high
prices. This is a relatively unusual phenomenon. In most cultures and
at most times there has been no special premium on old things; even
the most venerated images have been repaired and replaced as necessary, while outstanding artistry or craftsmanship has been appreciated more for its own sake than for any glamour attached to the
name of the person responsible for it."[31] Naturally, a global generalization such as this is modified by the specialized research of every
single period. Ancient objects were very much prized in the Middle
Ages, which the authors of old texts and pictures kept very much in
evidence. And while the forging of relics and documents were, for the
same reason, extremely common, art forgery did not exist at all; at
best, the "originals" of cultic representations were "recovered" occa-

sionally, or copies were proclaimed to be original, or St. Luke's *original* painting of the Virgin Mary and the Child was "identified" in various pictures. The then-prevailing notion of originality was different from the notions of artistic originality described above.

In his authoritative new monograph, Hans Belting clarifies this point. The title itself refers to the turning point that took place in the Renaissance: *Picture and Cult: A History of Picture Before the Age of Art.* It was characteristic of the medieval perception of pictures that the image was literally conceived as reality, the bodily representation of a sacred person. "The notion of originality is established by the uniqueness of the picture *itself.*"[32] This essentially amounts to the interpretation of originality as material identity (often in conjunction with the sacrosanctity of the location). Far from denouncing them, the authorities encouraged the cultic devotion of copies in the interest of enhancing their stature, placing them, incidentally, under the strict obligation of formal identity. According to the sanction, a formally identical but physically different copy could share in the privileges of the original, for example with regard to the performance of miracles. For this reason, copies were valued no less than the original works of accomplished artists. In connection with Antoniazzo Romano, a very late icon copier who worked in Rome in the 1460s, Belting points out that when Antoniazzo wrote words on one of his paintings claiming that *this* was the picture in front of which Pope Leo the Great prayed a thousand years earlier, then "these words cannot be interpreted as if Antoniazzo had tried to forge a late Antique original"[33]; he did, indeed, talk about the original painting and its miraculous power.

The new notion of originality emerged from the crisis of the cultic pictures. Following the natural laws of perception, pictures turned from reality into paintings, the emancipated products of the imagination. "Between the poles of the copying of nature and the artist's imagination, the new interpretation of *pictures* unfolds as the interpretation of art."[34] In a series of brilliant analyses, Belting shows how this new interpretation of pictures reflects on the old, all the while changing its character: how it complements the traditional form of icons with a landscape full of humanist quotations from indirect traditions in the background or a freely invented still life in the foreground; or, in reverse, how the material interpretation of the cultic pictures is evoked solely by the arrangement of drapery in the *Sistine Madonna.* "In the religious sense, [the picture] loses its significance as an 'original' that has power over the faithful by its physical presence. Instead, the picture becomes 'original' in the artistic sense, as the authentic reflection of the artist's idea."[35] In the words written in 1411 by Manuel Chrysolóras, the Greek literate who lived in

Florence: "In images we are admiring the beauty not of bodies, but of the maker's mind."[36]

To return from this grand subject to our more humble theme of forgery, we must see in the light of what has been said above that forgery, in its very existence, turns against its own progenitor, the modern concept of modernity, sabotaging all three of its components: individuality, novel solutions to artistic problems, and historicity. Regarding the trivial notion of originality as *physical identity* (trivial in itself, that is, when removed from the context of either of the previously mentioned concepts or—as was the case in the medieval age—of a theological norm), forgers are, once again in paradoxical fashion, greatly attached to it. However, this should not be surprising, considering that a forger's aim is to pass off his work as someone else's. This is the only notion of originality that forgers do not question and that they do not provoke with their gesture. When a forger has fooled the entire world he can deprecate the entire conceptual framework surrounding the works of art, but he cannot fool himself. He might think that he has proven his work to be just as valuable as Donatello's or Verrocchio's, Mino da Fiesole's (Dossena), Rembrandt's or Vermeer's (van Meegeren),[37] but he cannot think that his work is *their* work in the trivial sense. If, however, of all the possible notions of originality only that of physical identity is accepted, then the work of art becomes a copy (a beautiful copy as it may be), and when it hits the art market, the only question is whether it is a unique copy or, should there be more identical copies, whether it is *the* unique copy. This is the opportunity the forger fraudulently exploits. What is at stake here is not the sacrosanctity of the work of art, but its price, real or theoretical, in a scheme of self-justification or revenge. And success is seen as the justification for forgery's malicious criticism of the art world.

———— Forgery as the Criticism of Originality ————

We must ask the question, therefore, as to whether, and to what extent, forgery's criticism of originality is justified. Since forgeries are the parasites of the original, both in the logical and historical senses, the validity of the criticism should remain relative—with one exception. It is possible that the current crisis of art will eventually lead to the renewal of the rules of the game governing art, since the preponderance of intellectual qualities over beauty, of provocative elements over attractiveness, along with the uncertain status of the works of art, the irrational tendencies in judging quality, and the growing frustration of artistic taste have by now reached a critical value in contemporary art, both on the creative and receptive sides. It is possible that, instead of moving further towards the antiquation and museologiza-tion of art, with a parallel shift towards the continuing sectarianism of contemporary art, the crisis will be resolved by the birth of a new paradigm that could turn out to be—as certain signs already indi-cate—none other than forgery itself, rendering all concepts of origi-nality—individuality, innovation, and historicity—altogether mean-ingless and void, rather than merely weakening them. Later on I shall return to the examination of this possibility; all I wish to say for now is that although I fully appreciate the need to reform our notions about art, with regard to *this* possibility I remain skeptical. For the above reason, now I turn to the *relative* justification of the criticism.

When forgery criticizes originality as individuality, then its aim is to glorify the biography of an artist and to glamorize a certain group of artists at the expense of others. The deification of the artist's person-ality began in the Renaissance, and it was this tradition that the romantic and historicizing art-religions tried to revive at the begin-ning of the nineteenth century. In order to be able to refer simulta-neously to *several* chapters from European cultural history, I have chosen to mention the names of Raphael and Dürer. The works of both artists were copied by Marcantonio Raimondi, and until he was banned from this practice by a Venetian court order at the insistence of Dürer in 1506, the copying even extended to Dürer's famous monogram.[38] I have already mentioned the Dürer cult and the indus-try of Dürer imitations in the sixteenth and seventeenth centuries. It is well known what significance the genius-aestheticism of Romantic-ism assigned to these two artists in particular. The tendencies of the cult of the artist, as evidenced in various cultural contexts, have exerted a lasting influence on the institutional framework of art. For a long time art history was mostly equated with the biographies of artists. In the collection of art, but also in its appreciation, the fetishism of great names was taking hold.

By way of illustration, I would like to present two paradigmatic cases. The first features the art collector and connoisseur Morris Moore, who became obsessed with the idea of proving Raphael's authorship of an excellent Renaissance painting in his possession. Moore bought the *Apollo and Marsyas* in 1850, and for the remaining 35 years of his life the authentication of the painting remained his chief concern. He organized exhibitions and showings in the major European cities. Overcome by paranoia, he was in constant battle with the experts, most of whom refused to back him, preferring to cast their votes for people in Raphael's circle such as Francesco Francia, Timoteo Viti, and others, until the Sherlock Holmes of attributionism, Giovanni Morelli alias Lermolieff, concluded his long deliberation by deciding the issue in favor of Pietro Perugino. This has remained the accepted view ever since.[39]

Károly Pulszky, the buyer in the second case, was the director of Országos Képtár, a gallery in Budapest. If anything, it was the spell of quality rather than that of names that had bewitched him; yet in 1896, when he came under attack in a politically motivated campaign, "the charges—what is more, the major charges—included the accusation that the male portrait he had purchased from the Scarpa collection was the work of an insignificant painter called Piombo, rather than that of Raphael. It should be noted that at the time of the purchase the experts in general were already more inclined to accept Piombo's authorship, which was also the view shared by Pulszky. Of course, the painting remained just as good, regardless of the name associated with it. Unfortunately, at that time only very few people in Hungary had ever heard of Piombo, and even fewer knew that the works he painted in the 1510s would stand up in comparison with even the best of Raphael's works. More than that, it was in Piombo's masterpieces that the portraiture of the High Renaissance crystallized in its purest form.

The painting owned by the Budapest gallery represented a quite memorable moment in the history of art: The moment when the Renaissance was already, and still, at its purest—that is, already mature but not yet over-ripe. This was that "narrow edge" mentioned by Wölfflin, the—temporally extremely limited—consummation of the mature Renaissance. Nonetheless, Piombo's name in Hungarian public opinion became synonymous with dubious dealings and embezzlement. As Ferenc Herczeg (a well-known Hungarian writer) wrote in *The Gothic House*: "In Hungarian political vocabulary the word Piombo has developed a connotation similar to the word 'Panama' in France. Every time the self-appointed 'Chief Attorney,' Géza Polónyi, sardonically howled the name of Piombo in the House, the honorable members started to fall about laughing."[40]

To my knowledge, *attributionism* has remained an unexplored chapter in the cultural history of art. In the two cases above, the reader might find a vivid demonstration of one of its central principles, which might be called the *absorption effect*. But the same problem, which has obvious financial causes, is well known from art history, curatorial experience, and art dealership: The great names absorb, or try to absorb, the minor names from historically or stylistically associated milieu. According to the records of the New York

Customs Office, between 1909 and 1951 a total of 9,428 works by Rembrandt were imported into the country.[41] As a reaction to the above-mentioned absorption effect, we are now witnessing a reversal of attributionism and a dramatic revision of Rembrandt's oeuvre in particular; this is shown by the Rembrandt Research Project's work, which has been publishing its verdicts in huge volumes since 1982.[42] "Rembrandt" now seems to splinter into dozens of names: students, members of his workshop and people from his surroundings, painters under his influence, the juvenilia of later masters, etc. And although it would probably significantly help combat the fetishism of names if we were capable of respecting the work of other artists, known or unknown, in such wonderful masterpieces as *Saul Listens to David's Playing the Harp* in The Hague, *The Man with a Golden Helmet* in Berlin, *Daniel's Vision,* also in Berlin, and perhaps *Polish Rider* in New York, there are still some highly respected critics who are concerned with the hyperradicalism of the enterprise.[43] These concerns are bound up with the questions of *originality as novelty* and *originality as historicity.*

To provide a brief summary of the problem, we must first realize that the question of originality as individuality is linked to that of autography in a manner that historically changes, not only from one branch of art to the next, but also within the individual branches. Nelson Goodman is probably right in claiming that originally all art forms were autograph,[44] and that it was only later that the group of art forms indirectly transmitted through some medium (printed letters and musical notes) separated from the rest.

As it happened, however, even with regard to the directly experienced fine arts, the expression "by the artist's hand" was often meant to be understood not literally, but partially only or symbolically. In fact, it was precisely in the first centuries of the new system of art that such a meaning was predominant, when, parallel with the growing importance of individuality, the artist's intellectual pursuits began to clash with his craftsmanly qualities, while the guild system of his art was still to survive in many areas for some time to come. Total autography was a later myth, part of the mythicization of the artistic individual, and resulted from the backward projection of the norms of later generations. The recent restoration of the Sistine Chapel has dispelled the legend that Michelangelo painted the entire ceiling by himself, without the help of any of his assistants.[45] Corot's nonchalance towards autograph originality seemed bizarre only in his own age; Boucher's similar attitude never prompted such a response. Burckhardt rated the autography of Rubens's works on a scale of one to six. The only works that were entirely autograph were the portraits, his early pictures, the smaller compositions, and those made for his own pleasure.[46] The Dutch painters' guild in Rembrandt's age found nothing wrong with the assistants working in the manner of their master, nor with their filling in the details of lesser importance in pictures; these paintings then went on sale under the name, and often with the signature, of the master.[47]

In this case the master's originality meant the individuality and novelty of the artistic idea and style, as well as his supervision of the execution. The Rembrandt issue is of course a great deal more complex than this, and I do not feel qualified to venture to pass judgment on the work of the Rembrandt Research Project. Nevertheless, the investigation is likely to reveal that quite a few major artists were under the influence of Rembrandt in the early part of their careers. It will probably help disentangle the oeuvres and artistic ideals of a number of lesser-known but outstandingly talented artists; however, concerning a number of the almost four dozen students working under Rembrandt (and the much larger group of his imitators), Alfred Lessing's bon mot is, paraphrased with slight modifications, extremely appropriate: Paradoxically . . . it is as much a monument to the artistic genius of Rembrandt as are Rembrandt's own paintings. Even though it was painted by X, Y, or Z in the seventeenth century, it embodies and bears witness to the greatness of the seventeenth-century art of Rembrandt.

For this is precisely where the relativity of the criticism of individual originality lies: To denounce the mythicization of biography, or to criticize its endowment with aesthetic qualities, is justifiable; there are several great artists whose biographies are completely or partially unknown to us and whose names are mere conventions, as indeed we are often in the habit of naming them after their artistic creations. In that case, "the discovery of artistic individuality is usually epiphenomenal to the perception of the high quality of work."[48] Still, it is the greatest consolation of our culture that such individuals as Michelangelo or Rembrandt are possible.

When forgery criticizes originality as invention, then in the debate of creation versus imitation it rehabilitates imitation, at the same time relativizing the artist's identification with, or comparison to, the creator or the discoverer, two more attitudes that originated in the Renaissance. It questions the presumption whereby what comes before the work of art is "nothing" and the work of art itself is a "new world." It denies—in the name of some kind of aesthetic atheism, blasphemy, or the frivolous mockery of the attitude of the art lover— that works of art are created *ex nihilo*. It calls attention to the fundamental significance of imitation, of copying of models, of repetition in the arts.

This is a very important viewpoint, and the historically authentic continuity in which forgeries are placed right beside imitations, copies, replicas, variations, restorations, pastiches, and the like can indeed be reestablished only by taking this aspect into account. And this is also the viewpoint that might achieve the continuity between the new system of art and its entire history.

The criticism is nevertheless relative. The branch of art theory that most ardently emphasizes the importance of replication, effectively subordinating art history to archaeology by regarding it as the history of things (Kubler's "shape of time"), may be able to reduce the amount of artistic innovations and may suggest a new conception in which aesthetic determinism has greater significance in the majority of cases than do artistic decisions; yet even this art theory cannot deny that there are innovations, or "prime objects," in the history of art, which produce discontinuities.[49]

When forgery criticizes the concept of originality as historical authenticity, it addresses directly the question of the cult of antiquity and in a broader context broaches the relationship of historical authenticity and beauty.

The grievance already voiced in the anecdote of the *Sleeping Cupid,* whereby ancient works of art enjoy an unfair advantage in aesthetic judgment by virtue of their antiquity, is one of the most frequent complaints of artists. In fact, all that a self-confessing forger wants to achieve through his prank is to call attention to this injustice. The early avant-garde movements hoped to do something similar when they did away with the past for good in their manifestos and other symbolic gestures. Of course, the historical and sociohistorical picture of the retrospective and futuristic movements is extremely colorful, along with the increasing and declining authority of the past (with regard to the various periods in particular) and the relationship between contemporary and old art; nevertheless, historical reflection and historical normativity were undoubtedly among the main characteristics of the Renaissance artists' process of intellectualization, as indeed evidenced in the original meaning of word *renaissance* itself. And provided my analysis stands, the aura of historicity, in addition to that of beauty, *and often as an alternative to beauty,* has become the main basis of perception in the modern system of art.

The liberation of art history from connoisseurship, art criticism, and aesthetics is a reflection of this development in a new discipline and a new institution. And much the same way as the methodological predominance of artists' biographies at a given stage of development in this discipline demonstrated the interconnection of originality and individuality, the program of the judgment-free description of stylistic changes, initiated by Alois Riegl (and Franz Wickhoff) at the turn of the century, reflected the process in the course of which antiqueness, independently of the considerations of beauty, assumed the quality of originality in art. When Riegl chose to study a period, for example, the late Antique, the art of which appeared decidedly unattractive to his own age, he tried to achieve the ideals of disinterested scholarship and what they implied: The elimination of personal tastes and preferences. But what he accomplished was something different: He codified the *intrinsic value* of antiqueness as well as anticipating the coming reign of taste completely liberated from considerations of beauty.

With this turn of events (in view of its consequences, rather than that of Riegl's great work) the criticism of forgery finally came of age; and if up till now we have emphasized the *relative* justification of this criticism, from now on we shall talk about its relative *justification*. Artistic value is not necessarily associated with the individual or innovative originality of works of art. When we discuss a person's desperate attempt to be original, we register the individuality or novelty factor of this originality, albeit in a neutral or negative way. Nevertheless, there *is* individuality and there *is* innovation, which has artistic value. Originality as historical authenticity is not an artistic value, but a documentary one, or, in the most general sense, an ontological fact. For us, children of modernity, beauty and historical authenticity *together constitute* the artistic value.

In this broad interpretation, originality as historical authenticity simply means that it is man-made beauty that forms our subject matter. Beauty in itself is not associated with the quality of originality. Natural beauty is not original. Only in the physical sense can the word "original" be applied to a flower or sunset, as opposed to being artificial or painted; in the historical sense it has neither individuality nor novelty nor authenticity. By contrast, works of art have original beauty in the sense that they possess historical origin and individual fate.

These attempts to provide definitions have not been prompted by the futile ambition to capture metaphysically the notion of beauty. Beauty too has a history; beauty too is historical. Although natural beauty has no historical origin, its *discovery* forms part of our story, the same as our historically changing perception of what is beautiful in nature; that is, what types of landscapes or bodies arouse us. Nor is beauty innocent: only its interpretative perception is possible, not its pure comprehension. But the history of beauty is not identical with the history of art, just as our two historical sensibilities, of beauty and of art, are different, even though mutual interaction or interference between them is possible. The history of art might deeply influence the history of beauty, and vice versa. They can mutually document each other. Nevertheless, works of art are born from the tension between historical beauty and historical originality, and when this tension vanishes there will be, on the one side, pure decorativism, and on the other will be the intellectual rule of artistic originality, something that cannot be criticized on the basis of absolutized historicism—the purest form of relativism.

Hence the crisis of modern art. Nevertheless, suffice it to conclude at this point that originality—in and of itself, without beauty—is not the last word and the ultimate value in art in the modern system of art. In this respect the criticism of forgery is justified. And if we have up till now maintained that in the modern system of art originality and forgery complement each other, by virtue of which the latter's criticism of the former can only be relative, there is no need to disavow that statement now; rather, we might be able to elicit certain methodological benefits from the internal character of the criticism.

The ideological message of forgery can be summed up as follows: Who cares about originality if the copy is beautiful (equally beautiful, more beautiful)? Who cares about originality if the copy cannot sensually be discerned from the original? Who cares about the art theory of originality if the practical reality of aesthetics makes fun of it? Let us put aside for the moment those arguments that support the ontological extra of (beautiful) originality, along with the claim that, due to their individual fate, forgeries too become "originals"—in fact quite often nonbeautiful "originals" in the eyes of a later period. In the structure of the questions a certain control of historical beauty over historical originality is discernible; one might even call it the control of historical aesthetics over the philosophical history of art. This is not contradicted by the history of forgery, which could—at least until the second half of our century—have provided material for a historical sociology of beauty. If we take an inventory of the works of art selected by forgers in any particular period, we can more or less form a picture of what the people of that period found beautiful. This critical control does not belong to some higher jurisdiction, as beauty without originality in art is nothing but empty decorativeness, while the discovery of the beauty of originality often takes time. But the tension between the two derives from their mutual control and criticism. Rather than judging a historical entity from some metaphysical aspect, here we have two nonidentical historical aspects mutually controlling each other: The history of beauty and the history of artistic originality. Absolutized historicism is pure relativism, which kills off criticism with its tit-for-tat type of banalities. The formulation of relative critical positions is made possible by the juxtaposition of pluralized *historicisms*. In art, the confrontation of originality and beauty is justified.

Of course, the criticism of forgery is but a satire of all this. We deliberately derived critical conclusions from *forgery,* rather than talking about the criticism of *forgers.* Forgers often regard themselves as mere copiers, the imitators of old periods and styles, or at least that is how they try to excuse themselves. In another typical category of the cases—and this is what should concern us for the moment—the criticism is often no more than a history of grievances, the motifs of which happen to *coincide* with the aspects of originality, the very subject of the criticism. It all starts out from the forger's conviction that his own personality possesses considerable artistic originality, which he is not allowed to develop. The object of revenge: the cult of great names, artistic personalities of the past, with the corresponding cult of the old and the historical, and the cult of innovation even, which is directed however at the rediscovery of old processes—and the false presentation of all this in the present. There was originality in the past therefore, which is missing from the present, and forgery itself has the honor of effecting its nostalgic revival. The true spirit of the original reappears in the forged one: The personality, the novelty, and the history. The *conscious* criticism of the forger is directed at the institutions of the art world, rather than at the entire modern system of art.

The victims of forgery stories are people from the art world. The art collectors, the experts, the curators, the art historians, the art dealers, the art critics, the editors and journalists of art magazines, the art philosophers, the connoisseurs, the amateurs, the dilettanti, the (other) artists, the reproducers of works of art, the government officials working in the field of art patronage, the visitors to museums, the art enthusiasts and lovers, the audience. The forger's grievance is that he resents that all these people, or a group of them, should have the right to determine what is art and what is not; he wants to prove—to himself, to "them," to the world—that their decisions, which have the effect of producing art by "anointing" some objects to be works of art and excluding others from this honor, are arbitrary and unfounded.

What seems peculiar, however, is that art philosophy in a way anticipated this critical phenomenology of the art world, setting it forth positively, rather than critically, in George Dickie's institutional analysis of modern art entitled *Art and the Aesthetics.* His qualifying definition of a work of art is as follows: "1) an artifact, 2) a set of the aspects of which has had conferred upon it the status of candidate for appreciation by some person or persons acting on behalf of a certain social institution (the art world)."[50] Although not as formal, this is similar to the situation where legal status is conferred upon someone: the appointment to an office, the pronouncement of a sentence, the designation of an honorary title, the conferment of marital status, etc. When a product is exhibited in a museum, then that is to be taken as a sure sign of the conferment having taken place. Therefore the paintings made by chimpanzees and gorillas and exhibited in the Field Museum of Natural History of Chicago do not qualify as works of art, but had they been exhibited in the Art Institute only a few miles away, "the painting would have been art if the director had been willing to go out on a limb for his fellow primates."[51] And although in this particular case it was unlikely that the art world would have admitted these "painters" to its ranks, their work would still have qualified as the art of the art establishment and of the person responsible for the decision.

It was most likely due to its involuntary satire and unconscious criticism, as well as to a certain rough and unintentionally cynical realism of the phenomenology, that Dickie's work actually came to enjoy greater attention and exert greater effect than it would have deserved on the basis of the level of its theoretical foundation and productiveness. The theory is based on a contradiction, which has not been resolved or even addressed and which immediately becomes apparent in the context of our theme, whereby the author—in a wholly surprising manner—left the forgeries off the list of possible candidates for the art world's appreciation, that is, from the list of potential art works.[52] He does this simply by adding a further stipulation, which reserved institutional recognition strictly for *original* paintings. He approaches this with the familiar analogy of legality: Once a particular invention is patented, an identical invention is no longer eligible for patent protection.

Despite the fact that Dickie apparently reduces forgery to copying, something that is not borne out by the history of forgery, and although his conception of copies is not compatible with the history of art, we cannot turn a blind eye to the fact that he even contradicts himself when he claims that forgery is nonart, which people nevertheless think of as art. But what other specifications do works of art have in this theory beside the conventions and practices by which people in the art world decide whether something is art? Because if they only had substantive qualities, or even qualities based on diachronic rather than synchronic conventions, then the appointment, conferment, or qualification of the art world could never be the only ground on which to base the definition. But Dickie seems to start out from the claim that it was the appearance (i.e., acceptance and conventionalization) of unconventional works of art that revealed the true nature of art founded on conventions, demonstrating that mimesis and expression are not their essential qualities, and that in fact they have no essential qualities at all. Accepting this, works of art can only be defined on the basis of their actual social context. (Dickie's paradigm is Marcel Duchamp's objet trouvé, *Fountaine*, which is a urinal acquiring the status of work of art by virtue of having a title and being placed in a museum.) With the stipulation of originality (as first), however, a substantive and valuational element has slipped into the classification, contrary to the original proposition of the theory that set itself the task of separating classification and valuation. (This is why, according to the cunningly worded definition, a work of art can only be a *candidate* for appreciation.) Richard Wollheim's illuminating criticism of Dickie's work is based on the skepticism about the possibility of such a radical separation in art.[53]

In his incomparably more sophisticated, impressive, fully developed, and consistent theory (one that has also reflected more on the history of culture), Arthur C. Danto, whose ideas concerning "art world" and "art as an institution,"[54] along with his argument about originality,[55] seem to have exerted a great influence on Dickie, has bravely spelled out all the troublesome consequences of founding one's concept of art *only* on originality. The perceptual indiscernibility of works of art, which nevertheless have fundamentally different conceptual and historical originality, has become the paradigm of his concept of art, of which he has construed dozens of examples. He either eliminates the perceptual conditions of aesthetic reaction or puts it in the service of the *awareness* of a work of art (i.e., the awareness of whether or not something is art). In principle, *every* material thing might have a counterpart in a perceptually identical and indiscernible work of art. In the case of forgery too, everything hinges on the originality of causal historical authenticity, but since "objects do not wear their histories on their surfaces,"[56] the search and emphasis of perceptual differences do not serve the artistic interest. "The eye, so prized an aesthetic organ when it was felt that the difference between art and nonart was visible, was philosophically of no use whatever when the difference proved instead to be invisible."[57] Another radical consequence was the *barbarization* of the concept of beauty (i.e., the material beauty of the object defines the barbarian taste), or its complete elimination. Never before in the history of the humanities has art philosophy broken away from aesthetics so radically.

Forgery has its own criticism for this perspective too: The forger's work presented as something utterly easy, as child's play. The imitation of conceptual originality freed from all sensuality requires no invention whatsoever. In the famous example construed by Danto,[58] a painter, a forger, and a child produce three completely identical objects: three ties painted in a single shade of blue. In contrast with the other two ties, the work-of-art status of the painter's tie is established purely by its historical originality, as well as the reputation of the painter in the art institution. The child who is able to paint a tie blue would *obviously* be unable to copy Piero della Francesca's *Legend of the True Cross* on the wall of his room, Danto points out. Obviously!

Clearly, by introducing a child in this example next to the forger, Danto wishes to answer, in a rather provocative way, the vulgar criticism of modernism that is frequently encountered on the pages of museum guestbooks: *"Even a child could have done this."* Since works of art have history, *this* criticism is stale. I would have to admit, if the task of the reproduction or copying could have been carried out equally successfully by a trained expert (a forger) and an unskilled child, that would have damaged the artistic comprehension or reception. In the aesthetic destruction of indiscernibility the trade of forging becomes doubtful and forgery itself turns into a concept. In a way, the absolutization of originality could turn Dickie's nightmare into reality: criticism (the act of qualifying objects as works of art) would be forced to do the job of a patentor. In this case the *following of patterns*, the *repetition*, the *copying*—these secret upholders of the continuity of art—would be disqualified as potential works of art.

Notes

1. Adolf Furtwaengler, *Neuere Fälschungen von Antiken* (Berlin: Giesecke & Devrient, 1899), 1.

2. Peter Metz, "Echt oder falsch? Eine Studie über Grundsätzliches" in *Festschrift Karl Oettinger,* ed. Hans Sedlmayr and Wilhelm Messerer (Erlangen, 1967), 466. He claims in the same study that the nineteenth century could produce only Renaissance forgeries, because they were closest to its own traditions: ". . . any artist living after the close of the medieval age should be completely incapable of recreating the medieval's relationship towards the human body" (472). However, the catalog raisonneé compiled by him for a sculpture gallery that opened in Berlin-Dahlem in 1966 (*Bildwerke der christlichen Epochen von der Spätantike bis zum Klassizismus* [Munich: Prestel, 1966]) featured a number of small multifigural sculptures made of ivory under catalog numbers 279–281 (64), which a few years later came to be identified as the works of a major forger or a Romantic retrospective artist from the early nineteenth century, and subsequently were exhibited in the forgery exhibi-

tion of Essen. Cf. *Fälschung und Forschung*. Ausstellung Museum Folkwang Essen, October 1976–January 1977, Skulpturengalerie Staatliche Museen Preußischer Kulturbesitz Berlin, January–March 1977, 60. Cf. NS [Neil Stratford], "Gothic Ivory Fakes" in *Fake? The Art of Deception,* ed. Mark Jones (Berkeley: University of California Press, 1990), 180.

3. Furtwaengler, op. cit., 38. The compiler of Corot's oeuvre catalog, Alfred Robaut is said to have delivered the following attack on a particular expert: "Oh, the idiot of the idiots . . . this stupid expert deserves to have his eyes scratched out. . . . What fools! They are able to recognize not a single genuine and original work!" Quoted in Frank Arnau, *Kunst der Fälscher, Fälscher der Kunst* (Düsseldorf: Econ, 1960), 323.

4. Clive Bell, *Art* (London: Chatto & Windus, 1949), 37.

5. Cf. Guillaume Apollinaire, "Des Faux" in Apollinaire, *Oeuvres en prose completes II* (Paris: Gallimard, Pléiade, 1991), 74ff. (The article was published in the April 1, 1903 issue of *La Revue blanche*).

6. Cf. Heinrich Dilly, *Kunstgeschichte als Institution* (Frankfurt: Suhrkamp, 1979), 165ff. It was not the intention of the 14 art historians—among them Moritz Thausing and Wilhelm von Bode—to rule in a forgery case. They set themselves the task of deciding which one of the two versions of *The Virgin with the Mayor Meyer* was the original: The one held in Dresden or the one in Darmstadt? This incident, the object of great publicity, was mentioned by Apollinaire as well; only he emphasized the positive aspect of the verdict: The Germans did not throw out their *Dresden Madonna* (op. cit., 75).

7. Jakob Burckhardt, "Über die Echtheit alter Bilder" in Burckhardt, *Die Kunst der Betrachtung. Aufsätze und Vorträge zur bildenden Kunst* (Cologne: Du-Mont, 1984), 291.

8. Ibid.

9. Immanuel Kant, *Kritik der Urteilskraft. Werkausgabe* Bd. X (Frankfurt: Suhrkamp), 231ff., 42§.

10. Cf. Erwin Panofsky, "Kopie oder Fälschung. Ein Beitrag zur Kritik einiger Zeichnungen aus der Werkstatt Michelangelos," *Zeitschrift für bildende Kunst* 61 (1927).

11. Alfred Lessing, "What is Wrong with a Forgery?" in *The Forgers Art,* ed. Denis Dutton (Berkeley: University of California Press, 1983), 66.

12. Ibid., 74.

13. Ibid., 76.

14. Cf. Karina Türr, *Fälschungen antiker Plastik seit 1800* (Berlin: Mann, 1984), 184ff., 98f., and 85ff. There is an interesting hypothesis that tries to prove that *The Fortune-Teller* (Metropolitan Museum, New York), one of the most famous paintings by Georges de la Tour, is a twentieth-century forgery, using, among others, considerations of fashion history: "From the point of view of dress, or in broader terms, style, it is almost impossible for a painting to escape the fashion of the time in which it was painted." Christopher Wright, *The Art of the Forger* (London: Gordon Fraser, 1984), 63.

15. Max J. Friedländer, "Die Madonna mit der Wickenblüte," *Zeitschrift für bildende Kunst* 45 (1909): 278.

16. Should Christopher Wright's earlier-mentioned hypothesis turn out to be true, then, in addition to his *Fortune-Teller,* La Tour's *Magdalena* (New York, Metropolitan) and Sharper (Louvre) would also have to be ascribed to a twentieth-century forger, along with one of Petrus Christus' best-known paintings, *In St. Eligius' Goldsmithery* (New York, Metropolitan), as well as several of his lesser known works. Furthermore, through his choice of themes and provocative ideas, the same forger would give evidence of a singularly roguish mind: The second gypsy girl on the left in the group of characters in *Fortune-Teller* wears a neckerchief with the words MERDE written on it. Cf. Wright, op. cit., passim and 67. (At the La Tour retrospective of Paris in 1997 the word wasn't perceivable on the picture.) Also, it has recently been suggested by an art historian (Federico Zeri) that the *Ludovisi Throne,* held in Museo Nazionale of Rome—one of the most precious examples of Classical Greek plastic art and one of the favorite artworks of the author of this book— is actually the work of a nineteenth-century forger. Cf. Luigi A. Ronzoni, "Kopien antiken Originale im Wandel der Zeit," *Original Kopie—Parnass Sonderheft* 7: 34.

17. Cf. Bernard Ashmole, *Forgeries of Ancient Sculpture: Creation and Detection.* The First J. L. Myres Memorial Lecture (Oxford, 1961), 4ff.

18. Cf. Norbert Kunisch, "Antikenfälschungen" in *Fälschung und Forschung,* op. cit., 20ff.

19. Ibid., 273.

20. Hans Tietze, *Genuine and False: Copies, Imitations, Forgeries* (London: Max Parrish, n.d. [1948]), 72.

21. Cf. Hans Tietze, "Zur Psychologie und Ästhetik der Kunstfälschung," *Zeitschrift für Ästhetik und allgemeine Kunstwissenschaft* 27 (1933): 231f.

22. Cf. his oeuvre catalog: William Voelkle, *The Spanish Forger* (New York: Pierpont Morgan Library, 1978).

23. Cf. Harold L. Petersen, *How to Tell If It's Fake: Trade Secrets Revealed for Antique Collectors and Dealers* (New York: Scribner's, 1975), 159. "Have you ever thought of collecting forgeries? I know a man in Italy who collects them. First as a hobby, and now he sells them to other collectors at quite high prices." Patricia Highsmith, *Ripley Under Ground* (New York: 1st Vintage Crime/Black Lizard, 1992 [1970]), 61.

24. Cf. Michael Wreen, "Is, Madam? Nay, It Seems!" in *The Forger's Art* (Dutton, op. cit.), 213.

25. Erwin Panofsky, "Introductory (Iconography and Iconology: An Introduction to the Study of Renaissance Art)." In *Studies in Iconology* (New York: Icon/Harper & Row, 1974 [1939]), 11.

26. Cf. *Fake?* (Jones, op. cit.), 34 and 196ff.

27. Catalog: *Fälschung und Forschung* and *Fake?* (Jones, op. cit.). The other type of forgery exhibition is designed to be educational. See, for example, *Fakes and Forgeries* (Minneapolis Institute of Arts, 1973).

28. János György Szilágyi, *Legbölcsebb az idö. Antik vázák hamisítványai* ("Time: The Wisest of Them All. The Forgery of Antique Vases") (Budapest: Corvina, 1987). For its appraisal and criticism see section 3 of chapter IV.

29. Cf. Hans-Georg Gadamer, *Wahrheit und Methode* (Tübingen: Mohr [Paul Siebeck], 1975); and Hans-Georg Gadamer, "Die Universalität des hermeneutischen Problems," in *Kleine Schriften I. Philosophie • Hermeneutik* (Tübingen: Mohr, 1976), 102.

30. In 1980 there was a court trial in the case of forging old photographs, where the forger's defense was that he "had wanted to demonstrate that collectors and dealers in Victorian photography equate age with beauty." M. H. B. [Mark Haworth-Booth], "Howard Grey and Graham Ovenden's fake 'Victorian' photos." In *Fake?* (Jones, op. cit.), 244f.

31. *Fake?* (Jones, op. cit.), 119.

32. Hans Belting, *Bild und Kult. Eine Geschichte des Bildes vor dem Zeitalter der Kunst* (Munich: Beck, 1990), 492. It is not pertinent to my subject, nor does it come under my competence, to discuss what theological antinomies the undeniable representative and imitative realism of medieval cultic pictures lead to or express.

33. Ibid., 496.

34. Ibid., 524.

35. Ibid., 538. Also see 544f.

36. Quoted by Richard E. Spear, "Notes on Renaissance and Baroque Originals and Originality," in *Retaining the Original: Multiple Originals, Copies and Reproductions. Studies in the History of Art,* Vol. 20 (Washington, DC: National Gallery of Art, 1989), 97.

37. Compiled by Klaus Döhmer, "Zur Soziologie der Kunstfälschung," in *Zeitschrift für Ästhetik und allgemeine Kunstwissenschaft* 23, no. 1 (1978): 81.

38. An unpublished dissertation from Budapest sums up the incident and also provides a concise bibliography: Zoltán Csehi, *Albrecht Dürer és a szerzői jog* ("Albrecht Dürer and the Copyright"), 1992.

39. Cf. Francis Haskell, "A Martyr of Attributionism. Morris Moore and the Louvre *Apollo and Marsyas,*" in *Past and Present in Art and Taste* (New Haven, CT: Yale University Press, 1987), 155ff.

40. László Mravik, "Pulszky Károly müve" ("The Work of Károly Pulszky), in *Pulszky Károly emlékének* ("In Memory of Károly Pulszky"), ed. László Mravik (Budapest: Szépmüvészeti Múzeum, 1988), 12f. With the phrase of Francis Haskell, we can also name Pulszky a martyr of attributionism. Due to his persecution he had a nervous breakdown; later in 1899 he went into exile in Australia and committed suicide.

41. Cf. *Fake?* (Jones, op. cit.), 130.

42. Stichting Foundation Rembrandt Research Project: *A Corpus of Rembrandt Painting,* Vol. I (The Hague, Netherlands: Martinus Nijhoff, 1982; Vols. II–III, Dordrecht, Netherlands: Martinus Nijhoff, 1986, 1989).

43. Cf. [Caroline Elam] "The Rembrandt Re-Trial" (Editorial), *Burlington Magazine* 84, no. 1070 (1992): 285.

44. Cf. Nelson Goodman, *Languages of Art—An Approach to a Theory of Symbols* (Indianapolis, IN: Bobbs-Merrill, 1968), 121. This issue will be discussed in more detail in chapters 4 and 5.

45. Cf. Fabrizio Mancinelli, "The Problem of Michelangelo's Assistants," in

Michael Hirst et al., *The Sistine Chapel: A Glorious Restoration* (New York: Abrams, 1994). The cooperative nature of sixteenth-century workshops was absolutely prevalent. There was nothing peculiar about Veronese's work method, for example; after having determined the composition, he left the major artistic tasks to be carried out by his assistants and family members, reserving for himself only the execution of the finest and most important details. The problems began only after the master's death, with his workshop still continuing to produce "Veronese works." Cf. Beverly Louise Brown, "Replication and the Art of Veronese," in *Retaining the Original* (op. cit.), 111ff.

46. Cf. Burckhardt, op. cit.

47. Cf. John Gash, "Rembrandt or Not?," *Art in America* (January 1993): 58.

48. George Kubler, "Towards a Reductive Theory of Visual Style," in *The Concept of Style,* ed. Berel Lang (Philadelphia: University of Pennsylvania Press, 1979).

49. Cf. George Kubler, *The Shape of Time: Remarks on the History of Things* (New Haven, CT: Yale University Press, 1962), 40. See my essay on Kubler, "Vis a tergo. George Kubler Az idö formája cimü könyve—harminc év múltán" ("Vis a tergo. George Kubler's *The Shape of Time*—After Thirty Years"), which was published as the afterword of the Hungarian edition: George Kubler, *Az idö formája. Megjegyzések a tárgyak történetéröl* ("The Shape of Time: Remarks on the History of Things") (Budapest: Gondolat, 1992). In German: "Vis a tergo. George Kublers Buch 'Die Form der Zeit'—dreißig Jahre später," *Zeitschrift für Ästhetik und allgemeine Kunstwissenschaft* 39, no. 2 (1994).

50. George Dickie, *Art and Aesthetics: An Institutional Analysis* (Ithaca, NY: Cornell University Press, 1974), 34 and 179f.

51. Ibid., 46.

52. Ibid., 47ff.

53. Cf. Richard Wollheim, "The Institutional Theory of Art, I. Essay," in *Art and its Objects: With Six Supplementary Essays* (Cambridge, UK: Cambridge University Press/Canto Edition, 1992).

54. Cf. Arthur C. Danto, "The Artworld" (1964), in *Art and its Significance: An Anthology of Aesthetic Theory,* ed. Stephen David Ross (Albany: State University of New York Press, 1994), 470ff. Danto himself does not subscribe to Dickie's institutional theory, partly because of its sociologizing empiricism, and partly because of the fact that it yields a noncognitive theory of art that is fundamentally opposed to Danto's intentions. He thinks that Dickie must have misunderstood the following frequently quoted sentence from his study: "To see something as art requires something the eye cannot decry— an atmosphere of artistic theory, a knowledge of the history of art: an art world," Ibid., 477. Cf. Danto, "The Art World Revisited. Comedies of Similarity," in Danto, *Beyond the Brillo Box. The Visual Arts in Post-Historical Perspective* (New York: Farrar, Strauss, Giroux, 1992), 33ff. For Dickie's reply ("A Tale of Two Artworlds") and Danto's counterreply ("Responses and Replies") see *Danto and His Critics,* ed. Mark Rollins (Oxford UK: Blackwell, 1993), 73ff. and 203ff.

55. Cf. Arthur C. Danto, "Art Works and Real Things," *Theoria* 39 (1973):1ff.

56. Arthur C. Danto, Chapter 2, "Content and Causation," in *The Transfiguration of the Commonplace* (Cambridge, MA: Harvard University Press, 1981), 44.

57. *Beyond the Brillo Box* (Danto, op. cit.), 5.

58. Cf. Chapter 4 of this book, in which the modern philosophical discourse on forgery is discussed.

3

THE COPY

— The Historical Types of Pattern Maintenance —

What is wrong with copying works of art? The answer is not as obvious as it was in the case of the analogous question about forgeries (although even with forgeries, a prudent answer does not require the presumption that forgeries are always, and a priori, bad). The apparent reason for this is that copying has none, or at least fewer, of the moral connotations associated with forgery. Still, assuming that copying is "wrong," then it is obviously the lack of *originality,* and that in the sense of *novelty,* which elicits our disapproval. Another reason for our finding fault with copying is that it violates the principles of the individual artwork's incommutability, nonsubstitutability, and uniqueness. Although not as pronounced as in forgery, there is something provocative in copying. Who—or what—is being provoked? This is the subject I would like to address next.

For this purpose, I would like to summon the help of an art philosopher whose testimony is rendered all the more interesting by the fact that he is striving for a paradigmatic revolution in art: A revolution that is to be based on the advancement of copying and the priority of copies being mass-produced for the masses. I am talking about Walter Benjamin and his famous (and highly problematic) study, *The Work of Art—In the Age of Technical Reproducibility.*[1] We learn from this work that copies and reproductions (in general, rather than merely their technical types) undermine the *authenticity* of artworks, which is the same as saying that they subvert the "here and now" of the original, "its unique existence in the actual place it happens to be."[2] Benjamin's notion of authenticity (*Echtheit*) also encompasses the entire history of the artwork, laying special emphasis, of all its possible components, on the changes taking place in the physical state and conditions of ownership of the artwork. To this line of argument he appended the following important footnote: "Precisely for the fact that authenticity cannot be reproduced, the intensive advance of certain copying methods—of a technical nature—helped differentiate between the various grades of authenticity. One of the important functions of the art business was the establishment of such differentiation. . . . We might say that with the invention of woodblock printing the quality of authenticity was attacked at its roots, before it was able to burst belatedly into blossom. At the time of its making, a medieval Madonna was still not 'authentic,' and only became that in the course of subsequent centuries, in the last century perhaps more intensively than at any time before."[3]

Commenting on this particular passage, Hans Robert Jauß observes that it contradicts the definition of authenticity that Benjamin himself had given earlier and that therefore can have no general applicability in the history of art.[4] And indeed, when Benjamin, in his own aphoristic style, talks about authenticity, he does so at times in the ontological sense, as if it had general relevance to *every* object ("the authenticity of an object is inherent in the totality of all its intrinsically transmittable aspects, from its material permanence right down to its historical testimony"[5]), and at others in the sense of attributing a characteristic historical role to authenticity, one which is connected to the belated blossoming mentioned earlier, when the various techniques of copying undermine material permanence and in consequence also endanger the historical testimony of the works. According to Benjamin, this danger sparks off the consciousness of the works: This is why "authenticity" belongs to the modern world of art.

According to the crucial category of Benjamin's aesthetic theory, this concept of authenticity is *aural*. By endangering authenticity and uniqueness, and thereby threatening tradition itself, copies strive to annihilate the aura of the artworks as similarly reproductions do, which weaken the original production so to speak. The main effect of the aura is that, suddenly and in a revelatory manner, the distance inherent in all these notions—authenticity, uniqueness, traditions, and the like—is evoked in the aesthetic experience of the isolated individual. For Benjamin, the aura is the depository of aesthetic *autonomy*, the hallmark of classic bourgeois art. Ever since the Renaissance, works of art have been perceived on the basis of their *exposi-tional,* rather than their *cultic,* value. When art loses its special social functions it then becomes autonomous. For Benjamin, the premod-ern function of art is always cultic: To this extent he (along with Max Weber and, among his contemporaries, Karl Löwith) regards modern-ization as a form of *secularization.*[6] This, of course, amounts to the reduction of the premodern functions of art, since it altogether disre-gards the roles art had in entertainment, ornamentation, and play, and also fails to include all the tasks it performed in the representa-tion of the power structure, not to mention the fact that its functions in displaying normative lifestyles were not necessarily contained in the cultic and ritual practices. Nevertheless, in Benjamin's view, it is the aura that secures the continuity of art, insofar as it *reminds* us of the ritualistic functions art once had.

Notwithstanding the numerous clever reconstructions of "Benjaminology" in the past decades, we have to come to terms with the fact that Benjamin uses the notion of aura in a similarly contra-dictory sense—in terms of the philosophy of history and ontology—not to mention the fact that he occasionally applies it to cultic and ritualistic premodern art.[7] The gist of the above brief reconstruction is that Benjamin essentially regards the aura, within the context of the bourgeois *art-religion,* as the unique atmosphere of a work of art, which has the distinctive property of being destroyed by copying or reproduction. Benjamin's text has something of the flavor of a funeral oratory given by a resigned person of Romantic or conservative per-suasion, occasioned by the burial of modern ideas of art and beauty—a characteristic we cannot help noticing elsewhere in his impressive, albeit incomplete, oeuvre. Yet those familiar with Benjamin's line of reasoning know that after this point there comes a major turn in his essay, amounting to the questioning of beauty and other timeless val-ues, the defense of the primacy of anti-Classical culture (the counter-currents of classical culture were something Benjamin passionately researched throughout his life), and the earnest welcome of a barbaric new culture (the most widespread manifestations of which are the movies, which provide popular entertainment) opposed to the aes-theticism of contemporary culture.[8] From this perspective everything is dialectically turned upside down: The autonomy of art proves to be an illusion, the aura turns out to be "the 'spiritualization' of the com-modity fetishism,"[9] the expositional value appears as "the imago of the barter process,"[10] and authenticity and uniqueness and (contin-uous) tradition seem to be the private features (in opposition to the collective experience) of the bourgeois world.

It is not my aim to criticize Benjamin's critical analysis. I am not concerned with the disturbing illusion and—to the observation and experience of my contemporaries—terrible perspective that lies behind the idea of responding to the fascist aestheticizing of politics by the Communist politicizing and refunctionalizing of the arts. Instead, I am interested in Benjamin's cultural–historical (rather than ontological) starting point, which associates the destructive nature of copies with the modern system of art.

Of course, when one thinks about the extraordinary influence Romantic cultural philosophy exerted on the young Benjamin, one tends to identify the entire problematic of authenticity and uniqueness with the Romantic paradigm that is responsible for the cult of these notions and (allegedly—although this *itself* is a Romantic idea) is also responsible for the creation of the notions themselves. The historical truth is, however, that the notion of originality struck root not in the age of Romanticism, but during the eighteenth-century debate on imitation versus creation, reaching its climax in the genius-cult. The greatest influence was generated by Edward Young's essay entitled "Conjectures on Original Composition" (1759), with its complete rejection of imitation, not sparing such "imitators" and "copiers" as Pope, Ben Jonson, or Dryden. More precisely, "Imitations are two kinds; one of nature, one of authors: the first we call 'originals' and confine the term 'imitation' to the second."[11]

As is well known, the symbolic line of demarcation in the debate lay between the French dramatists copying the antique playwrights on the one hand, and Shakespeare on the other, whose distinctive "originality" was explained by his having eyes for nature only.[12] For one thing, this contrast mobilized a much larger segment of culture than could possibly be termed "Romantic"; in addition, and in total disagreement with the popular concept about Romanticism, the greatest Romantics had strong reservations about the pure types of "Originalgenie" and "Naturgenie," assigning too much importance to tradition to be able to accept uncritically the preconditions of the genius age, which were characterized both by the rejection of pattern-maintenance and, what is even more extreme (albeit plainly visible in the case of Young, and even of Lessing), by reservations about the limited potentials of teaching and learning. During the period 1795–1797, when Friedrich Schlegel described the characteristics of modernity in his essay "On the Study of Greek Poetry," he ridiculed equally the reverence towards unconditional originality as a mystical oracle and the rule of copying works of art sanctioned by authoritarian principles; but most of all he ridiculed the alternative itself.[13]

In view of the fact that the new system of modern art, which had been in the making ever since the Renaissance, was a theoretical construct of the great aesthetic debates of the eighteenth century, Benjamin's suspicions regarding the destructive influence of reproduction and copying on the art of the *entire* modern age do not seem unfounded; additionally, it was in this modern system that the uniqueness of the work of art acquired a distinctive significance. The complexity of this phenomenon—or the dialectics of it, if you like—was much greater than Benjamin had depicted: In copying and reproduction alike, destructivity and constructivity are present simultaneously and are often found to be trading roles. For example, it is undeniable that copying undermines the individuality of the original; equally undeniable, however, is that by their large-scale distribution, copies actually serve the originals by helping to found their individuality. The dynamics of modernity are based on the continuous corrosion of artistic conventions; contrary to Benjamin's views, copying disrupts this process to the same extent that it sustains convention. Reproduction and copying might have just as much importance in the dismissal of the aura as they have in its preservation.

The early reproductive techniques could hardly serve as *replacement* for all these processes. Benjamin's theoretical objective of opposing nonfunctional, aural art (which has replaced functional—or cultic—art) with another, politically functional and technological art leads to the unjustifiably close linking of otherwise unrelated technological discoveries (the early copying process, photography, and motion picture), not to mention the fact that in the case of those *art forms* that are *based* on reproductive techniques, the distinction between original and copy either makes no sense at all or is fundamentally different from what we are accustomed to in the case of the "one-off copy" genres—genres not *designed* for serial copies. (Marcantonio Raimondi, for example, did copy Dürer's original woodcuts. But the individual sheets of the series printed by Dürer are neither reproductions nor copies, in the sense that their original can be defined. The "original" in this case is the woodblock, which is still not an *artwork*, but becomes *that* in its capacity as a copy, and only as a copy. The same could be said about the negatives of photographs or motion pictures.)

By itself, however, this fact does not imply that a work of art that is originally intended to be copied should also lose its autonomy and aura. Even from a historical point of view, the argument establishing a close connection between the problem of authenticity/originality and the reproduction by printing would not hold: ". . . the workshop of production of replicas and flood of good copies raised the problem independently of prints."[14]

In other respects too the argument on which Benjamin founded his conjecture appears—to my mind at least—as a complete fallacy. "The individuality of a work of art is equivalent to its embedment in the interconnections of tradition," he claims.[15] I think precisely the opposite is true—that the growing awareness of individuality can be linked to the abandonment of the interconnections of tradition, while the *deliberate* cultural practice of pattern maintaining copying, replica, and reproduction is intimately bound up with the growing awareness of tradition. So much so that the *first* great coming-to-awareness of tradition was manifested in the copying of another culture. "This happened, first, when the Romans adopted classical Greek thought and culture as their own spiritual tradition and thereby decided historically that tradition was to have a permanent formative influence on European civilization. Before the Romans such a thing as tradition was unknown; with them it became and after them it remained the guiding thread through the past and the chain to which each new generation knowingly or unknowingly was bound in its understanding of the world and its own experience."[16]

In the literature on the Roman copies of Greek art, there has been an ongoing debate ever since the end of the last century about the extent to which lost originals can be reconstructed on the basis of copies, or—what amounts to an extension or theoretical generalization of the above problem—how much originality can be attributed to the Roman copies. "From Winckelmann to Furtwängler, Roman copies were used without hesitation as direct sources for our knowledge of Greek art."[17] If I read the situation correctly, the view that only attributes mechanical and exact copies to Roman art is to be regarded as outdated, and it is also debatable whether all the Greek masterpieces have been copied by the Romans. The next open question concerns the copiers' motives: Whether they were driven by pragmatic considerations or considerations of quality. In other words, whether their primary motive was respect for a particular work of art or its ready adaptability to the new context.

A new hermeneutics in the interpretation of copies has been gaining ground, according to which new, albeit assimilative, original works are created through the imitation, or emulation, of the prototypes.[18] Heidegger's exposition of the fundamental differences resulting from the Roman "translation" of Greek notions[19] can also be applied to the field of art, where Greek sculptures were "translated" (i.e., adapted) into the cultic statues of Roman gods.[20] The tendency of opinion towards the growing independence that Roman fine art maintained in relation to the Greek—whether we regard it as a critical revaluation or overvaluation—has gathered speed since the beginning of the century. Yet it cannot alter the fact that the extremely wide-spread custom of copying, which came as a consequence of the Hellenization of Roman culture and was practiced continuously for 500 years (and, of course, carried on with varying intensity throughout history, eventually being extended to the copying of Roman adaptations themselves, not just the Greek originals) initiated a pattern-maintaining cultural practice that was closely connected to a selective approach to traditions—that is to say, their *deliberate adaptation* as opposed to (or in conjunction with) their natural transmission.

The above quote from Arendt is applicable to this practice as well. In fact, one of the fundamentally important aspects of this new development, as a consequence of which tradition came to be seen as tradition, rather than an accustomed, natural procedure or some holy truth, lay precisely in the fact that Roman copies no longer had the same function as their Greek originals. Even when a copy kept its cultic purpose, it was a different cult; and when copies were invested with other purposes or interests, whether political, decorative, or merely extravagant, the purpose of forming a fitting arrangement with the building or the garden, the modified interest of the theme, the portraiture, and last but not least, the reputation of the original, themselves often redefined the functions of the artworks. In addition to the selective and deliberate method of pattern maintenance, there has, of course, prevailed throughout the entire history of culture a more evident, less deliberate, and more traditional method, which appears as an adjustment to tradition only from without, because from within it has no alternative. This was how a readily available form was imitated and copied for thousands of years, or a picture of cultic significance was repeated over many centuries. Copying and repetition has a sustaining role in preliterate cultures—cultures communicating only verbally. It is when copying means a choice between alternatives (and, consequently, when traditions are more or less looked upon as traditions) that we are badly in need of an extensive vocabulary of fine distinctions to differentiate between "servile" duplications and multiplications, or reproductions easily identifiable with the original. Such a vocabulary was put together by Georg Lippold (and has remained in use to this day), in which he drew a distinction between the copy, replica, repetition, type, original, change of stylization, transformation, change of creation, development, contamination, use, and reuse in the art of Roman copies.[21]

It follows from the above considerations that a distinction should be made between the *traditional* and the *traditionalist* forms of pattern maintenance. European traditionalism was introduced by Roman culture and has been in existence more or less continuously ever since; as for traditional pattern maintenance, this has fundamental importance in most premodern cultures, and has even survived into the modern age—often unconsciously, or as a form of learning, or as part of the conservative trends that view the past with unreflecting reverence. Nevertheless, as this respect diminishes and becomes the subject of criticism (this criticism always reflects the passing or impossibility of the evident trust and respect enjoyed by tradition), an increase can be observed in the role of the traditionalist movements that partake in the debate on tradition, which pick and choose among tradition's offerings but that ideologically approach the continuous existence of tradition. In this respect, modern art is different from premodern art not in that it copies less, but in that it copies from more numerous sources and, as a result, also from a much broader scale of variations. At the same time, the most recent period can be regarded—in the aesthetic sense as well—as the age of the mass-produced exact copy (designed industrial objects, tourists' souvenirs, and the like). Of course, there may also exist individually made exact copies of artistic purpose. With regard to these, it might not always be possible to determine whether their makers considered the model as something given or something to select; whether they were motivated by a naive respect for tradition or by the kind of intellectual relationship that characterizes the so-called "appropriation art"; but this difference exists and invariably becomes evident in a broader context.

The traditional and traditionalist forms of pattern maintenance together do not extend over the entire culture of copying, not even in the generalized sense that we are now discussing. The selection and copying of patterns has a radically actualizing mode, which somehow transforms the model into reality and is definitely antitraditional, yet at the same time is also opposed to all forms of traditionalism. On the one hand it does not share the premodern, natural, and a priori existing authority of the former, and on the other hand it definitely opposes the latter's attempts to create the continuity of tradition. This was how the French Revolution came to copy the forms of antique Rome, going about it in a manner that was, indeed, reminiscent of "a tiger's leap into the past," as Benjamin referred to the event in his famous theses on the philosophy of history. "The French Revolution saw itself as the reincarnation of Rome."[22] Smashing the fetters of tradition is a radical gesture that generally involves the forcible abolition of certain parts of the past, and people usually get more engaged in this than in the revived past.

In any case, the revolutionaries of art (and society) are distinguished from others in most cases not by their opposition to copying and pattern maintenance, but by that characteristic discontinuity that drives them to patterns ever more distant in either space or time.

In her essay cited earlier, Hannah Arendt considers the Renaissance itself as a radical and discontinuous backward leap and return to the past, since it was characterized not so much by designating a segment of history as history as by imagining the rebirth of that segment of history. "The discovery of antiquity in the Renaissance was a first attempt to break the fetters of tradition, and by going to the sources themselves to establish a past over which tradition would have no hold."[23] This clear-cut picture was modified by the more complex nature of the Renaissance, by the scenario in which the tradition of Christian religious culture was not abolished completely and in which, at least on Italian soil, the antique tradition continued to survive to a certain extent. Still, apart from the traditional and traditionalist components of Renaissance culture, there is this other element that Arendt mentions, that either abolishes the past or experiences it as present. If Panofsky's remark about sixteenth-century man's inability to recognize the fundamental difference between the "*buona maniera greca antica*" and the "*moderno si glorioso*" (and the copying of the two could evidently be combined in a single piece)[24] is correct, then the above-mentioned incarnation did indeed take place in the cultural imagination of an era.

No other theoretician or art critic has probably ever been as preoccupied with the problems of reproduction, copying, pastiche, and "nonoriginality" as Benjamin was; and it was his essay resulting from this preoccupation that placed this problem at the center of attention. A work of art consisting of nothing but quotes—copied texts—was his critical ideal. Benjamin's alliance with Brecht, the literary genius noted for his extensive copying, was not unrelated to his reception of the Baroque and Romantic revivals of earlier, and largely forgotten, nontragic drama of anti-Classical origins, concentrating on *poetae minores*. Brecht's anti-Classical ideas and antitragic approach, as evidenced for example in his preferring Lenz to Goethe, radically actualized, in the artistic practice, the hidden tradition that Benjamin exposed in theory and presented as having current relevance. However, the fragmentariness and incongruity that characterizes Benjamin's oeuvre can be explained, among other things, by his failure to separate clearly the radical choice of traditions intended to disrupt continuity on the one hand, and the traditionalism reconstituting continuity on the other. With the exception of the radical fundamentalist movements, traditionalism in the twentieth century cannot mean exclusive identification with any one of the available traditions, yet Benjamin's traditionalism became unmistakably tinted with Jewish mysticism and messianic expectations. (This is symbolized by his other great friendship and alliance: the one that bound him to Gershom Scholem, the classic twentieth-century author of Jewish scholarship and outlook.) His experiments often attempted to reconcile the "tiger's leap" into the past with traditionalism. This must have been the reason why, in the structure of his thinking, Benjamin remained close throughout his life to that historical school that had exerted the greatest influence on him in his youth: Romanticism. And this is also the explanation for the irreconcilable radicalism and conservatism in his reproducibility study.

——— Artistic and Referential Reproduction ———

The relevance of the three ways of relating to tradition that I have outlined above extends far beyond the specific problem of copying. Nevertheless, in view of the fact that in each of the mentioned types copying forms at least one of the representative cultural norms, the question arises whether we should assign a general interpretation to it. This was what George Kubler attempted to do in his book, *The Shape of Time.* According to it, copying (or to use Kubler's expression, "replication") fills history, "prolongs the stability of many past moments, allowing sense and pattern to emerge for us wherever we look. The stability, however, is imperfect. Every man-made replica varies from its model by minute, unplanned divergences, of which the accumulated effects are like a slow drift away from the archetype."[25] Copying is one of the most fundamental cultural pursuits (and it occurs incomparably more frequently than innovation), due to the "reproductive powers appearing to reside in things,"[26] whose protraction can be secured only by replication. The maintenance of convention is based on the method of copying.

Ever since the genius age (1760–1780), our awareness of the above "rule" has been gradually diminishing (almost to the point of extinction, so to speak), which is connected not so much to the declining practice of copying as to the custom of placing the major artworks of the past in public collections, as well as to the establishment and growing number of public museums and the eventual realization of the imaginary museum, the belated diagnosis of which being given by André Malraux. Paradoxically, the establishment of this museum without walls, which is to be put together by using the materials of various local museums and other monuments, requires as its precondition the availability and widespread circulation of the copies of the major works of the most diverse artistic traditions, allowing the high points of the entirety of culture to become visible, so to speak; the visual world of educated people, but increasingly also of the masses, should have an extremely trimmed catalogue, the entries of which they can retrieve from the mind. The pluralization and general spread of traditions loosen, or even sever, those threads that tie a major artwork to its antecedents or original context, reinforcing the false illusion that art is made up of monadic artworks. Copying and imitation, variation and the emulation of patterns, which make up the most important media of this context, all fade away, become peripheral, or vanish altogether from public attention. For this, too, copies and reproductions are responsible, since no one can actually see the original of each entry in the above-mentioned catalog, trimmed as it may be. These are circulated with the help of books and picture postcards, or formerly—when they were still fashionable—museums featuring plaster copies, which were then replaced by television documentaries, slides, and most importantly, the products of the advertising industry. The function of the picture postcards, including those sold on location, is to provide orientation: To provide advance warning at the railway stations, hotels, and souvenir shops regarding what *must* be seen.

I have assigned the term *referential reproductions* to the copies listed above. It is precisely the *referential* character that the individual copies made by the artists themselves lose. In the mind of the public, which can keep track of only a limited number of "originals," the connection between works of art held in museums located far apart mostly remains unnoticed, except for the case when the artist himself calls attention to this by his choice of theme. When this is the case, the quality of originality that used to be guaranteed mostly by the cult is now certified by the provocation. And if we now leave behind the construction or deconstruction of the canon and return to the humble art of copying, then we shall see that any of the cheap copies on permanent display in the intimacy of people's home museums—even the commercially produced series—preserve or acquire some kind of an individuality lingering between personal memory and aesthetic experience.

By contrast, a referential reproduction turns into a glass sheet that imperceptibly separates the viewers from the original. It gradually becomes neutralized, losing its individuality. We know that it is a reproduction, yet it puts us in immediate contact with the original. This has three conditions: The first one is the obvious difference in the medium or material. This was the case, for example, with the serially produced plaster copies of the nineteenth century. The second condition is the advances made in the technology of reproduction, their increasing faithfulness, and in part, our growing acceptance of the delusion of the deindividualization of the copy. The delusion in this case concerns not the lack of individuality, but the assumption that the deindividualization extends *only* to the copy and stops short of the original. In fact, as far as facture, depths, etc., are concerned, it even annihilates the works themselves.[27] The third condition is that the reproductions may not be assumed to have a separate creator. The development of the technology of mass-produced reproductions does, indeed, have a crucial role in providing these conditions.[28]

The distinction between referential reproductions on the one hand and copies retaining a certain measure of individuality on the other—although for a long while remaining relative—has been in existence ever since the spread of printed books. It is true that initially, equal importance was attached to the three genres of graphic arts—drawings, original prints, and reproduced prints—and it was not before the seventeenth century in France and the eighteenth century in the rest of Europe that the civilizing (i.e., the educational and memory-aiding) function of reproductions became primarily and deliberately emphasized.[29] But a print depicting the column of Trajan—regardless of the fact that as a work of graphic art it was considered on par with other graphic artworks of original invention—obviously reproduces something of the original or "prototype" that was to be found somewhere else. "There can be no doubt that the chief way by which knowledge of the most famous and beautiful statues of Rome was spread throughout Europe during the period of the High Renaissance was the print rather than the art," Francis Haskell and Nicholas Penny write.[30]

Following certain sixteenth- and seventeenth-century preliminaries, the first truly outstanding achievement in this respect was Bernard de Montfaucon's collection of 40,000 antique reproductions published in ten volumes (1719, 1724); in spite of Winckelmann's rebuke reserved for "*Scribents,*" in general (in all fairness it was a verdict he extended to *all* the preliminaries) this work was regarded as a reference source for over a century, which was to be followed by the great illustrated archaeological volumes of the eighteenth century. The first *modern* collection of reproductions, complete with commentaries, was published in 1724 through 1729 and came to be known, after its abbreviated title and its organizer, as *Recueil Crozat.*[31] The above quote from Haskell and Penny should be slightly modified in that, for centuries, the copies of the "Museum Chartaceums" (the paper museums) themselves formed important branches of applied art, whose creators were by no means nameless technicians, as has been the case with the reproduction experts of the modern book industry—or even book art. What was of a purely technical nature with regard to old books was their method of printing and distribution, which broadly affected people's tastes. It was of utmost concern to book editors to find the right copying artist. In the preface to the 1763 edition of *Geschichte der Kunst des Altertums* ("A History of Antique Art"), Winckelmann described Giovanni Casanova as the greatest Roman draftsman, praising him for accuracy, good taste, and archaeological knowledge.[32]

Another typical vehicle for the world-wide spread of knowledge about antique sculptures, in addition to engravings and prints, was plaster moulding (in the mid-sixteenth century still an expensive method) and the unique replica (for example, the small-scale bronze version of large statues). These made up the greater part of the collections at the various princely courts. The copies commissioned by the collectors were naturally not made for the same purpose as the originals. The purpose in the former case was the collection itself. To use Benjamin's expression, their value became an expositional value. This indicates that the process of their becoming autotelic began in the modern system of art. This is a slow process. From the viewpoint of the artistic *tradition,* it completed its course in the nineteenth century with the establishment, formation, and spread of public museums, where the artworks had but one function: being artworks. From the viewpoint of the artistic *practice* however, this process will probably never be completed, save for a few provocative "l'art pour l'art" gestures from the nineteenth and early twentieth centuries. In any case, in the early princely and aristocratic court collections the *representational* value both competes and mixes with the *expositional* value, and does so on two levels: As the representation of power (which is reflected in the possession of the collection's value, both material and symbolic), and the significance of the content represented by the works (for example, the portraits). There remains, furthermore, the mainly *decorative* function (the grandest undertaking in this respect was the execution of the numerous marble copies ordered in 1661 by the "Sun King" on the occasion of rebuilding Versailles).

The persons who make copies are artists. Yet although the copies made to order belong to the category of applied art, and although, as we know, this hierarchical distinction has been in place since the Renaissance, we could name a host of minor masters who regularly worked as copiers, with even some of the greatest masters joining in occasionally. Primaticcio and the young Vignola both were commissioned to make plaster copies for Francis I. David Teniers "the Younger" was in the service of the Archduke Leopold William as a copier, making gallery paintings and copies, as well as publishing *Theatrum Pictorium,* the illustrated catalog of the collection.

As can be seen from the above, the register of the high points of art, which became the single-most important factor in shaping "public taste" in the nineteenth and early twentieth centuries, has a long preliminary history. I have turned to the antique history of copying sculptures for examples (and will continue to do so in the following), because historically the Classical canon was established on the basis of antique plastic art, and came to be handed down to subsequent ages by analogy. This pantheon is fundamentally different from our imaginary museum in that its pluralism has definite, and only slowly extendible, limits. First it was antiquity, then came the Renaissance, and after the end of the eighteenth century, the medieval—this was how the limits of canonization expanded. (The eighteenth-century Japanese, Chinese, Moorish, etc., "revivals" enriched only the *decorative* possibilities and not the *stylistic* canon.) In addition to their value, the prominence of the major works of art was at times due to the fact that they happened to remain in a place that continued to be an important center of culture[33] (above all, Rome: The statue of the horse bridler, the equestrian statue of Marcus Aurelius, the wolf of the Capitoleum, Trajan's column,[34] the triumphal arches, the Pantheon), and sometimes to the sensational circumstances of their discovery (*Laocoön, Farnese Hercules,* the Pompeii excavations, the Elgin marbles, the group of statues of Aegina, etc.). The changes in this catalog, the rises and falls, reflect the major turns in the history of taste. (Take for example the Classical zenith of the *Apollo of Belvedere* and its subsequent nadir after Canova and Thorwaldsen[35]; the relatively modest interest generated earlier by Michelangelo's *David* in comparison to his *Bacchus* or *Moses,* and its continuous rise ever since the second half of the nineteenth century[36]; or Goethe's laudation of the cathedral of Strasbourg). One of the most important reasons for all these events is copying. In Kubler's words, it simultaneously guarantees the survival of historical monuments and records the changes in their popularity and the interest they generate.

Fidelity and Modification

Thus far we have discussed copying as a faithfully executed (or at least intended to be faithfully executed) reproduction, the main purpose of which is *preservation* and *circulation.* We progressed backward in time—relying on casual examples in our attempt to illustrate, rather than narrate, the full story—from the modern and late-modern catalog of the high points of art to the early modern canons. At this point we have to make two things clear: The institutional framework for the accurate copying of the universal canon is made up by the collections, the art academies, the publications, and the art dealers. But there are local canons also for which the institutions of faithful copying are the guilds and the workshops employing artists and apprentices. These were the crucial institutions of early modern art in which the characteristics of originality and autography did not overlap completely. In most cases a work of art was executed by apprentices and subordinates who followed the directives and guidelines of the master, making workshop copies, etc. These local canons gradually declined, the great workshops slowly vanished, and the relationship between the cultural canon and artistic practice became uncertain in late modernity. The fact that the canon became a catalog indicates that its copying no longer meant its artistic continuation. As a result of the technical advances in copying, the control of referential reproductions was no longer in the hands of artists.

Secondly, the notion of faithful copying is obviously a borderline category, and from the viewpoint of cultural history and aesthetics, those involuntary (or in some cases, very much voluntary) changes by which the originals, the prototypes, are modified have a greater importance. In the following I wish to discuss these cases.

"The attempt to preserve those values which have already become art historical leads to copying, not only within the museum but also in a broader sense, in their application in contemporary life. This application generally begins with associations from outside literature and art, and eventually becomes wasted in worthless use in applied art," Heinz Ladendorf writes.[37] In his book he goes through the entire history of studying and copying antiquity and, as seen also from the above quote, treats his subject with a certain amount of classicist rigor and aesthetic purism. In any case, his material provides an absorbing addendum to the history of taste. It presents stories about the copying of particular antique artworks. These stories are often surprisingly drawn out and eventful. Take, for example, the case of the famous *Spinario* ("Thorn-Puller"), the earliest plastic and miniature variations of which are dated back to the eleventh and twelfth centuries (initially the terracotta copies from the provinces formed the model, rather than the prototype from the Capitoleum): In the medieval period it was the symbol of March (March was the month when people started to walk barefoot); then it became a favorite subject for small plastics in the Renaissance; and the theme survived all the way into the eighteenth and nineteenth centuries, when it had special variations featuring, for example, erotic female thorn-pullers.

Could it be that this example from the history of copying was also linked to the process of canonization? In the majority of cases this is not so. "In the medieval age the purely aesthetic still had no intrinsic value, and hence in that age the theme, and thus the form-task as well, was kept alive by nothing more than the interest in the content."[38] The forms assume various contents, and vice versa. This is the observation that Panofsky later defined as the principle of the medieval separation and the Renaissance reintegration of form and content.[39] But even the post-Renaissance use of the theme was often aimed not at the emulation—and thereby the canonization—of Classical patterns, but at the exploitation of everyday, natural, and lyrical potentials, or at the theme's reinterpretation towards an erotic direction. Copying, or the application of the possibilities present in the arsenal of patterns, permits the execution of widely different thematic and form-tasks.

In addition to its applications in museum preservation and everyday utilization, copying also has an artistic-reflective interpretation. Copying is a hermeneutic task, in which the great contending paradigms of hermeneutics are at work such as understanding, understanding *better* than the original, understanding differently, or even demonstrating the impossibility of understanding. Even a student who acquires his master's or some other artist's conception of form by copying might find himself in the situation where he is able to *solve* something during copying that his predecessor was unable to do; in other words he understands the dilemma better than the master himself. There are several such instances from the apprenticeships of great artists.

But even more interesting perhaps is the case whereby for some reason a major artist in his mature period decides to copy with great accuracy the work of another artist, preserving the entire setting and composition; by modifying minor details, he achieves artistic solutions that make his version incomparably more valuable than the original. Perhaps the best illustration of such an incident took place during 1532–1533, when Titian painted his *Emperor Charles V,* which was a copy of Jakob Seisenegger's full-size portrait, *Emperor Charles V with his Ulm Mastiff,* which had been made in 1532 and is now displayed in the Viennese Kunsthistorisches Museum. Gustav Glück called attention to this incident in his otherwise rather affected and flaunty, fictitious dialogue between a "Princess" and the art historian. In his fine analysis of the differences, he showed how the pedantic and insignificant work of a Viennese court painter was turned into a great painting under Titian's brush: He painted everything the same, except for the excessively elaborate pattern of the background drapery and the floor, which he left out; the cropping of the dog's body, which he moved closer to the forelegs of the animal, thus restoring balance to Seisenegger's lopsided composition; the naturalistic and linear details in the representation of the face and the dog, which he replaced with artistic generalization and characterization, etc. In addition to the evidence of the available documents, Glück relied on considerations from the criticism of style to refute the suggestion that it had been Seisenegger who copied Titian, and not vice versa. As he pointed out, in Titian's work a large number of the specific details copied from nature either were left out or were freely invented from his imagination.[40]

Probably the most famous episode in the early history of modern copying concerns a replica that Andrea del Sarto made in 1525 after Raphael's work painted during 1518–1519 and entitled *Leo X with Two Cardinals*. It is unlikely that the copy was made in secrecy, amidst the kind of adventurous circumstances that Vasari suggested.[41] In any case, according to Vasari's account, even Giulio Romano was unable to recognize the copy, despite the fact that, as a student of Raphael's, he had taken part in the painting of the original version. When he was informed of the truth by Vasari, he made the following comment: "I do not value it less than I value the work that Raphael made with his own hand; on the contrary, I value it all the more highly, since it is supernatural that an excellent artist should be able to imitate someone else's style so well and that he should be able to make such a perfect copy."[42] By contrast, the modern art historian emphasizes the difference: "The copy is, in its faithfulness, a sincere compliment from one artist to the other, but in its occasional deviations it is also a criticism. Where del Sarto found weaknesses, from the Florentine point of view, he corrected him."[43] He made the section with the table bell and the codex look more like a still life; he composed the heads of Pope Leo and Cardinal de'Rossi in a more coherent unit; he enhanced the difference between the top and the sideboards of the table; the chair became more plastic; the hands look more powerful and bony, etc.

Titian, Rubens, Tintoretto, El Greco, and Poussin were all great copiers. If I may draw a conclusion on the basis of this hastily compiled list, I would say (borrowing the categories developed by Max Dvořák) that it is not so much the naturalist type of artist who *searches* for patterns in art, but the idealist type. But the patterns are in fact there for everyone. The nineteenth century was the great century of copying. The list of the Louvre's copiers include Delacroix, Géricault, Manet, Degas, and Cézanne.[44] Certain works (and certain artists) have been posing challenges over and over again for centuries:

Take, for example, Titian's *Bacchanalia with the Sleeping Ariadne,* which was copied by Rubens,[45] van Dyck, and Poussin; or his *Entombment,* which was copied by Géricault, Delacroix, Fantin-Latour, Cézanne, Chagall, and Derain.

Andrea del Sarto's famous copy of Raphael's work (made to order) or Titian's copy of Seisenegger's painting (made to land a job at court) provide examples not so much of a certain art-historical awareness and reflection as of the general practice of early modern art. These, too, of course, are based on a thorough understanding of the original work, yet they lack the kind of hermeneutic discernment that Van Gogh's remark displayed when he said that, in making oil paintings after Millet's drawings, he was not so much copying as translating from one language to another.[46]

Copying the works of an artist from the past is a typical gesture of choosing tradition. The sequence of traditions defined by the choice can be interpreted as the course of artistic progress pointing towards the inevitable truth, the alternate succession of problems and solutions; it can also be interpreted as the sequence of attempts to solve perennial problems (where the ideal solution is given and *unique*); furthermore, it can be interpreted as the successive stages in some essential reductive process (the "purification" of art); and finally it can be interpreted as individual solutions, or solutions regulated by the discourse-possibilities of the given age, the copying of which—in view of the fact that they are the works of another individual or age—necessarily results in another solution (or problem). Our hermeneutic age seems to support the latter view, and this is also how we understand the art of copying in the past.

From this follows the form of copying that regards the art of the past as a repertoire, the various elements of which are there to be borrowed. Naturally, this borrowing is one of the most important driving forces in the history of art, but parallel with the increasing awareness of it, grows the spirit of "counter-copying," the elaboration of the *difference* between the original and copy. And the greater this difference is, the more necessary it becomes to point out the original, to call attention to it. It is often the title, that ever-so-important element of twentieth-century art, that fulfills this role. At this point it suffices only to refer on the one hand to the destruction that was carried out in Picasso's series to the works of Velázquez, Poussin, Delacroix, Manet, and others, or to Velázquez's *Pope Innocent* in Francis Bacon's paintings, and on the other hand to the iconic arrangement of copies in one picture that Salvador Dalí experimented with several times in connection with Millet's *Angelus,* which he reinterpreted in paranoid fashion.[47] The processes at work in all these are "fragmentation and repetition," those two indivisible poles of late-modern art.[48]

The relationship that the artistic-reflective type of copying has with the canonization of the artworks of the past is twofold: It can constitute the pattern, or it can deconstruct it. By canon—in the modern sense—I mean a kind of arsenal of patterns that provides lasting models and standards. However, the concepts of models and standards might conceal certain tensions, or even contradictions. We have to distinguish between two kinds of artistic canons: One that is at work in the everyday practice of art, in which the model is also the *standard*; and the other whereby the canon of culture, the "catalog," sets the standard for the concept of art within the culture—whether or not it actually provides patterns for artistic practice and whether or not it is suitable for copying, imitation, and emulation. All the debates that concern old and new and that have accompanied modern aesthetic thinking derive from this tension: *What sets the standard does not necessarily provide the pattern.* "In the history of European art, the creation of traditions has, from the beginnings, been a process of mediation between present and past experiences, a never-ending *Querelle des Anciens et des Modernes*," Hans Robert Jauß writes.[49]

The transformation of past experience into contemporary experience can result from the absorption of Classical works as well as from the assimilation of contemporary works that integrate tradition. The balance between the two was for a long time maintained by the formula of copying and imitation, and only *later* by rivalry. This was reflected in the report of the House of Commons' Select Committee designated to make the decision whether to purchase the Elgin Marbles in 1816. The committee expressed their hope that the marbles would "receive that admiration and homage to which they are entitled, and serve *in return* as models and examples to those, who by knowing how to revere and appreciate them, may learn first to imitate and ultimately to rival them."[50] In the great nineteenth-century culture of copying—to a considerable extent as a consequence of the extraordinary spread of canonic works and copies—this optimism was severely disappointed, which eventually produced a frustrated feeling of unattainability and resulted in the radical criticism of the canon. The destruction of the balance is clearly shown by the increasing importance of the decanonizing function of copying, notably in twentieth-century modern art.

But the decanonizing function of copying is not a recent phenomenon. Attempts to shake off an exceedingly powerful influence, or criticism of a culture's canonizing direction (its inordinate respect for antiques), have often led to such copies. Forgery too has a decan-onizing function: Its typical form is distortion, earlier manifested in parody and caricature (for example, Titian's famous woodcut, *Monkey Laocoön*) and lately in destruction. Since 1919, *Mona Lisa,* the most frequently reproduced and probably the most canonic work in the history of painting, has been the subject of distortions and destruc-tions of unrivaled versatility (at the same time playing a fundamen-tal role in mass culture with its legion of reproductions, some designed to compliment and some to distort). That was the time when Duchamp made his mustached and bearded Mona Lisa, *L.H.O.O.Q.* It is one of the remarkable points of interest of cultural history that Andy Warhol's series of various Mona Lisas, including *Thirty is Better Than One* and *Double Mona Lisa* (1963), which eventu-ally relativized the difference between high culture and mass culture, was made almost at the same time as Duchamp's follow-up on his almost 50-year-old *L.H.O.O.Q., Shaved L.H.O.O.Q.* (1965), an unre-touched Mona Lisa reproduction.[51] Anyone engrossed in the prob-lematics of copying should find it intriguing that the basis of Duchamp's original deconstruction was a simple picture-postcard sold in galleries. Thus he manipulated a commercial copy to produce this work of art (or should we say artifact?), which ironically and playfully questioned the notion of artwork as formulated by the 500-year history of art beginning from the Renaissance. But then there was Francis Bacon, from whose profound art the radical questioning of the notion of art itself could not have been further; he too copied a picture postcard for his Velázquez variations. According to his own words, he never saw the original work, which he regarded as one of the most important masterpieces in the history of painting; when he was in Rome, he made sure to avoid it.[52]

The Imitation of Nature, the Imitation
of Art–Retrospective Art–Restoration

"It is well known that prior to the age of genius, the notion of origi-nality played a minor role. It was not uncommon for composers of the seventeenth and early eighteenth century to use whole sections of their own and other people's work for new composition. Similarly, painters and architects entrusted the execution of their sketches and designs to their pupils. Both phenomena prove that artists did not critically reflect upon originality, although it would of course be mis-taken to think that originality was totally absent. This difference could be documented easily by comparing Bach and his contempo-raries," Adorno writes.[53] This is the value-specific interpretation of the concept of originality, which, similarly to Benjamin's notions analyzed above (albeit without the contradictions of the latter), simultaneously refers to its historical genesis and its objective nature recognizable in older works of art. "Originality, the specificity of a particular work, does not stand in direct opposition to logicality, which is universal. Rather, it frequently comes into its own in the sort of syllogistic consistency and elaboration that is the prerogative of great artists only."[54]

However, it is the utopistic, the yet-to-be-born element in originality, which forms the origin rather than the ancient element, since the latter presupposes an emancipated subject. Since the ancient element in originality already presupposes an emancipated subject, it is the utopistic element in it that forms the origin. One cannot help noticing in this argument a certain fundamental suspicion towards all kinds of nonautonomous works of art (whether because they are from any of the nonautonomous artistic periods or because they are the works of a nonautonomous artist). This is the viewpoint of the musicologist, whose historical paradigm more or less coincides with the autonomous period in art, or of the aristocratic aesthete for whom art belongs to the realm of "consummated" masterpieces. Furthermore, one cannot help noticing the arrangement of the facts of art in this argument from the viewpoint of an utopistic future—but a detailed discussion of this topic would lead us too far from our theme.

What is more pertinent to my subject in the above passage is rather the misunderstanding it contains; the fact is that the independent emergence of the concept of originality in the terminology of genius aestheticism in no way means that the concept itself—together with its standing—appeared in the eighteenth century *ex nihilo,* in the same manner as the work of a genius was supposed to appear according to the aforementioned aesthetes. All three of its components—individuality, novelty, and historicity (the historical authenticity of old works of art)—represented obvious values in the Renaissance, although the three components may not have been united in one concept. It is also the time in which the distinction (and hierarchism) of the intellectual versus the craftsmanly concept of art dates back to. It generally holds true that whenever the notion, or accusation, of forgery comes up, its opposite (i.e., the original) is also present. But then the history of this notion has been continuous ever since the Renaissance, even if the accompanying self-reflection, the self-consciousness of the forger, originated much later. And the sporadic, noncontinuous impulses of forgery could be discovered even before the Renaissance, and even outside of Europe; for example, in ancient Rome or in China during the northern Sung dynasty

(960–1127), the Ming dynasty (1368–1644), and during the late nineteenth and early twentieth centuries.[55]

The new element in genius aestheticism was that it regarded originality as the predominant value, and consequently rearranged tradition and artistic practice in accordance with this value. The person of genius creating a new world *ex nihilo,* who has neither to learn nor to imitate, along with the work of art and myth of *natura naturans* has become—despite the early and profound criticism of this myth—one of the most important elements in the popular registers of artistic culture. The wild genius has made it into the intellectual wax museum. Copying and imitation, which up till then had formed an organic part of the artistic practice and had not necessarily been regarded as the antitheses of originality, suddenly had to find a justification—ideological as well as pedagogic and propagandistic—for their existence.

The views that I have quoted from Young, maintaining that imitation comes in two forms, one being the imitation of nature (which constitutes originality itself) and the other being imitation proper, the imitation of respected artists and artworks (the actual target of condemnation), are frequently echoed considerations nowadays. That both forms continue to be referred to as imitation is due to the copying of an authority. As for the Greeks in general, the essence of art for Aristotle lies in its mimic nature. The distinction is modern and it reflects, albeit negatively, on the point that, in addition to the resemblance to nature—not only actually existing, but also potentially existing Nature (i.e., that created by fantasy)—there is another frame of reference: This being the connection to the intrinsic nature of art tradition, its evolution, along with the sustenance of this evolution by the imitation of earlier works of art.

Nonetheless, the essential distinction between these two forms of imitation becomes apparent only in criticism. Shaftesbury, for example, did not distinguish between them, even though he took a favorable view of imitating works of art. "'Tis from the *many* Objects of Nature, and not from a *particular one,* that those Genius's form the Idea of their Work. Thus the best Artists are said to have been indefatigable in studying the best Statues: as esteeming them a better Rule, than the perfectest human Bodys could afford. And thus some considerable Wits have recommended the best Poems, as preferable to the best of Historys; and better teaching the Truth of Characters, and Nature of Mankind."[56] The last sentence recapitulates the point made in the famous chapter 9 of *Poetics* on the difference between poetry and historiography; and since in his parallels Shaftesbury brings up the example of the best statues, it can be assumed that he regards the imitation of characters, emotions, actions, and ideas as equivalent to the imitation of artistic tradition.

As for Winckelmann, he has no doubt that the task assigned to art is the imitation of Greek artworks. This is illustrated from the outset by his decision to insert the tract about beauty at the beginning of the Greek chapter in his great historical treatise, with the art of every other age and people being measured (and mostly found wanting) by the Greek standards. In the background of all this stands the normative/rationalistic conviction that, in its best (second) period, Greek art imitated the laws and truth of nature—in particular, of nature as it developed under the most fortuitous circumstances, weather and all. Therefore Winckelmann himself did not relate the requirement to imitate Greek art to the possibility that art could be made to refer to itself, to its own immanent development, and in fact expressed his aversion to such an eventuality. When he compares the old and strict Greek style, which came to an end with the appearance of Phidias, with the great style, he defines the difference precisely in this: "The older style was based on a system which consisted of rules derived from Nature; later this style moved away from Nature and became idealistic. Artists observed the requirements of the rules more than they followed Nature, which was the subject to be imitated: art has developed its own system. It was from this derived system that the reformers of art emerged and moved closer to the truth of Nature."[57]

Therefore the important recognition that art develops its own system is presented here as an unwelcome development. The alternative to this is the free imitation of the highest forms of nature; free in the sense that in accordance with Socrates's recipe—as echoed in the first sentence of the previous quote from Shaftesbury—it was based on selection and combination, rather than on direct copying from nature.[58] The result is a beauty of "noble simplicity," which is "like the perfect spring water: The less flavor it has, the healthier it is considered, since this means it has been purified of all alien parts."[59]

Why should anyone imitate the Greeks when the Greeks themselves imitated nature? Because this will lead to a closer imitation of nature. In part because the Greek natural world itself was the closest approximation of ideal nature, and partly because the Greek rules of beauty idealized the true nature, imitating its ideal essence. "Nothing could make the advantages of the imitation of old art over the imitation of nature clearer than taking two young men similarly abundant in talent, having one of them study antiquity and having the other study mere nature. The latter would represent nature, *as he finds it*. If he was an Italian, he would perhaps paint figures like Caravaggio, if he was Flemish and fortunate, he would paint them like Jacob Jordaens, and if he was a Frenchman, then he would paint them like Stella, but the former would *represent* nature as nature itself demands it, and would paint figures like Raphael."[60]

The paradox in Winckelmann's suggestion is that at the same time he considers the inimitability of Greek perfection as one of its epithets, and in fact strongly criticizes its imitators (in the fourth, declining period of Greek art, and also elsewhere). Still, "to become great, or even inimitable if possible, we have but one course of action: to imitate the old artists. . . ."[61] However absurd this might seem in terms of logic, all forms of modern classicism are based on this paradox.

The imitation of Greek works formed one of the main artistic movements of the period. The Neo-Classicism of the second half of the eighteenth century was the most canonical of the universal *retrospective* period styles in the modern history of Europe. This was followed by several retrospective movements that were present throughout the nineteenth century, but which either were not universal (the Gothic style was revived in Germany as a *national* art) or, taken individually, represented just one of the many trends active at the time, or whose historicizing eclecticism itself had a pluralist character, ascribing a peculiar, functionalist interpretation to the various period styles. Unlike the artists and theoreticians of the Neo-Classicist school, who turned to one particular period for their worldview, the disciples of the other retrospective movements found their world view in history in its entirety. Thus, with regard to the history of architecture, the Classical model was applied to museums and libraries (the worldly "churches"), while churches proper were built in Gothic style, castles in medieval style, palaces in the style of the Renaissance, public buildings either in Gothic or Renaissance, and synagogues in Moorish style. The debates preceding the construction of both the British Parliament and the Hungarian Academy of Sciences were debates on styles, in which the various period styles of the past became freely accessible sources for copying. An interesting illustration of the international habit of shopping around in the stylistic catalog occurred in 1896 when, in two distant corners of the world, the state of Tennessee celebrated its hundredth anniversary of its existence and the country of Hungary its thousandth. The exhibition buildings of various historical styles at both locations were built or copied according to very similar programs.[62] Similarly, the history of interior design can also prove that the different historical styles were functionalized: the salons of the haute bourgeoisie were designed in rococo style, and the drawing room, library, and dining room in "Old German" (i.e., Neo-Renaissance, etc.).[63]

The retrospective artist is an *artifex doctus,* in much the same way as Mengs, Piranesi, Cavaceppi, Canova, Flaxman, Thorwaldsen, and many others were. It is the more or less strict adherence to antique patterns, the close contact with them, which can explain the fact that Neo-Classicism was the last era in which Europe's leading artists could still be engaged in restoration. To be more precise, completion, restoration, replacement, the addition of new parts, and recreation all form part of the retrospective artistic practice. On the one hand, Neo-Classicism was still one of the high points of *free* restoration, but on the other, in its scholarly and scheming branch the embryo of modern purism was formed. Of its representatives, those who were still close to the baroque or rococo, or who were more naive, had no objection to reconstructing.

Although Winckelmann acknowledged this practice, he never stopped making fun of those scholars whose conclusions about antique art were based on modern appurtenances, and outlined the need to write a separate book on the restoration of antique works of art. In the second half of the eighteenth century, scholars had regular discussions about whether it was right and appropriate to complete antique works of art. Count Caylus, Christian Gottlob Heyne, Wilhelm von Humboldt, and many others took part in this discourse.[64] Canova's decision not to restore the Elgin Marbles was the cultural–historical turning point in this matter, although it took a while before creative restoration came to be considered improper altogether. Following Canova's refusal, it was only Elgin's shortage of funds that led Flaxman in his—admittedly unsure—decision not to undertake the restoration of the Parthenon sculptures. The Aegina marbles were, again, restored creatively by Thorwaldsen (the damage caused by World War II in Munich provided the opportunity to restore the original, fragmented condition of the marbles as they existed prior to Thorwaldsen's restoration).

With a few exceptions (the Vatican torso, for example) and one particular stylistic intermezzo (Mannerism), it can generally be maintained that until the middle of the eighteenth century, fragments were not regarded as works of art, and thus a kind of *horror fragmenti* was allowed to rule in aesthetic judgment. The restoration of fragments by the addition of missing heads, limbs, and figures was regularly practiced until the beginning of the nineteenth century; and while the existence of a very interesting range of tendencies was noticeable, with the purely aesthetic-decorative school at one end of the spectrum and the school striving for historical–philological authenticity at the other, the practice itself was never called into doubt for almost three centuries.

I am less concerned here with the otherwise extremely interesting problem of how much the hermeneutic task of restoration is subordinated to the concepts and preconceptions of the age concerned. These might became apparent even through the example of a *calf,* as was the case with the *Farnese Hercules,* which had been completed by Giacomo della Porta before the missing lower leg of the statue was found; now both are on display in the Archaeological Museum of Naples. Then there is the Venus of Arles, found in 1651 and restored in the same year by François Girardon (the Phidias of the age, according to Boileau), the results of which can be compared to a plaster copy made before the restoration.[65] The current condition of the Aegina marbles can be compared to Thorwaldsen's additions. All these provide excellent examples of the Renaissance, baroque, and Neo-Classicist concepts of antique art, where the emphasis is precisely on their reflecting their own concept of antiquity.

What here should concern us more, however, is that restoration too forms part of the artistic practice of pattern maintenance and imitation, and if the growing prestige and bid for hegemony of the individual greatly affected the cultural–historical fate of forging and copying, the same also applies to restoration. The same process was reflected in the growing concern about restoration in the second half of the eighteenth century: Whether or not it had been too extensive, whether the head was in fact original, etc. The so-called *Lansdowne Discobolus* was excavated in 1784 and—since the marble copy, which came to be known as the Lancelotti version and that was later identified, on the basis of antique descriptions, as a copy of Myron's *Discobolus,* had not been uncovered until 1781—its subsequent restoration was based an entirely different iconographic program, representing it as a Diomedes figure. In 1791 another copy was found, which was named *Townley Discobolus* after its buyer. The head, which proved to be antique but did not belong to the torso, was facing straight ahead. Both finds raised serious doubts.[66]

Without the changes in style and aesthetic judgment, as manifested in the appreciation of fragments, torsos, and ruins, the increasing prestige associated with erudition about originality and antiquity would not have been enough. These changes, the forerunner of which had been the eighteenth-century's sentimental cult of imitation ruins in landscape design and the historicizing melancholy of which was soon replaced by an anthropological realization (i.e., of the fragmentary nature of man himself), have combined to produce one of the most important turning points in the history of culture, the repercussions of which can still be felt today. The appreciation of a fragment as a fragment; the ability to mentally reconstruct the whole from the part; the admiration of fragments for their beauty and cathartic qualities, as opposed to the mere respect generated by their age: These comprise the new mode of reception, representatively demonstrated by the poetic experiences of Byron and Keats, as well as by Rilke and others. The literary rehabilitation of fragments, their promotion to an aesthetic program even, has been one of the well-known accomplishments of early Romanticism.

Nevertheless, the debate on the relative merits of copying/restoring versus untouched preserving continued among preservationists and aesthetes throughout the entire nineteenth century, even though, with regard to sculpture, it had symbolically ended at the beginning of the century. The practice of renovating historical buildings was so widespread that by the end of the century people joked about the epidemic of a certain *peronospora renovatrix*. The church of Zsámbék, Hungary, this valuable and magnificent example of Premontre-type Gothic architecture from the thirteenth century, was saved from creative restoration by the extensive decay it had undergone; therefore the decision was taken to preserve the existing condition on the site and to erect its replica at Lehel Square, Budapest. If the nineteenth century was called the "golden age of forgery," then to a large extent it was on account of that broad and blurred continuum in which restoration, renovation, new copies of old objects, old objects assembled into new ones, and the creative use of retrospective, historicizing fantasy to produce new objects were all lumped together. Respected professors of architecture, famous sculptors and forgers (Giovanni Bastianini, for example), goldsmith-restorers, and forgers (such as Reinhold Vasters [1827–1909])[67] of Aachen, who was unmasked only after his death) differed from one another more in their morality than in their artistic practice and accomplishments.

The debate on restoration can never reach a satisfactory settlement, since all forms of restoration and alteration amount to a new interpretation.[68] The school supporting the view that artworks should be preserved in the state in which they were found is opposed by the movement that wants to restore them to their original condition, thus trying to erase the evidence of their subsequent history of reception and—according to the conceptual framework I advocate—coming down on the side of the strictly interpreted historical authenticity assigned to the hypothetical moment of creation and against the concept of originality. The purists are quick to call attention to the slightest interference. The restoration of every major work of art fires up the debate, and every solution must be a pragmatic one, based on compromise. The recent restoration of the Sistine Chapel reestablished the faded reputation of Michelangelo as a great colorist, but left intact those famous veils that were added to the pictures a quarter of a century later upon the Pope's instructions, with the purpose of covering up the private parts.

The Tradition of Art

In contrast to the imitation of nature, art develops its own system—I quoted Winckelmann earlier. Edward Young contrasted the imitation of nature with the imitation of tradition. In this case, the "discours" of Aristotle forced the art writers standing at the opposite poles of eighteenth-century art-philosophy to express themselves in similar formulas. Nevertheless, the distinction points to something in the phenomenology of (modern) art, the validity of which depends neither on the original propositions nor on the framework of categories. A few pages back I already attempted to expound on this; now I shall try again. The point is that the relationship works of art have with the "world" is not entirely identical with the relationship they have with the world of art tradition. Something that can be posed as a question or formulated as a problem and perhaps can be solved in the context of the given period's system of beliefs (I use this expression here as the sum total of people's views and opinions about their own age) cannot necessarily be identified with, or translated into, the existing stockpile of artistic traditions. Conversely, the immanent development of art tradition—occasionally in forms that are extremely abstract or formal—might pose questions or encourage solutions that cannot be interpreted in the language of the given period's system of beliefs, worldviews, conceptual and social frameworks. Perhaps they only make sense either in a language that was used earlier, or in one that will be used later. Artists and their works are citizens of two worlds: The world of their own and the world of art history.

They have been the citizens of two worlds ever since our culture has been *pluralistic*, rather than *monistic*. The precondition of this twofold referential and interpretative system of artworks is an awareness both of the existence of various historical worlds and of the historical changes in the arts. To this extent the duplicity belongs to, and is the result of, our historical consciousness: in its mature form it is one of the characteristics of modernity. This twofold character explains why the artworks of the past do not fall to pieces with the passing of time; instead, they are, again and again, integrated into the subsequent worlds, as well as creating new worlds for themselves; nor are the artworks of the present assimilated entirely into the present, but continue to preserve a secret: A dialogue with the ancestors (which may or may not become apparent), as well as the prospect of a dialogue, kept open for the descendants.

In some sense, therefore, every work of art dwells in two worlds. It has a local value in the physical world, being in contact with the reality that belongs to all of us (insofar as it accepts or absorbs the selected norms of reality outside the realm of artworks) and forming part of that synchronic culture in which it was born; and it has a local value in the diachronic reality of its own artistic tradition, which is manifested in works of art in the form of quotes and copies, whether deliberate or unconscious. The two can interfere with each other: The early sixteenth-century representation of a 24-year-old lady with an inscrutable smile became the icon of fine arts in the twentieth century, occupying a permanent place in culture that is understood in the broadest sense: Everyone knows it and everyone responds to it. Whether an artist copies it or defaces it, parodies it, or even refers to it in the vaguest possible manner, the effect of sparking in the viewer associations with Leonardo's momentous creation is guaranteed. (A century earlier it was Raphael's *Fornarina,* and in the second half of the nineteenth century his *Sistine Madonna,* that had similar status, although neither of them were, of course, exposed to so much destruction.)

Most of the inspirations deriving from the art tradition are of a different nature, especially since the decrease in importance of schools and masters in the education of artists, and the formal possibilities of universal art history have, in principle, become accessible. Assuming that George Kubler is correct, then Frank Lloyd Wright, for example, "renewed an experimentation with Maya corbel-vaulted compositions that had lapsed since the fifteenth century in Yucatan."[69] And while this aspect might be of crucial importance from the viewpoint of a work of art's immanent nature, the chances are very small that this secret will be revealed to the (lay) audience. Those modern critics (Adorno or Panofsky, for example) who consider every aesthetic experience regressive if it is not based on a close familiarity with the history and tradition of the given artwork, miss the mark in their cultural criticism. With desperate gestures, they set specialized knowledge against the lack of cultural refinement and barbarization. Nevertheless, it would be wrong to suggest that if the discovery of the truth about something requires specialized knowledge, then this something—in this case the immanent development of art—itself must be specialized. It is often the case that artists are able to gain more universal inspiration from it than from the challenges of their own historical period, and their dialogues with past masters might be deeper and more compassionate than with their own contemporaries.

If I am justified in my attempt to draw the above distinction, then it can rightly be assumed that the two referential frameworks also have a different concept of reality. In the case of the earlier-mentioned eighteenth-century authors, this distinction still poses no problems: It is they who set the two against each another as opposites in terms of artistic school or approach, rather then presenting them as the twofold referential system of the same work of art; they claim that nature forms the reality to be imitated according to the one school, while the same role is assigned to art's own nature and system in the other school.

By the end of the eighteenth century this alternative—creation or imitation—had already become a common theme in educated conversations; I have quoted Goethe in this matter.[70] Rosalind E. Krauss has found an excellent illustration of this in *Northanger Abbey*, a novel written by Jane Austen at the turn of the nineteenth century but published only after the author's death; the book ridicules those "refined gentlemen" who look on the landscape as a painterly subject, a mere motif for the fine arts, rather than as the face of nature.[71] The justification for such mockery can nevertheless be questioned.

One-and-a-half centuries later an art historian could rightly claim about Constable, whose relationship with nature was so intimate that all he required for his work was the Suffolk landscape, that even he looked at this landscape through the eyes of Ruisdael and Hobbema.[72] In his classic essay entitled "The Philosophy of Landscape," Georg Simmel rightly regards the landscape to be a modern-age *artistic* creation: ". . . we look upon the landscape in the form of a painter's work. . . . To a growing extent and in a purified form, the landscape as a work of art continues the process, in the course of which the landscape, as understood in its ordinary sense, is created for all of us from the mere effects of certain natural objects." "Where we see a landscape, rather than just the sum total of various natural objects, is where we have captured the birth of a work of art."[73]

If we continue to use the example of Constable, then we might say that in his pictures the reality of the Suffolk landscape can be discovered in one referential system, and the reality of Ruisdale's or Hobbema's style of painting and approach to nature in the other referential system. On examining the first statement of the sentence, it immediately becomes apparent that when we identify the reality of a painting with the representation of the reality of the landscape it depicts, then we resort to a concept of correspondence, equation, with empirical vision, which might have reigned for a long time in the history of fine art, but still cannot be generalized. In Cézanne's pictures the Provence countryside is turned into an individually interpreted landscape (the consciousness of individual interpretation increases), while in Mondrian's works the correspondence with the empirical experience of space is gradually lost.

The unified truth of picture and reality is not an immutable law of aesthetics. This is not to say that an artwork's relevance to "reality" (the reality of life-experience) is meaningless. Instead of being some objective and external circumstance, this reality is always determined by the work of art: *It is what it sets itself apart from,* either by imitating and copying it, or by contrasting it with the freedom of imagination, or by maintaining an idealistic distance from it, or by approaching it in a realistic manner. The difference can be maximized or minimized, but its existence, the dialogue with "reality," is a precondition of art. Artistic creation and appreciation alike start out from that evident and tacit knowledge by which we know that a man can play "the Wall" (in Shakespeare's *A Midsummer Night's Dream*), the same as we know that the person playing the part of the lion is no savage beast. There can be several external causes and explanations for the kinds of notions of reality that might exist in the art of a given period, yet it is up to every single work of art to carve out that area in which it wants to function as the counterpart of reality. (With more complicated works, or even genres, the level of reality is varied. The kneeling donors painted on the closed panels of the Gent Altar obviously have a level of reality that is different from the level of reality associated with the simulated sculptural representation, using grisaille technique, of both St. John the Baptist and St. John the Evangelist; similarly, the interplay between the different levels of reality of the various mural sections of the Sistine Chapel is incredibly rich and complex. Shifting the levels of reality in a novel—for example, in relation to the writer and narrator—is among the familiar devices of the genre.)

What is the situation concerning the notion of reality in reference to the immanent nature of art? In my opinion, the reality of art in this case is formed by Ruisdael's and Hobbema's approaches to nature, together with the contemporary reading of the artistic views of earlier generations, and the possibilities in variation and innovation. It is at this point that copying, deliberate and unintentional alike, plays a fundamental part in art: ". . . to copy a model by rendering its likeness is actually to copy a set of preexisting representational models for such depiction—representations must refer to other representations."[74]

In this respect, therefore, the reality of art is a given domain of representational and compositional possibilities. To a very large extent, these possibilities are determined by tradition, which enters the present in the form of pattern maintenance, reproduction, and copying. And while perfect replicas do not exist even in the most traditional societies, the differences can remain so minute and unnoticeable that series spanning across thousands of years might have a direct link to the archetype. In nontraditional cultures the strict attachment to the archetype—full-fledged copying—has, ever since the Renaissance, been less frequent in high art, although, as we have also found out, it has still been practiced a great deal more frequently than is admitted by public opinion, conditioned as it is to fetishism towards the original and keep copies out of its conscious awareness. By contrast, the modern classics occasionally realized the principle of adequacy with art patterns, the same as the principle of adequacy with nature. The idea behind Giulio Romano's sentence quoted earlier, in which he valued the author of the copy more than the author of the original, might have been the conviction that there could be only one perfect and faithful representation of the subject of the painting, in view of which it was truly remarkable that someone was able to realize it once again. He regarded the perfect copy as the triumph of *aemulatio*.

Today, we are on the lookout for the differences in a copy. We regard the perfect copy (and the perfect fake) as the scandal of the intellect.

Notes

1. Walter Benjamin, "Das Kunstwerk im Zeitalter seiner technischen Reproduzierbarkeit" (Zweite Fassung), in *Gesammelte Schriften* I/2 (Frankfurt: Suhrkamp, 1974).

2. Ibid., 475.

3. Ibid., 476.

4. Cf. Hans Robert Jauß, "Spur und Aura: Bemerkungen zu Walter Benjamins 'Passagen-Werk'," in *Studien zur Epochenwandel der ästhetischen Moderne* (Frankfurt: Suhrkamp, 1989), 196.

5. Benjamin, op. cit., 477.

6. For the criticism of this argument see Hans Blumenberg, *Säkularisierung und Selbstbehauptung* (Frankfurt: Suhrkamp), 1983.

7. "For instance, an antique sculpture representing Venus had a different relation to tradition in the Greeks' case, who made it the object of their cult, than in the case of the medieval priests who saw an idol evoking disaster in it. The one thing shared in both cases was the individuality, in other words the aura, of the sculpture." Benjamin, op. cit., 480.

8. "The characteristic extravagances and crudities of art, produced in the so-called periods of decline, in fact derive from the richest historical power center of art." Benjamin, op. cit., 501.

9. György Márkus, "Walter Benjamin and the Commodity as Phantasmagoria." Unpublished manuscript.

10. Theodor W. Adorno, *Ästhetische Theorie. Gesammelte Schriften VII* (Frankfurt: Suhrkamp, 1972), 73.

11. Edward Young, "Conjectures on Original Composition," in *The Complete Works*, ed. James Nichols (London: William Tegg, 1854 [reprint, Hildesheim: Georg Olms, 1968], Vol. II.), 551.

12. Cf. Jochen Schmidt, *Die Geschichte des Genie-Gedankens in der deutschen Literatur, Philosophie und Politik 1750–1945* (Darmstadt: Wissenschaftliche Buchgesellschaft, 1988, Vol. I), with the chapter "Genie-Paradigmata des 18. Jahrhunderts," 150ff.

13. Cf. Friedrich Schlegel, "Über das Studium der Griechischen Poesie," in *Kritische Schriften und Fragmente [1794–1797] I* (Paderborn: Ferdinand Schöningh, 1988), 69.

14. Jeffrey M. Muller, "Measures of Authenticity: The Detection of Copies in the Early Literature on Connoisseurship," in *Retaining the Original: Multiple Originals, Copies and Reproductions. Studies in the History of Art*, Vol. 20. Washington, DC: National Gallery of Art, 1989, 146.

15. Benjamin, op. cit., 480.

16. Hannah Arendt, "Tradition and the Modern Age," in *Between Past and Future* (New York: Viking, 1968), 25.

17. Margarete Bieber, *Ancient Copies: Contributions to the History of Greek and Roman Art* (New York: New York University Press, 1977), 1. In the first chapter of the book the author presents the findings and opinions concerning the research of Roman copies (between 1889 and 1970). For a comprehensive history of Roman copying see chapters 15 and 16.

18. Cf. Brunilde Sismondo Ridgway, *Roman Copies of Greek Sculpture: The Problem of the Originals* (Ann Arbor: University of Michigan Press, 1984), 82 and passim.

19. Cf., for example, a discussion of the differences between the Greek ψευδοζ (pseudos) and the Latin falsum(!). Martin Heidegger, *Parmenides*. Gesamtausgabe, Bd. 54 (Frankfurt: Klostermann, 1982), 57ff.

20. Of the so-called replica series, and restricted to the Venus representations, Praxiteles's *Knidos Aphrodite* had more than 50, the *Medici Venus*-type had thirty-three, the *Capitolium Venus*-type had 101 surviving versions. Cf. "Copying in Roman Sculpture: The Replica Series" (Miranda Marvin, "Copying in Roman Sculpture: The Replica Series," in *Retaining the Original*, op. cit., 36f.

21. Cf. Georg Lippold, *Kopien und Umbildungen griechischer Statuen* (Munich: Beck, 1923), 83ff. To all this Ridgway adds the pasticcio, stylistic mixture, eclectic rendering. Cf. Ridgway, op. cit., 82. Another division used in early modern fine art distinguishes between the original, the replica, the variation, the version, the copy, the pastiche (a collection of motifs from borrowed sources), the plagiary, the paraphrase, the parody, and the persiflage. Cf. Heribert Hutter, *Original–Kopie–Replik–Paraphrase*. Ausstellung 8.9.–5.10., 1980. Bildhefte der Akademie der bildenden Künste in Wien. Doppelheft 12/13.

22. Walter Benjamin, "Geschichtsphilosophische Thesen," Thesis XIV, in *Schriften I* (Frankfurt: Suhrkamp, 1955), 503.

23. Arendt, op. cit., 25f.

24. Cf. Erwin Panofsky, *Renaissance and Renascences in Western Art* (New York: Harper & Row/Icon Editions, 1975), 41. Cf. chapter 12.

25. George Kubler, *The Shape of Time: Remarks on the History of Things* (New Haven, CT: Yale University Press, 1962), 71.

26. Ibid., 62. Here Kubler refers to a work by his master, Henri Focillon, entitled *Vie des formes*.

27. Edgar Wind has noted how its influence also extends to artistic practice, and how painters have started to imitate the coarser effects of the reproductions by adjusting their palette to the mechanical color spectrum of prints. Cf. Wind, *Art and Anarchy* (London: Duckworth, 1985), 68f. André Malraux has noticed that the various artworks lose their colors, texture, and dimensions in reproduction, and that at the same time their family resemblance and shared style stand out clearly precisely for this reason. Cf. Malraux, *The Voices of Silence* (Princeton, NJ: Princeton University Press, 1978), 21. For a history of prints, see William M. Ivins, Jr., *Prints and Visual Communication* (Cambridge, MA: Harvard University Press, 1953).

28. A detailed study of this topic would probably reveal that even the most advanced methods of technical reproduction are "imperfect" and likely to produce unintentional dissimilarities—subordinated to the style or styles of that period. The popular, gold-trimmed Stengl picture postcards of the early twentieth century placed the entire universe of art history in a syrupy late-Biedermeier milieu, while the "hard," black-and-white reproductions of the 1930s are related to constructivism, etc.

29. Cf. Caroline Karpinski, "The Print in Thrall to Its Original: A Historiographic Perspective," in Muller, op. cit., 101ff.

30. Francis Haskell and Nicholas Penny, *Taste and the Antique: The Lure of Classical Sculpture 1500–1900* (New Haven, CT: Yale University Press, 1981), 2.

31. Cf. Francis Haskell, *The Painful Birth of the Art Book* (New York: Thames & Hudson, 1988).

32. Cf. Johann Joachim Winckelmann, *Geschichte der Kunst des Altertums* (Vienna: Phaidon, 1934), 22.

33. Cf. Heinz Ladendorf, *Antikenstudium und Antikenkopie. Vorarbeiten zu einer Darstellung ihrer Bedeutung in der mittelalterlichen und neueren Zeit* (Berlin: Akademie, 1953), 52.

34. On its history of copying, see Werner Haftmann, *Das italienische Säulenmonument* (Leipzig: N.p., 1934).

35. This was related both to the discovery of the Elgin Marbles and to the recently introduced practice of distinguishing between Greek, Greco-Roman, and Roman art. Canova's student, the sculpture and illustrator John Flaxman (himself a major copier of antique art) thought that the *Apollo of Belvedere* was a dance teacher in comparison to the *Theseus* representation of the Elgin Marbles (a sculpture from the eastern group of the Parthenon, which is now thought to be a *Dionysos* representation). Cf. William St. Clair, *Lord Elgin and the Marbles* (Oxford, UK: Oxford University Press, 1983), 167. Hegel also con-

firmed this change in attitudes since the age of Lessing and Winckelmann, quoting from a travel diary written in 1825 by an Englishman where *Apollo* was described as a "theatrical coxcomb." Cf. Georg Wilhelm Friedrich Hegel, *Vorlesungen über die Ästhetik* II. *Werke*, 14. Theorie Werkausgabe (Frankfurt: Suhrkamp), 431. Also cf. A. D. Potts, "Greek Sculpture and Roman Copies I: Anton Raphael Mengs and the Eighteenth Century," in *Journal of the Warburg and Courtauld Institutes* 43 (1980) and Éva Kocziszky, "A görögség ideálja a XVIII–XIX század fordulóján" ("The Ideal of the Greek World at the Turn of the Nineteenth Century"), *Holmi*, Budapest (March 1994): 415.

36. Cf. Haskell and Penny, op. cit., 117. We might also add that this was true not only in connection with certain works by Michelangelo, but also with his entire artistic personality. He was Vasari's choice, while Giovanni Pietro Bellori (1615–1696) already favored Raphael, and the latter view dominated public opinion for more than two centuries.

37. Ladendorf, op. cit., 20.

38. Ladendorf, op. cit., 21.

39. Panofsky, op. cit.

40. Cf. Gustav Glück, "Original und Kopie. Ein Gespräch," in *Festschrift für Julius Schlosser zum 60. Geburtstag*, ed. Arpad Weixelgärtner and Leo Planiscig (Zürich: Amalther, 1927), 237 and 224–42 passim. Actually, the debate as to whether it was Titian who copied Seisenegger or the other way around, has still not been settled beyond doubt, although in the recent literature the view that Titian's work is the replica has been gaining ground. Cf. Harold E. Wethey, *The Paintings of Titian*, Vol. II (London: Phaidon, 1971), 85ff.

41. Cf. S[idney] J[oseph] Freedberg, *Andrea del Sarto*, Vol. II (Cambridge, MA: Belknap/Harvard University Press, 1963), 133. Raphael's picture is displayed in the Uffizi, Florence, while Sarto's is held in the Galleria Nazionale di Capodimonte in Naples.

42. Giorgio Vasari, *Le vite de' piu eccellenti pittori scultori ed architettori* (Firenze: Sansoni, 1906), Tom. V, 42f.

43. John Shearman, *Andrea del Sarto* (Oxford, UK: Clarendon Press, 1965), 125.

44. Cf. the great Louvre exhibition in 1993, and its catalog, *Copier Créer. De Turner à Picasso: 300 oeuvres inspirées par les maîtres du Louvre* (Paris: Réunion des Musées Nationaux, 1993).

45. The impressive oeuvre of Rubens the copier covers the works of Rogier van der Weyden, Pieter Bruegel the Elder, Raphael, Mantegna, Michelangelo, Andrea del Sarto, Leonardo, Primaticcio, Correggio, as well as a number of classical sculptures. For a summary review of the problem see Jacques Foucart, "Rubens: Copies, répliques, pastiches," in *Copies, répliques, faux. Revue de l'art* 21 (1973). In a 1988 exhibition of copies, a nice copy of the *Spinario* was also shown. Egbert Haverkamp-Begemann with Carolyn Logan, *Creative Copies: Interpretative Drawings from Michelangelo to Picasso* (New York: Drawing Center 9 April–23 July 1988), 77.

46. Letter to Theo van Gogh. Quoted in K.E. Maison, *Themes and Variations* (London: Thames & Hudson, 1960). The illustrated book, which was published shortly thereafter in German as well (*Bild und Abbild. Meisterwerke von*

Meistern kopiert und umgeschaffen (Munich: Droemersche Verlagsanstalt Th. Knaur Nachf., 1960), was among the earliest popular works to draw attention to the fundamental importance of copying in the history of art, a point amply illustrated by the nearly 300 reproductions included.

47. Cf. Salvador Dalí, *Le Mythe Tragique de l'Angelus de Millet* (Paris: Société Nouvelle des Éditions Jean-Jacques Pauvert, 1978).

48. Cf. Kirk Varnedoe, "Fragmentation and Repetition" (chapter 3), in *A Fine Disregard—What Makes Modern Art Modern* (New York: Abrams, 1990).

49. Hans Robert Jauß, *Ästhetische Erfahrung und literarische Hermeneutik* (Frankfurt: Suhrkamp, 1982), 793.

50. "Report from the Select Committee of the House of Commons on the Earl of Elgin's Collection of Sculptured Marbles." Quoted in St. Clair, op. cit., 263. My emphasis. Felicia Hemans, a fashionable poetess at the time, expected no less from these models than the appearance of the British Michelangelo, "What British Angelo may rise to fame." Quoted in Christopher Hitchens, *The Elgin Marbles* (London: Chatto & Windus, 1987), 86. During his London visit in 1815, Antonio Canova too talked about the Elgin Marbles' opening a new era in sculpture. Cf. St. Clair, op. cit., 227.

51. Cf. *Copier Créer*, op. cit., 421f., and also Tillmann Osterwold, "Die trivialisierte Mona Lisa," in *Mona Lisa im XX. Jahrhundert*. Wilhelm Lehmbruck-Museum der Stadt Duisburg, 24. 9.–3. 12. 1978, 119ff. The stealing of the *Mona Lisa* in 1911 and its sensational recovery one-and-a-half years later more or less introduced its twentieth-century career.

52. Cf. David Sylvester, *The Brutality of Fact: Interviews with Francis Bacon* (London: Thames & Hudson, 1987), 38. Velázquez's *Pope Innocent X* is on display in a separate little cabinet in the Doria-Pamphilj Gallery in Rome, alongside Bernini's sculpture of Pope Innocent.

53. Theodor W. Adorno, *Aesthetic Theory* (London: Routledge & Kegan Paul, 1984), 246.

54. Ibid., 246f.

55. Plinius's remark in his *Naturalis historia* about *real* Corynthian bronzes might refer to Roman forgeries (34, 5–7), according to Ridgway (op. cit., 22). Speaking less rigorously, or with the purpose of emphasizing the positive historical significance of forgery, some authors often refer to the copying industry as forgery. János György Szilágyi, a monographer of the Italian copying industry specializing in Corinthian vase painting (*Etruszko–korinthoszi vázafestészet* ["Etruscian–Corinthian Vase Painting"] [Budapest: Akadémiai, 1975]), for example, wrote the following: "Thus, art historians do not lose sight of the fact that their task-list *per definitionem* includes the persecution of forgeries; nevertheless, they do not like to stop at the unmasking of forgeries, but precisely in their capacity as historians, they also bear in mind the positive historical significance of forgeries and forging: no matter how unintentionally, but by their existence and by their inevitable exposure, they bear witness to, and unveil if necessary, the system of values which created them and justified their existence. This equally applied to the Graecophil Etruscans, who made the local 'forgery' of mass-imported Greek vases a

worthwhile project and the Roman nobility who, without truly compre-hending it, fell in love with Greek art, trying to fight their intellectual inferi-ority complex by commissioning the forgery of Classical Greek works with a vehemence and lack of taste characteristic of the *nouveaux riches.*" Szilágyi, *Legbölcsebb az Idö. Antik vázák hamisítványa* ("Time: The Wisest of Them All. The Forgery of Antique Vases") (Budapest: Corvina, 1987), 38. In his book on the moral history of the classical period of Imperial Rome, Ludwig Friedlaender, while unable to come up with positive proof, thinks it almost impossible that, with the great demand for old and famous works and given the high level of virtuosity in copying, there would have been no lack of unscrupulous artists and dealers to exploit the situation (*Sittengeschichte Roms.* Besorgt v. Georg Wissowa [1919], Stuttgart: Parkland, Ungekürzte Textausgabe, n.d.). However, to substantiate this claim he mentions an epi-gram by Martialis (IV/39) and the introduction to Phaedrus's *Fabulorum lib. V.* The latter reads as follows: "I hardly mention the name of good Aesop/Although I have already paid my debt/. . . ./Those who enhance the value of their works/By adding Praxiteles's signature to new sculptures, Myron's to silverware/Zeuxis' to painting/For it is the . . . antique/That our . . . age prefers to the good stuff of its own." For the Chinese forgeries, see Craig Clunas, "Connoisseurs and Aficionados: The Real and the Fake in Ming China (1368–1644)," in *Why Fakes Matter: Essays on Problems of Authenticity,* ed. Mark Jones (London: British Museum Press, 1992).

56. Shaftesbury, "An Essay on the Freedom of Wit and Humour," in *Characteristicks of Men, Manners, Opinions, Times,* Vol. I (Birmingham, UK: Baskerville, 1773), 145.

57. Winckelmann, op. cit., 216f.

58. Socrates tells Parrhasios, "When you copy types of beauty, it is so diffi-cult to find a perfect model that you combine the most beautiful details of several, and thus contrive to make the whole figure look beautiful." Xenophon, *Memorabilia,* III, 10. The individualistic view of the chief villain of modern art, Bernini, who claimed that a given part or limb fits only its own body, has been regarded as "extremely unfounded" by Winckelmann. Cf. Winckelmann, op. cit., 155f.

59. Winckelmann, op. cit., 150.

60. Winckelmann, *Gedanken über die Nachahmung der griechischen Werke* (1755).

61. Ibid.

62. Cf. Wilbur F. Creighton, *The Parthenon in Nashville: From a Personal Viewpoint,* Rev. Ed. (Nashville, TN: N.p., 1991). The winner of the competi-tion to design the building complex of the Millennium Exhibition (Ignác Alpár) announced the following: ". . . in accordance with the different his-torical periods, the historical exhibition should be set in a Gothic, a Renaissance and an Eastern-style block of building . . ." Quoted in János Gerle, Attila Kovács, and Imre Makovecz, *A századforduló magyar építészete* ("Hungarian Architecture at the Turn of the Century") (Budapest: Szépiro-dalmi-Bonex, 1990), 19f.

63. Cf. Joachim Petsch, *Eigeinheim und gute Stube. Zur Geschichte des bürgerlichen Wohnens–Städtebau–Architektur–Einrichtungsstile* (Cologne: DuMont, 1989), 82ff.

64. Cf. Heinz Ladendorf, op. cit., X. Exkurs B. "Ergänzen," 59f.

65. Cf. Maria Neusser, "Die Ergänzung der Venus von Arles. Ein Beitrag zur Geschichte der nationalen Klassizismus in Frankreich," *Belvedere* 13 (September 1928): 51ff.

66. Cf. Gerard Vaughan, "The restoration of classical sculpture in the eighteenth century and the problem of authenticity," in *Why Fakes Matter* (Jones, op. cit.), 43f. The head of the *Townley Discobolus* indeed does not belong to this torso, even though it is also antique and is made of the same marble. Cf. *Fake? The Art of Deception*, ed. Mark Jones (Berkeley: University of California Press, 1990), 140f.

67. Cf. Hugh Tait, "Reinhold Vasters: Goldsmith, Restorer and Prolific Faker," in *Why Fakes Matter* (Jones, op. cit.), 116ff.

68. "No restoration is well-directed if it does not make stylistic assumptions, which are of course open to debate. The belief that in any phase of his work the restorer can divest himself of this uncertainty is not only illogical; it is dangerous." Wind, op. cit., 130.

69. Kubler, op. cit., 108.

70. Cf. chapter 1, note 56.

71. Cf. "The Originality of the Avant-Garde," in Krauss, *The Originality of Avant-Garde and Other Modernist Myths* (Cambridge, MA: MIT Press, 1993 [1985]), 162f.

72. Michael Ayrton, "Introduction," in Maison, op. cit.

73. Georg Simmel, "Philosophie der Landschaft," [1913] in Simmel, *Das Individuum und die Freiheit* (Berlin: Wagenbach, 1984), 130ff.

74. Richard Shiff, "Phototropism (Figuring the Proper)," in *Retaining the Original,* op. cit., 163.

4

THE PERFECT FAKE

There is an extreme case of copying that is generally, but not necessarily, approximated by copy-type forgeries: The case when a copy is *indistinguishable* from the original, or more generally, one copy from another. Indistinguishability is an extreme situation in the sense that it is mostly an *idealization*, the result of a thought experiment. In practice, indistinguishability usually turns out to be retrospective: It is normally thrown into relief only in the—often comic—moment of distinguishing ("unmasking"). Only when we have distinguished do we realize what was indistinguishable before. It does happen, not inevitably but quite frequently, that we know about the need to distinguish, yet we are unable to do it. This can lead to embarrassing and comic situations. One of the eternal themes of comedy is that of mistaken identity and subsequent misunderstanding, all traced back to persons or things indistinguishable. Also, it is not uncommon in everyday life to find ourselves in the uncomfortable situation of not being able to tell which one of the two twins we are actually addressing, or mistaking a person not seen for some time for somebody else. There was an excellent chamber exhibition on forgery in Baltimore in 1987 (unfortunately, unaccompanied by a catalog), in which originals and forgeries were exhibited in pairs and the viewers—in the true pedagogical spirit of American museological traditions—were asked to decide. Only when they made their choice were they able to learn the truth about the exhibits. It happened more than once that the author of this book pressed the wrong button.

What are the cultural and artistic practices in which the problem of indistinguishability plays an important role? I would like to refer to the following three types.

Type One

There are two legends in circulation in the field of fine arts. Both have several versions and both can fundamentally reflect (determine?) the possibilities in our relationship to art. According to the one, a work of art was made so perfect that it turned out to be indistinguishable from reality, from nature, from the real world. For example, the sparrows try to land on the painted image of grape clusters. According to the other, a work of art was made so perfect that it itself became reality, nature, the real world. In a Chinese legend, for example, a painter sets out on the road in the picture he has painted and gets lost in the maze of his own creation.

When we stop and think about it, only in the first case can we talk about indistinguishability in the narrow sense—when there is a difference and, consequently, there is also a similarity. There is a difference between the real grape and its painted image displaying an extreme likeness—a difference that anyone can feel. The naive form of feeling the difference is the delusion, the state of being mistaken—and its reflected form is art appreciation (or one form of it). The road in the earlier-mentioned painting does not resemble a real road—according to the legend, it is *the* road; it has no counterpart in the real world, from which it could appear indistinguishable and from which we ought to distinguish it. In the first case we might relate the artwork to something, to a reality independent from it, and might regard its task to be in the *miming* of this reality, in its simulation or copying. In the second case we regard the artwork to be such a separate world, which cannot be related to the external world.

The first case relates to one of the most important historical traditions of art: Namely, the one that regards art as the imitation of nature. This idea has often been expressed by using the metaphor of a "mirror." Its origin is traced back not to Marxist aesthetics, but to Plato (*The State* X, 596d, e)—or in a positive sense to neo-Platonism—and has been in frequent use ever since the Renaissance (see, for example, Alberti, Leonardo, Shakespeare, etc.). "As late as the middle of the eighteenth century important critics continued to illustrate the concept of imitation by the nature of a looking-glass. Dr. Johnson was fond of this parallel, and found it the highest excellence of Shakespeare that he 'holds up to his readers a faithful mirror of manners and life.' In 1751 Bishop Warburton glossed Pope's line that 'Nature and Homer were, he found, the same' with the comment that

Virgil 'had the prudence to contemplate nature in the place where she was seen to most advantage, collected in all her charms in the clear mirror of Homer.'"[1]

My readers should know by now (if from nowhere else than from the previous chapters of this book) that what has been placed side by side in peaceful harmony in this comment—i.e., to hold up a mirror of nature in the manner of Homer and to imitate the best imitator in the manner of Virgil—was about to cause a major rift in the intellectual world. The mirror metaphor turns out to be an unsatisfactory analogy, one that is often found wanting in connection with many artistic problems, and is completely inappropriate with regard to some movements, periods, and genres. This might lead to the dethronement of the general validity of the theory of imitation, thus relativizing the intellectual accomplishments of important periods, which strictly distinguished between things and their representations, between the world of nature and the world of imitation, so as to bridge the gap with the principle of adequacy. But this cannot eliminate its role in artistic practice, in which the act of recognizing— or causing someone else to recognize—"nature" (the world, the things) shaped by artistic conventions might have an artistic function, along with the extreme case of playfully probing the idea of indistinguishability from nature (in fine art, it is called *tromp-l'oeil,* the deception of the eye).

However, not only nature can be reflected, but art as well. The extreme case in the maintenance of artistic patterns is the probing of the idea of indistinguishability from another work of art; in an ideal situation, the result is the perfect copy or the perfect fake.

Type Two

The above (mimetic) model of cultural practice is based on the existing difference between *depiction* and *depicted*; on the *similarity* and, in extreme cases (usually achieved retrospectively by way of thought experiments), on the virtual merger and apparent indistinguishability of reality and its representation. By contrast, the road on which the painter vanishes does not resemble the real road, nor does it identify with it: it *is* the road; that is, they are self-identical. In its own context and age, the medieval cultic picture did not so much represent the sacred person surrounded by respect and reverence, did not so much simulate reality, but rather embodied or at least resembled that person: What we see in this case directly expresses something of his or her reality. The notion of indistinguishability cannot, in any meaningful way, be applied to these cases. All the less so because these works distinguished themselves from "reality," not in the sense of the final unity of similarity, of adequacy, of depicted and depiction, but in the sense of providing evidence of a *different* reality, one that belongs to a higher and more sacred dimension.

When, however, the principle of identicalness returns in a later period, contrasting itself with the principle of similarity, then in this struggle and dialogue the notion of indistinguishability once again becomes meaningful. The "thing" is itself, but where is the distinction that elevates it to art? How can a mere thing be distinguished from a work of art? The entire range of the banal and conservative attack on modernity in the twentieth century can be summarized in the denial of this distinction and distinguishability. The scratches that we see, the cacophony that we hear, the meaningless heap of words that we read—these are all indistinguishable from the reality of scratches, of noise, etc., and can have therefore no artistic reality. This period abounded in philosophically inclined artists, or artists highly esteemed by philosophers (i.e., artists of radical outlook or artists whose works lent themselves to radical interpretation) who made this idea the basis of their experiments, either meditatively or provocatively, either ironically or pathetically. An illustration of this phenomenon, one that has been quoted on many occasions, is provided by the ready-mades, first put on display in 1913 by Marcel Duchamp. Here the artistic act is conceived to be in the placement of everyday, manufactured objects into a new context, as well as in the provision of titles (bicycle wheel = *Bicycle Wheel*; urinal = *Fontaine*; bottle dryer = *Bottle Dryer*, etc.).

A counter-example of *Fontaine* (1917), but also its counterpart in a different context, can be found in René Magritte's oil painting made in 1929 and entitled *Magic Mirror,* probably representing a bedpan[2] with the words "corps humaine" written inside. But Magritte's entire oeuvre can be conceived as the inversion of Duchamp's gesture, while all along probing *the same issues* with the same tenacity. While Duchamp's ready-mades experiment with the artworks' indistinguishability from everyday objects, Magritte's illusionistic art transfers the picture into the domain of similarity: He turns it into a *mirror*, only to withdraw it immediately from the realm of sense experiences through his *concettis,* his scintillating ideas of unfailing ingenuity. He suggests that the picture has no pattern. Rather than trying to copy, imitate, or represent, his paintings only resemble themselves: In his pictures a pipe is not a pipe, an apple is not an apple or, in his painting entitled *Not to be Reproduced* (1937–1939), the mirror does not reflect, as the mirror image of the man with his back turned to the viewers also shows him with his back turned to the viewers; the eye is *The False Mirror* (1928); nature uninterruptedly spills over into the picture space of canvasses erected on easels; the shirt front assumes the shape of the breast, the shoe assumes the shape of the foot; the clipped-out human shape becomes transparent; according to the inscription of the picture showing two identical drawings of a tiny house, the *objet réel* and the *objet représente*, "everything tends to make one think that there is little relation between an object and that which represents it."[3] In his superb Magritte study, Michel Foucault refers to this simulacrum, which resists all references and can identify only with itself, as *similitude,* as opposed to *resemblance,* the likeness that represents.[4]

Finally, by way of the third type, I name the re-creation of everyday objects requiring indistinguishability, as manifested in Jasper Johns's beer cans and *Flag* (the latter made in 1954, the idea of which was no more than serialized by Andy Warhol, the first mega-star of fine arts by the standards of popular culture). The representative interpretations, which Max Imdahl collected, went something like this: "this is not the painting of a flag"; "in the case of a painted flag, painting is painting, and the flag is a flag"; "is it a flag or a painting?"; "the flag's identity as a flag and the concrete painting's identity as a concrete painting—since they exist independently of one another—mutually exclude each other. This paradox makes it impossible for the viewer to orient himself firmly and to make positive decisions. The vacillation of perception between the flag and the concrete painting, of which Jasper Johns himself spoke, never stops the viewer's confusion and indecision: 'I am interested in that which is not what it was; in that which becomes different from what it is; in the moment when we clearly identify the thing, as well as in the passing of this moment; in the moment of seeing and saying, as well as in the way we come to accept this.'"[5]

The model types I have selected form some extremely radical experiments on the subject of indistinguishability from things in modern art. (The first example, Duchamp, was also the most radical of them all.) Nevertheless, in all these types we cannot help noticing one of the basic themes of this art. It is the same theme that Piet Mondrian referred to when he noted down in his Parisian diary the following sentences: "The natural surface of things may be beautiful, but their imitation is already lifeless. The things give us everything, and their representation gives us nothing."[6] And indeed, there is probably nothing that could show the conceptual shift from natural reality to abstract reality more clearly than the trees he created in the 1910s: after the gradual disappearance of resemblance, imitation, and representation, nothing more is left but color and line—the Platonic idea.

Despite all claims to the contrary, the various art theories have been in a mutually fruitful dialogue with artistic practice throughout the twentieth century. The theoreticians reflected on the above problem (or encouraged the new experiments) by putting forward their comprehensive *reductive* proposals, decreasing or bracketing the *comparable* elements in art—the elements that represent, or integrate into, the worldly experience—and at the same time increasing the importance of the artwork *as a world* (a new world, a possible other world, a world on par with the life-world). From the fact that they conceived of artworks as planes, spaces, or lines, or literary works as texts (these were to vary frequently in the wake of the early twentieth-century experiments of Alois Riegl and the Russian formalist literary critics), it follows that in the debate on *similarity* versus *identity* the art theoreticians came down on the side of the latter.

However, perfect self-identity has its sensual, perceptual limits. What puts the self-identity of the urinal, the flag, Robert Rauschenberg's *Bed* (1955), or Warhol's Brillo and Campbell boxes into focus is precisely the point that the artists close in on perceptual indistinguishability from a "real" object, a thing from the real world. (Or to put it in a different way, they distance themselves from indistinguishability, not perceptually but through a mere gesture of philosophical importance.) If we were to accept such extreme experiments as the paradigms of modern art, then the resulting conclusion would be that the function of the optical sensory organ, of visual perception, would have to be suspended. A prominent art philosopher did not recoil from drawing this—to my mind extremely problematic—conclusion: Namely, that in the case of two—physically, sensorially, perceptually—perfectly indistinguishable objects, one is *not* a work of art and the other *is*; or that two indistinguishable objects are two different works of art, with the difference lying exclusively "in the mode of production of these objects."[7] Without trying to exclude the possible emergence of such a situation under certain circumstances (especially with regard to the duality of artwork versus nonartwork), I very much doubt the possibility of founding an art on this new paradigm.

Type Three ——————————————————————————————————————

For the third cultural/artistic practice associated with indistinguishability, I have designated the name *quotation*. The question immediately arises whether it is justified at all to regard it as a separate entry. Would not the precise copy of an artistic pattern qualify as a quotation? Do not the Stars and Stripes quote the *Flag*? As for the second question, it is relatively easy to answer it in the negative. The readymades, as well as all other artistic devices aspiring to similar effects, usually dislodge the "original" objects from their respective class or sequence, and do so in such a way that these objects lose their original function and acquire a new, artistic one (ready-mades are often used to relativize or destroy the notion of art). The ready-mades' relationship to the "original" objects is characterized by negation, and if there is anything still left from the original context, then this tends to invoke what Imdahl called "vacillating perception," which eliminates the possibility of regarding them as quotations. As with the optical games, we see either a *flag* or a *painting*. Nevertheless, there exist ready-made objects that are inserted into the context of an artwork in accordance with their original function: *These* are quotations.

The problem concerning the quotations' relationship to the copying of artworks is much harder to tackle. This issue itself can arise only in connection with copying the patterns of art traditions, since not even the most naive ideology can propose that holding up a mirror to nature (to the human body, to a landscape) could result in a quotation characteristically more direct and objective than a conjuration or a reminiscence. Nature cannot be quoted and—save a few insignificant exceptions such as the direct outlining of shadows or the drawings made with the perspectival apparatus used in the Renaissance—cannot be copied, only imitated. By contrast, the question whether the accurate copying or imitation of an *artwork* also qualifies as a quotation is far from irrelevant.

It is worth illustrating the problem with the help of an extreme example contrasting two forms of morally deviant behavior: What is the difference between a forger and a plagiarist? This has been answered clearly by Monroe C. Beardsley: In the case of plagiarism one concerns oneself in "passing off another's work as one's own"; in the case of forgery, in "passing off one's own work as another's."[8] The distinction can perhaps be formalized even legally: one classifies as fraud, the other as theft. In the first case somebody fraudulently alters the pedigree of his own property, while in the second case somebody misappropriates someone else's property. Now, if we were to leave behind the mischievous practices of forgery and plagiary for the time being, then the question seems justified as to whether the same distinction could not meaningfully be interpreted in the broad cultural practice of imitating/repeating/copying tradition? To a very large extent, these practices serve the maintenance of tradition and the continuity of art. The more extensive the (often incognizant) imitation or the deliberate copying is, the more apparent it becomes that the work is someone else's. This is a trivial issue with regard to copying codices, manuscripts, or music scores, in which case there are clearly defined, pragmatic limits within which we decide whether to take notice or to disregard any divergence from the original: The typographical errors do not entitle a typist to a share in the copyrights of a novel, while a codex copyist, in harmony with the rarity and antiquity of his pursuit, might preserve valuable—linguistic and other—information for posterity. But as to the practice of *artistic* copying, the fact that an artwork is not mine not necessarily means that it is someone else's. It might belong to convention. Since the perfect individual copy is an impossibility—impossible in the world of objects, that is, where the subject of copying is not limited to signs (letters, musical notes), and even the most servile form of copying requires skills of execution—it can never belong *entirely to someone else*; but given that an entirely original work (that is, a work completely independent of all patterns) is also impossible, the existence of an artwork belonging to *no one but its author* is just as much of an impossibility.

Another group of copies and replicas is always deliberate. Their source, at least for the copier, is obvious. This is shown—again, within pragmatic limits—by the accuracy of copying. This deliberateness means that the copier has a definite, rhetorical purpose for his act. Most frequently, such a purpose in the history of culture is the enlisting of an authority in support of my cause. Such a reference strengthens the cause to which I have committed myself. The choice, precisely because it is deliberate, aligns the source with my cause, helping me to appropriate, if not the source itself, at least its spirit. The gesture of inserting a replica or copy of a segment of one's tradition into one's works is a gesture of *appropriation,* or, increasingly more often in its more modern versions, of *expropriation.* Therefore the quotation (because this is what we are talking about) can be seen as one particular form of repetition/copying, which paradoxically goes the furthest in the appropriation of the most precise and most deliberate copies.[9]

Another point not to be neglected is that copying approaches the conceptual generalization of repetition from the direction of craftsmanly or artistic re-*making,* while quotations do the same from the direction of verbal repetition. The verbal or literary origin of quotations is clearly shown by their current usage. We treat it as an obvious precondition of the quotation that anyone wanting to use quotations in his text has to copy the quotation first, or in the case of live speech, he has to perform the corresponding procedure of memorizing. With regard to fine art, we *transpose* the notion of quotation by using the experiences of literature and rhetoric. And although such transpositions are often legitimized by the historical changes of culture, yet in the field of fine arts it often proves a great deal more difficult to decide whether the case in point is about the preservation of tradition and convention, the sustenance of its continuity, that is about another's work in one's own, or about its decidedly deliberate revelation, illumination, quotation, about one's own work in that of another. There could be works that can be interpreted both ways, or at least the interpretation of which is open to both approaches.

With regard to twentieth-century art, in which the pattern-maintaining function of the canon has been called into question at the expense of its standard-providing function, these decisions are easier to make. When Salvador Dali inserts a faithful copy of Millet's *Angelus* in his various pictures or repeats the same painting in various other media, then we do not necessarily need written documents about the extraordinary influence this painting has made on him in order to realize that the *Angelus* is a quotation. And when we discover that one of Magritte's male figures has a black spot on his back that displays one of the female figures from Botticelli's *Primavera* in faithful colors, then once again we need not hesitate much.

The problem, which brings the quotation back to the difficulties regarding indistinguishability, concerns the *quotation extended to, or filling in, the entire work*. This is a modern problem. In the medieval period, "the four methods of making books"—i.e., by copiers, compilers, commentators, and authors—still formed a continuum.[10] In characteristic fashion, the primary literary example of this modern issue is provided not by a work of art, but by a thought-experiment narrated in a work of art: Borges's famous short story, "Pierre Ménard, Author of the *Quixote*" (1939), much loved by literary theorists. According to the story, Ménard's version—although it repeats Cervantes's novel (or rather, a few chapters of his novel) verbatim—is a perfectly original creation, since the 300 years that have passed between the publication of the two books have placed the latter work into an entirely new context. In the field of fine arts, the basic example has already been mentioned in this book—Duchamp's *Shaven L.H.O.O.Q.* from 1965, which is 100 invitation cards featuring an unretouched photographic reproduction of *Mona Lisa*, referring not only to Leonardo's work but also (and even more directly) to Duchamp's 1919 version of *L.H.O.O.Q.* (repeated seven times altogether over the decades!), in which the artist retouched a picturepostcard reproduction of *Mona Lisa* by adding a moustache and beard.

Over the past decades, the fictitious literary–historical event and the ironic art–philosophical gesture of a fine-art character have exerted an influence of unparalleled power on the respective practices of literature and fine arts. The great stylistic trend-setter of Hungarian literature, Péter Esterházy, devised a formula that has been repeated by many authors: "The book contains among other things quotations, verbatim or modified, by X.Y.Z." Esterházy has incorporated in his work *Bevezetés a szépirodalomba* ("An Introduction to Literature") a short story (from Danilo Kiš) with the following footnote: "The text ~~contains among other things~~ quotations~~, verbatim or modified,~~ from Danilo Kiš."[11] Of course, all forms of radicalism are alien to Esterházy's mentality; he saw a stylistic device in the frequent use of quotations. A short story of four pages inserted in a 700-page book was nothing more than a charming and somewhat narcissistic diversion: The hero of Kiš's story was one of Esterházy's ancestors.

The radical paradigm based on the ultimate case of the total quotation, which strives for complete indistinguishability, eliminates the difference that I tried to outline in my earlier attempt to extend the contrast between forgery and plagiary. In line with its ideological premises, it eliminates the subject itself, without which the distinction between its own self and anything else becomes meaningless. To avoid the endless prattle that characterizes this subject, I would again like to refer to a fiction, one that resembles Borges's invention in that it outlines the future tendencies of artistic practice with prophetic foresight: The novel I have in mind is Italo Calvino's *If on a Winter's Night a Traveler*. The central character is a writer named Silas Flannery, who (in the words of Hans Robert Jauß) "discovers the lofty, and hitherto unsuspected, aesthetic values of plagiary. He learns from his literary agent, Marana, that a Japanese company has come into possession of the essential formula for his plots, and has been turning out first-rate new Flannerys on the basis of this information. Once his initial outrage has subsided, Silas is overcome by a strange excitement: He imagines his Japanese alter ego in the process of inventing one of his stories, and he is forced to admit that these cheap imitations 'contain such refined and secret wisdom, the likes of which the genuine Flannery works completely lack.' Instead of simply being its disguise, a forgery is more like the final formula of fictionalization, the mystification of mystification, 'truth raised to the second power, so to speak.' This is Marana's argument, the secret seducer and herald of the electronic age, who believes that the difference between authentic and reproduced reality, nature and art, the technological lifestyle and the artistic world of the media, will vanish."[12]

By now this ironic fiction of indistinguishability has become the basis of deadly serious experiments. I am, however, of the opinion that Duchamp's life-philosophy still applies: It is possible to reach— once or twice or three times—the final frontiers of art, the place where an artwork dissolves into an art-philosophical gesture, the same way as the highest peaks can be scaled more than once by a mountaineer. But it is impossible to set up shop there for the continuous production of artworks. The fact that Duchamp walked away, and only rarely returned, followed from the insolent depths of his gesture. Every single one of his more serious followers, after having reconsidered the possibilities of artistic creation, toned his wonderful and cynical radicalism down a little.

So are there any limits to art, someone may ask? There are no limits, at least not in the kind of prestabilized sense that might enable us to say: Here is where reality ends and art begins. But every work of art, every form of artistic creation defines its own counterpart as the segment of "reality" from which to distinguish itself, and with which it cannot form an indistinguishable whole.

The Debate on Indistinguishability

Goodman

Let us assume that an authentic work of art (a painting) and its perfect forgery are hung side by side. We are *aware* of the distinction, because the authenticity of the first work is uninterruptedly documented, while the act of forgery in the second case can be proven beyond doubt with the help of scientific methods. The forgery is perfect in the sense that perceptually the fake cannot be distinguished from the original. Although there do exist a number of distinguishing factors with regard to authorship, period of origin, physical and chemical characteristics, and market price, these distinctions are not *visible*.

This thought-experiment, originally devised by Nelson Goodman, has generated a great deal of excitement among Anglo-Saxon philosophers.[13] This is one variation of the twin paradox originally proposed by Wittgenstein and reformulated by Jerry A. Fodor as follows: Two things, which are for all other appearances identical, might differ in a property *P*. In this case the difference is concealed, and *P* must be a relational quality. Wittgenstein's famous twin paradox focuses on the difference between motion and activity (my hand is raised–I raise my hand), whereas Danto's indistinguishable objects, one of which is an artwork and the other is not, explore the nature of artistic creation, with the concealed relational quality here being the intention. It appears that the puzzle of the true and false twins is not as fertile, or at least Fodor lists it among the philosophically—i.e., epistemologically—less interesting cases: ". . . it's not very interesting that there could be twins one of whom is a baker and the other of whom isn't; or even that there could be twins one of which is a genuine Da Vinci and the other of which isn't. It's obvious that bankers and genuine Da Vinci's are constituted by their relations (to banks in the one case and to Da Vinci in the other). . . ."[14]

Nevertheless, Goodman's dilemma addresses anew some of the classic questions of aesthetics. Assuming that the adjectives "original" and "forged" conceal opposing aesthetic value judgments, then the impossibility of perceptual distinguishability questions the *aisthesis*, the perceptual nature of aesthetic experience. It might be suggested that the aesthetic experience should somehow incorporate *knowledge*, at least as a guiding force. We could, however, turn the question around and accept the testimony of our perceptual experience, in which case the traditional aesthetic value of originality must be reexamined. Similarly, the notion of forgery could also be reviewed, since—as anyone will admit—the term "forgery" can easily be substituted in the hypothesis with terms like perfect reproduction, imitation, or copy, even if not all forgeries are copies and not all copies are forgeries. Also, we must be able to answer the question as to why it is possible to construct such an idealization in the field of fine arts, and why it is so complicated (if not impossible) to bring similar examples from the area of literature and music. This question shakes the foundation of the concept of unity of the arts.

However, one could point out that the hypothesis is somewhat feigned. Goodman's solution itself (as we shall shortly see) emphasizes the isolated, point-like nature of the example in the time dimension. A rather amusing point about the entire debate is that almost everyone participating in it decides to modify, shift, or otherwise change the original hypothesis. Nevertheless, it should not necessarily be accepted as a starting point. We might say that its universality is only superficial: A mere *symptom* of the situation in modern art. Then again, we might approach it from the other direction, claiming that the example fundamentally subverts tradition, although, in the majority of the cases and in its own context (and given enough time), tradition can—as a rule if not on every single occasion—solve the dilemma of distinguishing between the original works and forgeries/copies.

Goodman's answer to his own question ("the question is . . . whether there can be any aesthetic difference if nobody, not even the most skilled expert, can ever tell the pictures apart by merely looking at them"[15]) combines the aisthesis with the cognitive elements of the aesthetic experience. The fact that even an expert cannot distinguish between the original and the fake by merely looking at them does not necessarily mean that no one will ever be able to do so. And in the learning process of acquiring this skill, the nonperceptual knowledge that there is a difference between the two artworks plays a prominent part. Goodman shares Ernst H. Gombrich's view that the innocent eye is a myth—*perception* and *interpretation* are inseparable. In this case interpretation is guided by a piece of initially imperceptible knowledge, although this is not sufficient in and of itself. The aesthetic difference is constituted by knowledge and opportunity combined—opportunity allowing this knowledge to initiate processes, as a result of which we (or someone else) can become able to develop a perceptual ability to distinguish. For it provides evidence that the difference exists and that we might learn how to distinguish it. Our present perception in this respect can be regarded as an exercise in distinguishing. The knowledge instigates us to change our present aesthetic experience. The aesthetic qualities of an artwork not only constitute what we see, but also determine how we see it.

In Goodman's opinion, therefore, learning and practicing (these cultural practices with extended temporal dimensions), when they are driven by knowledge, form a primary aesthetic activity. And this is true not only with regard to one of the paintings, but to both of them. The information that a picture is original or forged cannot, by itself, guide us in the question as to whether there is a difference in *value* between the two, and if so, which one is to be considered more valuable. Titian copied Seisenegger's painting and created a more valuable work in the process. According to Goodman's original example of a Rembrandt composition and its copy, Rembrandt's work was likely to be the more valuable of the two, but if Rembrandt copies his master Lastman's work,[16] then the copy will probably be more valuable. The study of the "referential classes" of original and authentic works—for example, of the Rembrandt "class"—and the parallel development of the ability to distinguish between authentic and nonauthentic works, is also a matter of learning and practicing. This extends and generalizes Goodman's original example: There the cultural practice was connected to the familiarity with a fact, a piece of information—this one is forged, that one is not—while here we are talking about the learning *process* in the study of the class of original works.

Goodman's proposed solution continues, or revives, the classic views about the consensual nature of taste, about its attainability through practice. "But though there be a naturally wide difference in point of delicacy, between one person and another, nothing tends further to increase and improve this talent than *practice* in a particular art, and the frequent survey or contemplation of a particular species of beauty," Hume writes.[17] Although he was among the first ones to suggest that pictures should be interpreted as linguistic signs, Goodman was in fact not concerned with the growing skepticism about taste, nor with the suspicion towards the testimony of the eye, nor with the exclusiveness of the artwork's rhetorical interpretative unit, nor with that typically modern hermeneutic preference characterized by the tendency to regard artworks as art-philosophical statements. The advocates of the above views, as we shall shortly see, will come forward one after the other in the debate on Goodman's theses. But before coming to that, I would like to accompany our author in his attempt to clarify the position with regard to the second of the two fictitious pictures, the *forged* one.

Van Meegeren's forged Vermeers were authenticated even by the experts. As a result of the shock and the subsequent learning process that followed van Meegeren's announcement of his own forgeries and the verification of his claims, not even a layman could have confused the two anymore. In Goodman's view it was not our aesthetic sensibilities that changed in such dramatic fashion and in such a short period, but rather the new erudition and knowledge that brought about this turn. It happened not by itself, but by removing the obstacles standing in the way of practicing the differentiation between the Vermeers and the van Meegerens. As a consequence of the new information, the forgeries, which had up to then been classified as entries of the Vermeer class (mutually reconfirming one another in that status), now founded for themselves a new class of precedents, the van Meegeren class. The fact of the unmasking, in conjunction with the training it instigated, taught us to *see* the difference.

Goodman's definition of forgery goes as follows: "A forgery of a work of art is an object falsely purporting to have the history of production requisite for the (or an) original of the work."[18] This is a rather opportune formula in the sense that it avoids all moral complications: Instead of the intentions of the artist, it speaks about the "assertions" of the work of art. It includes the masses of copies and workshop material that eventually *became* forgeries, not in accordance with the original intentions of authors but due to faulty attributions, whether willful or inadvertent, of later times. It avoids discussing the issue of forgery in "the language of the morality of art."[19] On the basis of my investigations into the matter so far, I accept this definition with one modification: A forgery of a work of art is an object falsely purporting to have both the history of production, as well as the entire subsequent *general historical fate* requisite for the (or an) original work. Without the general historical fate—which includes aging and accidental wear and tear, and also the natural history of the artwork—the statement about the history of production does not have credibility. It was about the paintings of Lord Duveen, who was perhaps the most famous art dealer of our century, that his sister once maliciously remarked that his antique pictures stank with the smell of fresh oil painting. Forgery has as much to do with construction for the sake of the illusion of the history of production as with demolition for the sake of the creation of the illusion of the subsequent general historical fate (mostly for the sake of antiquity).

If we were to identify the precondition that an object should wear its history on its sleeve with the physical history of its production, this would limit the possibility of forgery to only a fraction of artworks: to those that are "autographic." To solve this problem, Goodman proposed a very interesting distinction between the *autographic* and the *allographic* forms of art. In the case of the autographic genres (this class includes the "one-stage" painting, and the "two-stage" engraving and print, but also sculpture, which might belong to both categories—in other words, the majority of fine arts), the prerequisite of authenticity is that either the work of art (painting, sculpture) or its first stage (woodblock, copper-plate) must bear the evidence of the artist's physical touch. Even the most perfect copy by any other hand cannot be authentic or original.[20]

As to the allographic arts (whether literature, usually one-stage, or music, transmitted by performing artists, therefore two-stage), they are mediated by signs (letters and notes) rather than by their physical reality. Every one of their allographic copies (books, musical score sheets, etc.) is authentic, provided that it meets the qualification of the "sameness of spelling." Therefore, such a definition allows for the possibility of someone trying to forge Shakespearean dramas or "discover" a previously unknown Schubert symphony; however, a fake *Hamlet* or a forged Great Symphony in C Major as the analogy of the copies or forgeries of known Dürer compositions is unthinkable. The emphasis in the earlier-mentioned story by Borges is precisely on the authenticity of Ménard's copy of *Don Quixote*. And Goodman's definition confirms this, since Ménard's work, although it is a word-for-word replica of Cervantes's book, never purported to have the history of production of the latter. While Cervantes "in a clumsy fashion, opposes the fictions of chivalry, the tawdry provincial reality of his country; Menard selects as his 'reality' the land of Carmen during the century of Lepanto and Lope de Vega."[21]

Our intuition undoubtedly makes a distinction between forgeries, copies, and imitations of objects—and of works of art in particular—on the one hand, and the more complicated issues concerning the forgery, imitation, and copying of artworks of nonmaterial media on the other, as indeed the notion of authenticity is interpreted differently in the case of, say, a sculpture and a musical performance. The same distinction is also preserved in language, as the authentic work of art of material media is the work of art itself, while an authentic performance meets the (historically changing) norms of faithfulness to the original work.

As Goodman has emphatically pointed out, he was led purely by considerations of convenience in introducing the above distinction; and indeed from an analytical point of view, this might be true. These categories, however, reflect the historical facts surprisingly well. It seems likely that initially all forms of art were autographic. In cases where the work of art is impermanent (a fleeting sound) or when the production requires the cooperation of a large number of people, the boundaries of time and individuality are breached by signs. In the case where an originally autographic (performed, recited) art form, literature, is still transmitted to the audience in two stages, as in a theatrical play, there a sovereign, autographic art has flourished—i.e., acting. The art of an actor can literally be copied, imitated, or "forged."

The paradox of the performing artist who has, even within the limits of "the sameness of spelling," a wide scope (one that is getting ever wider in the last century) for sovereign artistic creation and expression, takes us back to the problems of imitation, copying, and forgery in the (broadly interpreted) fields of fine art. After all, in discussing van Meegeren as someone who, rather than forging Vermeer's pictures, filled a hiatus in the painter's mysterious early period, Goodman himself extended the dilemma of forgery, formerly reduced to the problem of indistinguishable imitation. Umberto Eco classifies the van Meegeren affair to be a case for "forgery *ex nihilo*," with van Meegeren's pictures qualifying for not one but two of the postulated species of the class: His pictures were at the same time paintings executed *a la manière de* and creative forgeries.[22] Van Meegeren's distinctive relationship with Vermeer survived even after the former's works became established in their own precedential class. His whole adventure could be regarded as an (admittedly misguided) form of "performing art" in which he applied Vermeer's oeuvre as a method of writing to which he introduced new variations. It also resembles the widespread practice of writing sequels, the continuations of famous novels, in which the signs are, of course, not identical to those of the original, but on a more general level there is a common "spelling" to connect the two.

Goodman's twofold criterion of authenticity is, of course, also relativized by the activities of the apprentices, copiers, imitators, and forgers of great masters, as well as by certain tendencies in modern fine art. The canons of painting, along with the individual workshops, had distinctive hallmarks and schemes that could be regarded as signs or signals, while complete autography has never been a general rule in the history of painting. On the other hand, the idea of a picture being the construction of linguistic signs has very much become generally accepted in the art theory and practice of the past few decades.

As a radical nominalist, Goodman would, of course, dismiss a number of the objections. For him, the extension of his concept of "spelling" I have just indicated would obviously be unacceptable. But the ease with which the dichotomy of autography versus allography can be relativized itself suggests that this is a category that is readily adjustable to cultural practice.

The question is: What kind of cultural practice corresponds to Goodman's ideas about forgeries and authentic works of art? He assigns major importance to knowledge, or to new knowledge. For this reason, in his view the central character in cultural practice must be the expert, whose perception is trained by knowledge. And it is for this reason that slight and barely noticeable changes acquire great importance, providing firm holds for the eye to explicate the aesthetic difference. "Extremely subtle changes can alter the whole design, feeling, or expression of a painting. Indeed, the slightest perceptual differences sometime matter the most aesthetically; gross physical damage to a fresco may be less consequential than slight but smug retouching."[23]

Sagoff

Since in Goodman's theory a major, albeit not exclusive, role is assigned to the cognitive elements of the aesthetic experience, the debate is likely to focus on the actual balance—the relative importance of the knowledge about a work of art and the perceptual experience it provides. In Mark Sagoff's view, the aesthetic experience is based purely on knowledge. He is of the opinion that when the original and a forgery are perceptually indistinguishable, any comparison between them is wholly inappropriate. He considers such statements as "one picture (the forgery) is just as masterful or beautiful as the other (the authentic)" to be based on improper linguistic usage. In the same way as the adjective "masterful" has a different meaning when used to describe a fourteenth-century Florentine portrait and a jailbreak, it is also used in a different sense in connection with a portrait and its perfect fake. The adjective "masterful" becomes an aesthetic statement only in reference to the substance predicate (a fourteenth-century Florentine painting, Mondrian, etc.). "A forgery will not have relational aesthetic qualities, then, in common with the original no matter how closely it resembles it or how difficult it is to tell the two paintings apart."[24] They do not belong to the same referential class: ". . . original paintings and forgeries have radically different *cognizable* properties and for that reason are not equally valuable as works of art. . . . But great art works offer a more important and most profound kind of knowledge."[25]

The time factor plays no part in Sagoff's interesting analytical reasoning—and neither therefore does historicity—which in Goodman's case still had an important role. According to Goodman, for example, the van Meegeren pictures belonged to the referential class of Vermeer right until the referential class of van Meegeren was founded by recognition and the new piece of information. The realization of the existence of the two classes and the aesthetic distinction resulting from the subsequent learning process are therefore manifested in the historical dimension of cultural practice. In Sagoff's view, however, both distinctions are given, knowable facts; not knowing about them is a shortcoming, not a problem. This however distorts his relationship to historical culture.

As for Goodman's thought-experiment, it was also characterized by a certain degree of arbitrariness, when he confined it to studying the dilemma of forgery and authenticity through the example of the precise copies of known works. This is only one type of the several existing forms of forgery, while there are numerous copies that are not forgeries at all. Even Goodman himself surpasses this category with van Meegeren's case. By contrast, Sagoff treats the example of copying as a definition. When he sets out to prove that the original and a forgery cannot belong to the same referential class even with regard to the point that they both represent the same object (the same clouds are floating in the sky in the original and the identical forgery), then he distinguishes between forgery and reproduction: "A forgery copies another painting; a reproduction is not a painting but a print, photograph, or something of that sort, which represents a painting."[26] While a reproduction denotes the picture, the relationship between a forgery and the original is not one of representation but of identicalness. A reproduction represents the picture depicting the cloud; the forgery, on the other hand, stands in place of the original, and in such a way that it merely repeats the problem solution of the original (the representation of the cloud). While the original picture searches for a solution, the forgery repeats an already existing solution. To this extent it has a heuristic as well as a pedagogic value, but it cannot have the same aesthetic value as the original.

By contrast, we shall see later on that, in a hypothetical construction, Arthur C. Danto is prepared to allow for identicalness even in the case of wholly independent works of art, while he regards forgery and copying to be the kind of representations that Sagoff reserves for reproductions. Although for completely different reasons

Danto's criticism of forgery in one way resembles Sagoff's: Danto, too, rejects forgeries for their substitutionary and epiphytic character.

In his reasoning, therefore, Sagoff identifies copying with forgery. In order to be able to counter the obvious objection, whereby not every copy is a forgery, he labels as forgeries those copies that do not easily lend themselves to any other classification: Primarily copies of belated origin. He also wants to exclude the identity of period, provenance, school, and artist so as to avoid the possibility of having to place a work of art and its copy/forgery in the same referential class on that basis.[27] This is, however, wholly arbitrary. A forgery cannot be identified with a copy; rather, both should be regarded as the overlapping section of two intersecting circles. There are copies that are not forgeries, and there are copies that are; and then there are forgeries that are not copies.[28]

Equally untenable is the following conclusion: The fact that "an artist cannot forge his own work but creates an original work with every copy suggests the truth that paintings are not classified as forgeries or as fakes if they can plausibly be counted is some other way."[29] But at the same time, it is entirely plausible that a painter might produce or copy a work in the manner of his earlier, more successful period, which would thus be "falsely purporting to have the history of production requisite for the original of the work." Giorgio de Chirico is known to have done so. Less well known is the letter written on November 9, 1964 to Lajos Kassák by Victor Vasarely, which provides evidence for the wide occurrence of such practices: "I am certain that Denis [René, one of the famous gallery owners of contemporary Paris] will soon perform his great act for you. Naturally, he will greatly regret that the works of the past are so few and far between. He will not understand why you are not willing to 'recreate' a few collages, using old paper, after the existing photographs. Chagall, Braque, Miro, but most notably Arp are all playing this game, only they do it wholesale and without dating their works. The publication of the chronology only takes place in the catalog."[30] This is, I believe, quite plain talk. And to also bring in an example from outside the world of art, there is Mussolini's recently discovered diary, which the experts accepted as original in the sense that it was written by Mussolini himself between 1943 and 1945, antedated to the period between 1935 and 1939, in order to diminish the author's wartime responsibilities.[31] Now that is a classic case of self-forgery!

Generally speaking, it probably holds true that two barely distinguishable paintings cannot be regarded as two copies of the same work; but even with regard to prints, the situation is far too complicated to follow Mark Sagoff in regarding copies traced back to the same plate or woodblock as identical works of art belonging to the same referential class, "not simply because they look like each other but more significantly because they are struck from the same plate."[32]

In two-stage art, not only the plates have their own history of production, but so do the resulting prints. The so-called *Hundred Guilder Print,* one of Rembrandt's most popular copper-plate engravings during the eighteenth and nineteenth centuries, which shows Christ healing the ill, could well serve to illustrate the rising complications. The same copper-plate is known to have been used at the beginning of the eighteenth century, well after Rembrandt's death, to produce prints, the aesthetic status of which was very different from that of the early prints due to the wear and tear on the plate. Then, at the end of the eighteenth century an amateur restored the plate, thus introducing further changes in the aesthetic status of the artwork. (In the nineteenth century the plate itself was copied and forged, but that is beyond the scope of our current topic.[33])

Even when it has been heavily damaged, a fresco is thought to be identical with the original work of art and, to a certain pragmatic limit, the same goes for restoration; that too poses no threat to the work's identity. By contrast, the situation is thoroughly different with printed works. In that case, precisely because the early prints made during the lifetime of the artist and preserving the original intention are available, we have no reason to consider the copies printed on damaged, belated, restored, or new paper as works of art identical with the early, contemporary prints. Quite often these are forgeries, even when the plate used to print them is original in the sense of physical identity. There is a museum in Budapest where anyone can use the original print machine and typesetting to make his or her own copy of one of the greatest relics in Hungarian history, the proclamation known as the Twelve Points (1848). Nevertheless, it would be foolish to think that we are actually taking home one of the original issues. Sixty years after Rodin's death, a copy of his *The Gate of Hell* was cast again: The authenticity of this copy is dubious, regardless of the fact that even the first copy was made posthumously, and irrespective of the point that Rodin, who showed a marked nonchalance towards the "second stage"—or ultimate realization—of his sculptures, deeply believed in "the ethos of reproduction."[34]

How can the aesthetic distinction of perceptually indistinguishable works of art be established? Sagoff argues that no visual foundation is needed for the knowledge about this distinction; what is more, it is this knowledge that enables us to distinguish the different qualities as being the different qualities of the two pictures. It is this knowledge that helps us separate the referential classes and makes it plain that one picture is a masterpiece of art, the other a masterful forgery. "We understand a work of art, just as we understand an experiment in physics, not when we attempt to judge it out of every context, but in so far as we place it within the questions, problems, expectations, etc., which characterize the state of a continuing system of inquiry. Thus a painting and a forgery, no matter how they may appear on the screen of an oscilloscope, or to critics who cannot apply the appropriate framework, may still be the sources of very different kinds of cognitive response."[35]

We can certainly agree with that part of the above passage that constitutes the criticism of the perfect-forgery case. The problems of culture cannot be presented out of context, on the basis of the static, as opposed to the dynamic model of aesthetic experience. The strange thing is, however, that this is precisely the area where Sagoff leaves himself open to criticism when confronted with the questions, problems, and expectations connected either to the aesthetic status of forgery or to its historical authenticity. In identifying the aesthetic conception with cognitive responses to works of art, the author himself is found guilty of overlooking the cultural context.

In both of his quoted studies, Sagoff looks down with sarcasm on everything that in the aesthetic experience pertains to feeling, enjoyment, and sensuality, as opposed to knowledge. These he considers analogous to stimulation responses, to which no aesthetic significance should be attributed. He accepts as standard the theoretical confession of a single artist, Constable, whose views can safely be considered to constitute but one option of aesthetics (and certainly a rather ideological one at that): "Painting is a science and should be pursued as an inquiry into the laws of nature. Why, then may not landscape painting be considered a branch of natural philosophy, of which pictures are but the experiments?"[36]

We might try to identify the counterpart of this option in current cultural practice. Although I am of the opinion that Sagoff's studies cannot provide the aesthetic status of forgery with a conceptual framework in which the large number of cultural facts pertaining to forgery could be interpreted, I do not think that these studies should not be used for the interpretation of certain of these facts. It appears that Sagoff takes the norm from that decidedly experimental, detached, and scientific form of modern art that no longer concerns itself with questions of beauty and has Marcel Duchamp as its founding father. Secondly, by rigorously segregating the class of forgeries from the class of historically authentic works, and by excluding any common features, stylistic or thematic, that could possibly be shared by even two visually indistinguishable paintings, Sagoff in a way established the autonomy of forgery and imitation. He claims that the reason why nobody can produce a Vermeer or an Impressionist painting is that the classes of forgery and imitation have priority over both the Vermeer class and the Impressionist class with regard to all works of art that do not satisfy the necessary conditions, temporal, spatial, and the rest. It is nevertheless possible to break out from the forgery and imitations classes and thus to establish the class of Neo-Impressionism or the class imitating a certain painter, provided that a certain form of the imitation proves successful: ". . . the labels 'Impressionist,' 'Gothic,' and 'Baroque' started as terms of critical derision but eventually came to refer to celebrated styles. Perhaps the same thing will happen someday to paintings we now classify derisively as 'Fakes.'"[37]

The autonomy of the indistinguishable, the fake as original, the deliberate archaism and anachronism or the deliberate denial of "originality," the appropriation of styles, painters, and pictures (or photographs), both past and contemporary—or to use the title of an exhibition held in New York in 1985, "The Art of Appropriation"—all these do indeed characterize a loosely aligned movement and a heterogeneous group of otherwise unconnected oeuvres: Elaine Sturtevant, Giulio Paolini, Sherrie Levine, Richard Prince, Mike Bidlo, Philip Taaffe, Richard Hamilton, William Xerra, Jeff Koons, and others. The examples could be continued by mentioning the extensive graphic copies of the German Horst Janssen, or the Caravaggism of Tibor Csernus, a Hungarian artist living in France.

Even if a connection that we claim to have discovered between one of the fertile spin-offs of Sagoff's line of reasoning and an existing cultural practice turns out to be well founded, it will not change our firm belief that his answer to the philosophical problems of forgeries is unsatisfactory. In his earlier quoted writing, William Kennick analyzes an art-historical fact or well-established assumption: If a known copy of one of Caravaggio's paintings was made by his contemporary imitator and forger, Angelo Caroselli, then this is obviously not an original Caravaggio. Yet the question remains: Is it an original Caroselli? The positive answer would correspond to the autonomy of indistinguishability and also to the facts, provided that the painting was, indeed, executed by Caroselli's own hands. But if we regard as necessary preconditions not only the execution but the creation as well, then this work is merely a copy of Caravaggio's painting, made by Caroselli.[38] It is these two poles, invention and execution, that mark the boundaries between which cultural history, aesthetic outlook, taste, and reception ebb and flow.[39] Anyone who disregards the historical dynamics of the tidal motion between these poles could easily fall into contradictions. Sagoff's proposal about the autonomy of indistinguishability also contradicts his other statement, which we might call the "thesis of cognitive creativity." According to this, the copy/imitation repeats an already-discovered solution; it evidences no new knowledge and has no cognitive significance. Therefore it has limited aesthetic value: ". . . the process of making a forgery is the reverse of creative."[40]

Danto

Is it really possible to subordinate the perceptual and sensory circumstances of the aesthetic experience to knowledge? I believe that the true rival of Goodman's moderate solution is not Sagoff's radical, albeit self-contradictory, answer, but Arthur C. Danto's art philosophy expounded in *The Configuration of the Commonplace*, probably the most interesting art theory of the 1980s. In this book, central importance is assigned to the doubt as to whether the aesthetic response constitutes a form of perception. Goodman's belief that every aesthetic distinction can be traced back to some perceptual difference is called a "secret prejudice" by Danto. This is why he regards the condition of indistinguishability to the naked eye to be characteristic merely of a given moment, only to give way to the distinctions that sooner or later become apparent.

Without denying the importance of learning and practice, Danto assigns a lesser significance to these phenomena in cultural practice than does Goodman. (This has already been evidenced in the new interpretation of the van Meegeren affair.) He claims that it is indeed our aesthetic sensibility that has gone through changes since the 1930s, at least in the sense that the distance in time has helped to enhance the historicity of style and conception. Therefore, in the same painting that the contemporary viewers saw a Vermeer, we now witness the mannerism of the 1930s; and in the same painting that made contemporary viewers rejoice over the gains of seventeenth-century Dutch painting, we now lament the impotent anachronism of twentieth-century Dutch painting. The same incalculable changes that have rendered a tendency into a historical (i.e., a proper) style, have also brought hitherto invisible signs to the surface, thus unmasking a forgery, quite independently of the forger's actual self-confession in this particular case. In Giotto's paintings the contemporary viewers saw humans and angels (according to Boccaccio's testimony); what the contemporary viewers of today see is how Giotto saw the people and the angels. We might add to the above analysis that in the modern era, an age characterized by a pluralism of style of which people are extremely cognizant, it is precisely historical forgery—i.e., the imitation of a historical style—that can best serve to conceal from one's contemporaries one's own style, one's choice from the arsenal of styles available at the given time; but it is also this historical forgery that can best serve to reveal the same to the audience of the next period.

Although it is guaranteed by logic that two nonidentical things should be different, the possibility that they are indistinguishable as far as their perceptible qualities are concerned cannot be excluded, Danto claims. Whether or not something is a forgery depends on the *history* of its production; obviously there is no disagreement in this between Danto and Goodman. But in Danto's views—and this is where one of their disagreements comes into focus—the study of the receptive and perceptual differences ignores the artistic problem, because the exploration of the minute differences that do exist leads to the territory of psychophysics. Of course, in order to make his criticism apparent, Danto has to abandon the artistic tradition, where the objects do wear their histories on their surfaces,[41] and where the power of the expert eye enables one to make enormous discoveries by noticing and examining seemingly minute differences.[42]

Danto's philosophical hunting ground—the terrain, the cultural practice of which he samples—is the art of the second half of the twentieth century, primarily of New York. Andy Warhol's *Brillo Boxes,* the counterparts of the "commonplace" Brillo containers, exerted an extraordinary philosophical influence on him in the 1960s. This is remotely connected to the problem of forgery: "There was a certain sense of unfairness felt at the time when Warhol piled the Stable Gallery full of his Brillo boxes; for the commonplace Brillo container was actually *designed* by an artist, an Abstract Expressionist driven by need into commercial art; and the question was why Warhol's boxes should have been worth $200 when that man's products were not worth a dime."[43]

The particular art forms that have exerted the greatest philosophical influence on Danto—Concept art, Minimal art, and Pop art—all throw light on the following problem: If in theory *everything* can be art, then how is it possible to distinguish between art and nonart? In a world of disintegrating conventions and artistic instability, Danto is able to make this distinction by the simultaneous undervaluation of conventionality and overvaluation of banality. Copying must lose the significance it once possessed as one of the most important paradigms of art, while the trivial, the banal, the commonplace must go through an almost theological metamorphosis, a glorification, a transfiguration—hence the title. The great questions of art no longer concern the ways tradition continues or strikes roots, renews, or even disintegrates; now the great questions of art concern the ways by which the artistic counterpart of any one of the real, "mere" things can be created.

This is why the presentation and comparative study of perceptually indistinguishable objects through thought-experiments (in other words, the examination of the twin paradoxes) plays a crucial part in Danto's art philosophy. On the one hand he accepts that *anything goes,* that anything can be turned into an artwork, while on the other hand he sets certain preconditions to the admittance of mere things or representations into the Eden of art. (The rule of "aboutness": a work of art is about something; it has a subject; it conveys a viewpoint; it requires interpretation; its interpretation appears in the context of a historical art theory; it is rhetorical; it is metaphorical.[44]) Once again, we have an art philosophy that places the artist, and not art, at the center of attention in the maneuvering space of modernity; an art philosophy that, once again, focuses on masterpieces as opposed to the great tendencies encompassing individual artworks (and artists) in which the *minores,* the imitators and the copiers too, have a rightful place. In addition to the contextualism of art, the significance of its causal history and content is also emphasized. Another one of its consequences is that in the interpretation of artworks, a distinguished role is now being attached to the "intentional fallacy."[45]

This is a surprising development, since one of the characteristic features of modern art is seen in the artist's extensive loss of control over the interpretation of his own work. Nevertheless, when we consider the paradox that never before had the desire to control been as strong as in modern art, then it is not such a surprising development anymore. If Warhol is right in claiming that *everything* can be turned into an artwork, then the creation of artistic context cannot be linked—not decisively anyway—to tradition, while the *intention* to create a context will assume a fundamental significance. Danto is the art philosopher of this new experience, and the paradox of perceptually indistinguishable artworks, or artworks and objects, serves to strengthen the theoretical foundations of this. Anything can be art, provided that it has meaning, that it is not merely being itself—art converges with its own philosophy here[46]: "To seek a neutral description is to see the work *as a thing* and hence not as an artwork: It is analytical to the concept of an artwork that there has to be an interpretation . . . to see [an artwork] as an artwork then is like going from the realm of mere things to a realm of meaning."[47]

It is easy to recall one of the more radical slogans of twentieth-century modern art: The denial that artworks have any meaning at all, the insistence that they are nothing but themselves. A "pipe" is not a pipe but a painting; by contrast, a pissoir is nothing but a pissoir. On the point of content, Danto admits in connection with several modern works of art that they *do not have any*; yet there is a grave difference between answering a question in the negative and denying the question. A hundred years ago it would have been impossible within the dimensions of the art world to inquire about the content of a tie covered in paint; in other words, it would not have been accepted as a work of art. Today, inside the dimensions of the art world and within the context of an artist's oeuvre, we accept it as a work of art, and by doing so, we assign content to it, albeit a negative one. Instead of being devoid of content, its content is that it has no content. This reasoning has such a general importance in Danto's art theory that he picked the following lines from *Hamlet* for the motto of his book: "HAMLET: Do you see nothing there?/QUEEN: Nothing at all, yet all that is I see."

In this way Shakespeare's mannered pun has become the distinctive feature of modern art: Of the twin statements "I see nothing at all" and "all that is I see," the latter contains that imperceptible difference that is the distinguishing mark of art. Richard Wollheim quite rightly poses the question whether this indistinguishability is initial or definite.[48] Accepting the first alternative would mean that what we are witnessing is the cultural process of familiarization, appropriation, and learning that inevitably accompanies every artistic innovation. The second alternative would, however, imply an *encampment* in the realm of extremities, the possibility of which I very much doubt.

At the end of the second chapter, I mentioned the most famous of Danto's twin paradoxes, which, in the best picaresque traditions of forgery stories, tells the fictitious story of three indistinguishable ties painted in monochromatic blue: one made by Picasso, the other by a child, and the third by a forger. Following a kind of a comedy of errors, the ties are mistaken for one another: The child's necktie is displayed in a museum, Picasso puts his signature on the forgery, and the original is confiscated by the police. These are three truly indistinguishable objects, so crude and primitive that even the passing of time would not make them perceptually distinct. But Danto firmly believes that Picasso's version is a work of art, as opposed to the creations of the child and the forger, which are not. It is the internal structure of Picasso's lifework alone that can provide a framework for interpretation; only in the context of this oeuvre can the content of the monochromatic necktie be interpreted, and not just described. (We know already that even the nonexistence of any content can form the content of an artwork.)

The child's tie is an ordinary thing—it can perhaps be conceived to convey some kind of a meaning; nevertheless, quite unlike in the case of an artwork, it cannot be the meaning *itself*. And what is the situation regarding the forger? "The status of the forgery, in this perspective, perhaps is only this, that it too stands in the wrong relation to its maker to be supposed a statement of his: It only pretends to be a statement of someone else's, namely Picasso."[49] According to this view, therefore, a forgery is just as irrelevant for artistic appreciation as a childish fabrication is.

This is not to say that Danto actually denies the possibilities of cultural practice that Sagoff mentioned; he acknowledges that a forger too can make sovereign statements. Compared to Picasso's, the forger's necktie is rendered an ordinary object, as opposed to an artwork, by its nonexistent (or undisclosed) content—its *copy status*. (It is quite a different matter that, in my view, it would be possible to add to Danto's ties in the spirit of Danto still another tie, one with *artwork status,* constructed in such a way as to have a causal history that would suggest the intention—which would be its content—that the resulting artwork be completely indistinguishable from Picasso's tie, under a title such as "Picasso's Tie." This would be repetition, but not copying—it would not have the false aura of identicalness.[50])

In all those efforts, which span the entire length of Danto's book and prompt him to devise several thought-experiments similar to the tie-paradox, all in order to demonstrate either the artwork versus ordinary-object status of completely indistinguishable things or the point that these could be independent works of art, *it is precisely the copy that is excluded by the fiction of indistinguishability.*

In constructing the fiction of indistinguishability, both Goodman and Sagoff equated, quite unjustifiably, forgeries with copies. By contrast, in Danto's theory copies in general are banished from the world of art, with forgeries only included by implication, as being *a version of copies,* for the copy "merely replaces an original and inherits its structure and relationship to the world."[51] The copy of an artwork cannot be a sovereign work of art: "The copy merely shows the way the artwork presents its content, without itself especially presenting this in a way to make a point of it; a copy aims at a state of pure transparency, like an idealized performer."[52]

The question is whether we are talking about a statement made by the artwork itself, as was the case with Goodman's definition of forgery, or a statement made by the artist (the copier, the forger). Danto's forgery definition suggests the latter. And so does the fact that indistinguishable works of art that are *not* copies might have very different structures, very different relationships to the world, depending on the authors' intentions. It follows from the above that the sensual elements of the aesthetic experience—and, very revealingly of the latest trends in modern art, art appreciation as well—are losing ground, since the *precondition* of the aesthetic approach is the cognitive realization that what we are dealing with is an artwork, as opposed to a commonplace object; for the rest of the way, crucial importance is attached to the cognitive distinction on the basis of which we are able to interpret and judge perceptually indistinguishable artworks differently. It is a path of discovery, which means that it is not the aesthetic approach that formed the object.

In his earlier-cited essay, Noël Carroll brings up several examples to show that works of art can conceivably exist even without qualifying for Danto's conditions. It is not true that every artwork requires interpretation, nor that every artwork has content. There are, at the same time, didactic and nonmetaphorical artworks with direct content. Furthermore, "artworks may lack points of view in so far as they lack *aboutness*, which implies that they have no subject about which a point of view might be expressed. Or, artworks may be without points of view because the artist in question is incapable of formulating one in his medium."[53] Although this reasoning is debatable, because even the lack of a point of view or the inability to formulate one can be interpreted as a point of view and the discourse of a period is unavoidably absorbed into its artworks in the form of a point of view, it is undoubtedly true that an *existential* point of view is not a necessary precondition of an artwork. It is the copier that I have in mind, not the forger, since one of the main purposes of this book is the reconstruction of the possible existential points of view of the forger. The art of copying, which I earlier declared to be one of the main sustainers of art, is accepted as art by Danto only if it has a definite existential point of view and content, both allowing for interpretation: "*Marilyn x 100* . . ., like *Thirty is Better than One*, incorporates repetition, so the repetition of the images constitutes an image of repetition."[54]

Aside from everything else, Danto's tie-paradox is also an excellent joke for art criticism: The art critic and philosopher Danto's answer to the art dealer and philosopher Goodman's question. (For a period of time, Goodman did in fact work as an art dealer.) Picasso did not, of course, create a monochromatic tie—although he could have done so, because for some reason the tie acquired a cultic significance in the art of the 1970s—but in the case of his famous sculpture *Babuin with her Baby*, he did replace the monkey's head with a toy car.[55]

To illustrate the conflict between the ahistorical concept of culture prevalent in the United States and its historicizing counterpart predominant in Europe, I know of no more illuminating example than the fact that Danto saw the great artist of the glorification of the ordinary and commonplace in Picasso, while Richard Wollheim saw the same artist as the borrower and identifier par excellence. According to Wollheim, copying the works of the great masters, old and recent alike, or borrowing from them, has a fundamental role in artistic practice. With his series of variations on Manet's *Le Déjeuner sur l'Herbe* (200 drawings, 27 paintings, 5 linos) as well as with his other borrowings (from Cranach, Velázquez, and others), Picasso disclosed a great chain, reaching back not only to Manet (himself a great borrower and a passionate copier), but through him to artists like Giorgione, for example.[56]

Wollheim's Reply and
Possible Answer in Hermeneutics

Challenging Danto and his dozens of examples constructed to support the fiction of indistinguishability, it was Richard Wollheim who, in the debate on the "perfect forgery," called attention to the artificial and subversive character of the original paradox, as proposed by Goodman.[57] When the debate is confined to the point that the difference between the original and fake has not been revealed, then this could only rock the foundations of the faith we had in criticism, or not even that if there was, as in the case with Ossian or van Meegeren, a satisfactory historical explanation. When, however, the possibility arises that there is no difference at all, then that could shake the foundations of our expectations about art. Goodman uses the "weaker" notion of forgery when he essentially identifies it with *execution,* Wollheim claims. This notion could however be strengthened by assuming that the forger equals Rembrandt not only in execution, but in *invention* also. In fact, Goodman used the weaker notion of forgery in the original example, but he already modified it when he analyzed the van Meegeren case, without clarifying the difference. In a copy-type forgery the perfection of execution might be sufficient, while a non-copy-type forgery also requires the perfection of invention. The indistinguishability of a Rembrandt painting and its "strong" forgery could seriously undermine our view of Rembrandt and of art in general. Although Wollheim is skeptical about the possibility of such an event, one is forced to admit that in the history of art forgeries, there have frequently been dramatic or carnivalesque developments that were able to undermine the reputations not only of the experts, but also of great artists or historical art categories.

Furthermore, Wollheim regards as subversive the particular characteristic of the example that eliminates the affect that one's belief of the authorship has on *perception*. Knowledge can affect perception in two ways: It can affect both *what* we see, and *how* we see it. Beliefs as well as knowledge can put the viewer into a receptive mood for certain things that he would otherwise have passed by unnoticed. From the viewpoint of critical relevance, equally important is the second way, which teaches us to take in the entirety of the artwork. If *ex hypothesi* there is no visible difference to support the different authorship or the fact of forgery, then this could question the possibility of any knowledge ever being able to influence what we see. It was for the sake of this thesis that Wollheim decided to modify the original example and talk about Rembrandt and his student. Knowledge of this fact could influence perception. The viewer "could look at the Rembrandt differently from the way he looks at the Aert de Gelder, just because he has the evidence of his eyes to tell him that Aert de Gelder, in a certain frame of mind, could paint indistinguishably from his master."[58]

This is not so much a criticism of Goodman's answer to the problem, but of his hypothesis (since Goodman too comes down on the side of learning and practicing discrimination). At the same time, as evidenced from the above quotation, Wollheim's answer is not entirely free of inconsistencies either, since he too permits the two paintings in question, Rembrandt's and Aert de Gelder's, to be visually indistinguishable. Thus if we are still able to look at them differently, then this is only possible because we take into account the entire careers of the two painters, which at this hypothetical point in time happen to overlap. It is this unstated possible resolution of the inconsistency that might provide the clue to Wollheim's reasons for rejecting the starting point, the thesis of the perfect forgery.

The problem with this thesis is that it sabotages comprehension and critical perception because it treats them in an *atomistic way*: "Certainly, in seeking to understand a particular work of art, we try to grasp it in its particularity, and so we concentrate on it as hard as we can: but at the same time we are trying to build up an overall picture of art, and so we relate the work to other works and to art itself."[59] The joint operation of these two plans establishes critical relevance, but it might happen that we have certain information that, despite having critical value, only contributes to the second way of perception. In that case this will show "that there are concepts which have a fundamental role to play in organizing our experience of art—in this case, the concepts of autograph and forgery—but which might, in certain special and altogether insulated circumstances, have no influence upon our perception of individual works of art."[60]

These remarks clearly outline the vast difference that separates cultural practice as envisaged by Wollheim, from Danto's conception of it. The examples of indistinguishable paintings also suggest this. Goodman's choice was Rembrandt, Danto's the eight red squares and the three ties. He also compared Rembrandt's wonderful *Polish Rider,* owned by the Frick Museum (the authenticity of which has recently been questioned), to a wholly randomly executed action painting, where the statistical miracle of the color molecules resulted in a painting entirely identical to Rembrandt's. And now Wollheim returns to Rembrandt. His protests against the isolatedness of the forgery hypothesis show that he regards tradition as a living thing. I am inclined to agree with Wollheim.

It is a great surprise that the philosophical discourse on forgery took place in an analytical rather than hermeneutic environment. It appears that forgery, and most notably the unmasking of forgeries, could provide an excellent illustration for Gadamer's universal hermeneutics (although Gadamer himself never discussed the problem). The three paradigms of the hermeneutic method are as follows: To understand the author's intentions; to understand them better than the author himself; and finally to combine these elements into a circular understanding, which Gadamer calls the "merger" of the respective horizons of the author and the interpreter—in cases where the author is of the past and forms part of the tradition, this means the merger of historically different horizons.[61] The classic forgery of the stronger type employs either the first paradigm or the second or some combination of the two. Quite often the copy-type forgeries correspond to the complete reconstruction of the author's intentions, that is, the first paradigm, while the variational-type forgeries comply with the program of understanding the original intentions better—the second paradigm. Every unmasking amounts to the triumph of the third paradigm, insofar as the understanding is of a historical character and effects a shift; the activity of the interpreter is corrected by the general cultural development of interpretation; a new horizon opens up; and the merger of horizons, which was the guarantee of the forger's success, is eliminated. With this unmasking, the historically operative consciousness (*wirkungsgeschichtliche Bewusstsein*), which Gadamer considers to be an experience, scores a victory over an unhistorical and normative idea of knowledge. This triumph is all the more spectacular because under the given circumstances it would be falsity par excellence, the perfect forgery, that would be manifested in the truth of normative perception.

To the best of my knowledge, Ian Mackenzie has been the only one to try to steer the debate in the direction of Gadamer's hermeneutics. He wrote the following: "With the passing of time, as the interpreters' horizon diverges from the forger's, the latter's prejudgment become evident (though not those of a new generation of forgers), and his intention is flouted."[62] This corresponds to the art-historical experience, discussed earlier, whereby the actuality of forgeries—at least of one type—is limited, and the expiration of this actuality is automatically accompanied by the unmasking of the forgeries in question; also, the more effectively a forgery works on one generation, the less effectively it will do so on the next. (To which Gombrich sarcastically replied that this was a circular argument: The truly successful forgeries have still not been unmasked.[63]) In the debate that Eric Donald Hirsch—a disciple of the first paradigm, according to the earlier classification—initiated against universal hermeneutics and "in the defense of the author," Mackenzie himself has pointed out that the forgery stories provide strong evidence against Hirsch's view claiming that the correct interpretation of the *contemporary* text is more likely.[64] Mackenzie made the point that it was precisely the prejudices shared by contemporaries that stood in the way of interpreting forgeries as forged "texts."

In its classical form, forgery is indeed the area in which Gadamer's hermeneutics works well. I must emphasize the term "classical forgery," because those modern versions of forgery that we discussed earlier in our attempt to identify the various cultural practices correspond more to a possible fourth paradigm of hermeneutics: The *appropriation* of tradition, the formulation of a new perception without any regard to the original context. This is how Pierre Ménard perceives *Don Quixote,* and how Duchamp understands *Mona Lisa.* Nevertheless, this is not the only direction in which the classical notion of forgery turns out to have a limited validity. In those traditional cultures where the main forms of artistic practice are based on copying, distinguishing with the help of the naked eye between objects made at times separated by extremely long intervals—we might even be talking of several thousands of years, rather than just a few generations—often poses difficulties, the same way as the products of the archaizing tendencies of the ancient high cultures (the Egyptian, the Chinese) cannot easily be told apart from the "originals." The classical notion of forgery is linked to a specific concept of art: The concept of classical European art with a continuous tradition.

In one of my earlier writings questioning the universal validity of Gadamer's hermeneutics, I argued that his theory remained within the bounds of this concept of art.[65] In an indirect way, the limited validity of the universal-hermeneutic model of forgery as an interpretation provides evidence to this effect.[66]

The Fake as Original?

Is it possible to go beyond these limits? One of the most interesting attempts to achieve this came from an unexpected corner and from an unexpected intellectual environment. I refer to the Hungarian classical archaeologist János György Szilágyi's essay, "Time: The Wisest of Them All. The Forgery of Antique Vases." Regarding the point of the unexpectedness of the place, it should be sufficient to say that, although the Hungarian cultural world is also concerned with the disintegration of the concept of classical European art (Szilágyi mentions the "pseudo" works of Gyula Pauer[67]), one cannot expect the cultural peripheries to offer the same profusion of stimuli with regard to the latest trends that one witnesses in the case of the center. But if Arthur Danto feels obliged to count his blessings for his good fortune to be able to live in New York in the second half of the twentieth century, with its art world offering him a "philosopher's wonderland,"[68] then perhaps it will neither be seen as an act of self-delusion if a great Eastern-European art historian, Jan Bialostocki, actually talks about the advantages of cultural peripheries.[69]

Similarly unexpected is the fact that it is a scholar of antiquity, a specialist in classical archaeology and philology, who should be asking these questions, since the first centuries of the formation of the modern (i.e., beginning with the Renaissance) concept of art were inextricably entangled with the history of origin of his fields: With the humanist reception of antique art, the foundations of the authority of classical artworks, and their canonization. However, the actualization of tradition, that key category of modern hermeneutics, has always been fundamentally important to Szilágyi, to the same degree that his penetration in research has been.

And indeed, without being thematically related to philosophical hermeneutics or influenced by it in any other way, Szilágyi formulates his questions in a manner that is characteristically hermeneutic, rather than historicist. His method of inquiry reflects the same spirit that Gadamer described as follows: "In order to understand the message that tradition has specifically for us, we are required to place the reconstructed question in the openness of its questionability, so that the question should be modified to conform with the question tradition poses for us. When the 'historical' question comes to the fore for its own sake, then this always means that it will never again be posed as a question. It is the residue of understanding lost, a roundabout way where we got stuck. As to real understanding, this should contain the reappropriation of the concepts of a historical period, in such a way that we also retain our own concepts."[70]

In connection with an Athenian black-glazed amphora, to which the figural and ornamental decoration was added in Goethe's age, Szilágyi wrote the following: The painter "produced one of the true masterpieces of Antique forgeries. He translated the archaic forms of expression of the Gela painter into the language of late-eighteenth- and early-nineteenth-century Classicism, as most notably evidenced by the slight simplification of the facial features, the omission from the picture space of the ivy branches which disturbed the purity of the composition, but above all else by the alleviation of the original scene's tension. But he lived and worked face to face with the original works, understanding and preserving through his own creations a great deal more of archaic and early classical Greek art than was the case with the contemporary vases patterned on Augustian Classicism and produced according to the tastes of secondary Classicism in the workshops of Wedgwood under the guidance of Flaxman or in the workshops of Sèvres under the direction of Lagrenée. Demolishing the walls of secondary Classicism and catching a glimpse of the Classical Greek art behind it (however small the horizons were that this glimpse encompassed)—that was precisely the greatest discovery this age made about the Antiquity, even if the practice itself was neither deliberate nor widespread."[71]

Therefore the forgery of antique works of art and the formation of the view of Antiquity are closely interlinked. And the discovery and actualization of a genre or a movement is interconnected with their encounter with modern modes of expression, with the "recovery" of the historical past. In connection with another forgery, Szilágyi has demonstrated that the master responsible for it "was working for those who saw antique art through the color filter associated with the Neo-Baroque, historicizing, and eclectic tastes of the fin-de-siècle, for those whose tastes inspired the Art Nouveau and the Jugendstil. . . ."[72] The author associates the first Renaissance of the Attic white-figure pottery design—and what necessarily accompanies it, their imitation and forgery—with Degas's and Toulouse-Lautrec's graphic art and the linear qualities in their painting, and the second Renaissance with the nostalgic feelings of the late 1920s towards Classicism.[73]

And as for the eight decades that passed between the first great wave of forging the painted decoration of Corinthian vases and their scientific unmasking, this simply recorded the fact that forgeries preceded the recognition of the artistic value (in hermeneutic usage, the actualization, the reappropriation) of these works. To use Gadamer's terminology quoted above, this was a historicizing practice, a practice of *bygone understanding*; the historical value appeared in the forgeries for its own sake. Then came the 1930s and with it a certain sensitivity for the demonized symbolics of animal friezes, carnivores, and monsters. This started a new wave of forgeries, this time a hermeneutic rather than historicist one, while the understanding also mobilized sensitivity towards forgery.

The view that regards forgery as a way of understanding or form of translating, appreciating in it the high standard of technical, stylistic, and iconographical knowledge—assuming this to be the case— as well as its actuality understood in a profound sense; this view means a new perspective, the consistent application of which had been utterly foreign to earlier generations in Szilágyi's profession. Previously, the sensitivity for the color values of forgeries was mostly noticeable outside professional circles, as well as in *museological practice*—in the latter case probably not entirely independently from the motives of self-justification. In his essay entitled "The Anatomy of Snobbery," Arthur Koestler delivered something of a philippic in repudiation of those nonaesthetic arguments intended to lower the value of unmasked forgeries.[74] As early as the beginning of this century, Apollinaire was already calling attention to the Saitaphernes tiara's value independently of its actual date of origin; also, as I have already mentioned, in 1864 the Victoria and Albert Museum of London knowingly purchased a work by the famous forger Giovanni Bastianini. (It is currently displayed in the museum's collection of forgeries, along with other of Bastianini's forgeries.)[75] Speaking about Alceo Dossena's forged tombstone attributed to Mino da Fiesole, the director of the Museum of Fine Arts in Boston said the following in 1935: "Forgery, or no forgery, the work was . . . far too beautiful for basement dust."[76]

By contrast, forgeries were, as far as classical archaeology was concerned, obstacles to overcome and to despise because they supposedly distorted our knowledge about antiquity. They were to the original work what the evil sisters were to Cinderella, as Adolf Furtwaengler put it at the end of the last century.[77] This opinion too has its own hermeneutic truth: Quite often, forgeries were popular variations, effectively making our knowledge about the age or artist in question shallower rather than deeper. But more recent generations of classical archaeologists (and art historians) had to come to terms with the idea of having to learn to live with forgeries; they had to accept the fact that forgers, and their advisors too, benefit from scientific advances and the growth of information; and with regard to that certain faculty of irrational comprehension, which according to Furtwaengler belonged exclusively to the realm of the eye, this could be deceived, over and over again, by the genius of forgery. "In possession of new arguments of stylistic and iconographical nature, Ludwig Curtius showed half a century after his beloved and respected mentor Furtwaengler's monumental Gemma monograph had been published that all the items reproduced on one of the tables were forgeries," Szilágyi writes.[78]

If I am not very much mistaken, the consequences of this observation were drawn at roughly the same time that János György Szilágyi published his corresponding views. In his book on Italian sculpture, Sir John Pope-Hennessy, for example, dedicated the last chapter to the forgery of Renaissance sculptures. And while he did not apply the hermeneutic interpretation to forged sculptures, he did associate the practice of forging with the immense influence the Quattrocento's sculpting exerted on nineteenth-century sculpture, thus placing forgeries *next* to academic and nonacademic imitations and borrowings. His thesis could be summed up as follows: "The history of forgery is part of the history of Italian sculpture."[79]

Even more importantly than this, it appears that ever since Furtwaengler's age, the scientific purpose of unmasking forgeries *has become an end in itself*. Not only does the neurotic form of distinguishing between originals and forgeries lack hermeneutic understanding, but the scientific practice of this distinction in general tries to replace the hermeneutic understanding of works of art with a historicist viewpoint[80]: "It appears that in the forgery issue an important aspect of the polarization of the contemporary culture of European artistic tradition—and perhaps nonartistic culture, too—can be comprehended. On the one side there are those, and clearly they are the majority, who lack any living bond to art—be it contemporary art or art from the past—and try to fill this vacuum with some kind of a historical understanding, or at least with the historical placement of artworks. They primarily identify the message of an artwork with its historical dating and its attribution to a school, a circle or, most notably, to a master. This is that critical point of our culture where the dilemma of 'original or fake' acquires a distorted representation and a significance blown out of all proportions: Where the data of origin of a work of art are expected—quite hopelessly—to provide the clue to the understanding of reasons why we should like it."[81]

Up to this point we have remained within the bounds of universal hermeneutics in our discourse. To a certain extent, the cultural criticism summed up in the above quotation—the criticism of modern artistic culture—receives reinforcement from Gadamer's theory on the alienation of the aesthetic sphere and on aesthetic distinguishing. Works of art are becoming more abstract, losing their original embedment in their living environment: "Works of art lose their place and the world to which they belong as they become part of the aesthetic consciousness."[82]

This reasoning, besides being helpful in demonstrating the possible correspondence between the paradigms of hermeneutic interpretation and the various practices of forgery, can also help in the evaluation of forgery. Clearly, the naive dictum of "original in place of forgery" corresponds to the ideal that the original intention can be fully reconstructed; the problem of "forgery or original" offers the possibility of understanding more thoroughly or "better" than the original intention; and the acceptance of "forgery and original at the same time" broadens the interpreter's horizon, allowing him to embark on a thoughtful course of understanding.

Universal hermeneutics would not go beyond this point. Szilágyi, however, goes one step further, calling on the fourth, heretical, paradigm of hermeneutics. Originally, this postulated the interpreter's total freedom in practicing absolute power—independent of the original context and also of the question as to whether this context is retrievable or not. Its place on the list of forgery interpretations can be outlined as follows: "Starting out from the demand of 'forgery in place of original,' passing through the contemplation of 'forgery or original,' and even surpassing the dialectics of 'forgery and original at the same time,' we finally arrive at the viewpoint of 'forgery as original,' which at the moment offers perhaps the greatest perspectives: In an age when the confidence and trust in authenticity has been shattered, to direct a beam of light at the twilight concealing the distinction between forgery and original, with a painful brightness that provokes clarification and reaches the most secret corners of personal existence, with a brightness to which we cannot close our eyes. This is perhaps the most that art can do."[83]

From this beautiful idea (incidentally, the closing sentences of his essay) it should immediately become apparent that the author *limits* the validity of the fourth paradigm. If he was to extend it to scientific investigations as well, then he would, in a way, invalidate his results, which, although proposing to affect a major turn in the perception of forged works of art, do not abandon the perspective of the retrievability of the original context—whether it is the archaic forms of expression used by a vase painter of Gela or the Classicist forms of expression used by a late-eighteenth- or early-nineteenth-century forger. Szilágyi could not be further from an anarchistic theory of science of the kind Feyerabend represents.[84] Szilágyi has carried out his own scholarly investigations from the viewpoint of "forgery and original at the same time," reserving the possibility of "forgery *as* original" for *modern* art. Similarly to Mark Sagoff, who published his study approximately at the same time, Szilágyi too regards forgeries as a possible "category" of modern art.[85]

Assigning to art a special status—in other words, permitting things in art that are not permitted elsewhere. This impels the man of Classical studies to tolerate art movements that are surprisingly anti-Classical. He might also have been encouraged in this direction by the circumstance that he happened to eye-witness the classicizing of that wonderful period in fine arts that encompassed the first half of the twentieth century, and was even extended through the fifties, and that notoriously vexed the Classical tastes. The difference, however, which might be symbolized by Picasso's and Duchamp's trading places (in the sense that while the former's art went through classicization in the period beginning with the 1960s, the latter's heritage was actualized and became paradigmatic to an extraordinary degree), is one of essential importance. While the avant-garde movements and the great masters of the century demolished certain traditions, the representatives of the new art questioned the tradition of art and the notion of a work of art—and, in the case of its most consequential disciples, did that with an impressive philosophical radicalism.[86] Szilágyi either fails to see this difference or does not flinch from it: In his eyes, environmentalism, actionism, fluxus, concept art—or antiart in general—are all new and legitimate forms of art. While I find this openness admirable, I cannot help thinking that the reverence felt for a work of art that is manifested in his attitude itself forms part of the Classical heritage. Even if we have grown accustomed to the idea that art is no longer "beautiful," it can at least remain "sacred."

But is it not inadequate to try to extend that concept of art to this artistic practice? Is it not an inadequate, albeit very respectable, task—one that is carried out almost as homework in contemporary art—to try to find the same function (such as the "directing a beam of light," say), which characterizes tradition? Should we not assume that the art culture that has traded in the maintenance of a living bond with works of art for their historical understanding, extended its influence to the works of art themselves, imposing on several tendencies such coldness and aloofness; such indifference towards beauty and total self-absorbedness; and interventions reducing, or even eliminating, sensuality, which might perhaps be the source of some important experience, but does not resemble the classical aesthetic experience? To put it bluntly, is this art still art? (*Les Demoiselles d'Avignon* has gone through classicizing, *Fontaine* has not.)

In connection with this problem there is a very interesting document to consult. Arthur C. Danto, who is a significant critic of contemporary art as well as a philosopher and who cannot seriously be accused of having conservative views, writes the following on the same pages that he discusses the extraordinary philosophical challenges of modern painting: "I am . . . a lover of fine painting, and I cannot claim that I love the art that has occasioned my philosophy with anything like the intensity or in anything like the same way in which, for example, I adore the Dutch masters. I suppose I might be willing to trade it all for Giorgione's *La Tempesta.*" Then there is another, similar confession: "*Fountain* is not to every art lover's taste, and I confess that much as I admire it philosophically, I should, were it given me, exchange it as quickly as I could for more or less than any Chardin or Morandi—or even, given the exaggerations of the art market, for a middling chateau in the valley of the Loire."[87]

Coming from one of the most competent sources, this confession too poses the problem of *equipotentiality* of "old" and "contemporary" works of art. This has long been evident in the case of music, where the segregation of old and modern music in the concert programs has institutionalized it, so to speak. It is possible that in *fine arts,* the kind of complete aesthetic experience, which we all know, cannot be expected from contemporary works. It is also possible that such an experience can be expected only from certain great artists, rather than from tendencies. If this is the case, then János György Szilágyi's recommendation with regard to his own discipline—"the Antique works of art should be seen and enjoyed, as if they had been created today"—could almost be turned around. This optative had a clear function in the philological traditions associated with the names of Friedrich Nietzsche and Károly Kerényi. Philology, when understood in a broader sense, should not be historicist; it should not be "the field of knowledge concerned with things not worth knowing." In the present state of artistic culture, however, the recommendation could be modified that we should see and enjoy contemporary works of art in the way that today we see and enjoy the antique works of art or Giorgione's *La Tempesta.*

I would like to dwell on the subject of this modified formula a little longer. Inferring from personal experience as well as from other sources, I take it for granted that such a desire exists in a considerable number of people who are responsive to art. Szilágyi's essay also serves to confirm this, because, while I willingly accept that in the case of the Corinthian animal friezes his aesthetic reception was deeply influenced by Picasso—who himself has already become a great artist of the past—I cannot, with all due respect, believe that "Allan Kaprow's melting constructions made of ice, the German Wolf Vostell's action performance meant as a political allegory, which involved a car crashing into a tram, or Tinguely's famous self-destructive machine entitled 'Homage to New York'"[88] could have offered him a reception *model* for the perception and enjoyment of antique works of art. Obviously it is the other way around: He wants to convince his readers that the reforms of the concept of art, however radical they may be, cannot alter the essence of art.

But is this really true? It appears to me that it is in contradiction with an important sociocultural reality—the fact that we live with the art of the past, and it quite simply occupies a larger part of our culture than does contemporary art; in other words (and making use of Danto's turn of phrase), we love the former with a different intensity and in a different way that we love the latter. It is self-evident that the perception of old art is itself a modern perception, so much so that in the arguments of a powerful branch of cultural criticism—the one Gadamer belongs to—the loss of function associated with the old works of art, their removal from their natural habitat and placement in museums, forms one of the favorite examples. When Edgar Wind, for example, contrasted the art world that has a direct bearing on our existence, capable of arousing an anarchic and sacred fear (Plato's *theios phobos*) and providing a total experience, with the domesticated art world toying with alternative forms and driven to the peripheries of the great existential questions, then he also included in the latter category modern-art practice and the modern—mass-consumed and superficial—perception of old art alike.[89] Unlike the Romantic cultural critics, however, Wind has all along been conscious of the fact this process, which is over a hundred years old, tracing its origins back to the Renaissance and that has opened up new areas of sensibility, separating the artists from the everyday world of the viewers, is the product of enormous artistic efforts and achievements. And as for the old artworks having been refunctionalized in museums, it appears that, independent of all justified concerns on the part of Wind and other keen-sighted critics, and without regard to the relentless caricaturing of art tourists, they have not lost their "sting." At least they still have the capacity to mobilize in the viewer such immense energies of committed search for meaning, the likes of which can only rarely be associated with contemporary works of art.

This is not entirely caused by natural selection, which is the work of passing time. Also instrumental in it is the *added meaning,* which is the compensation that old objects and works of art gain in modernity precisely for losing their own world and natural habitat, their embedment in history and original function. This added meaning is the revitalizing memory of various traditions, histories, and human fates. Art cannot be limited to that frightening, demonic, and anarchistic formation, avoiding all safety zones, which was Wind's idea of a great work of art. On the other hand, memory can lend to an artwork that was primarily intended for entertainment, decoration, illustration, narration, or illustration, or even to an old and carefully manufactured utensil, a peculiar significance of pathetic or gentle feelings.

By contrast, the perception of contemporary works of art is very often accompanied by aloofness. In the case of several movements and artists this is intentional, but even where we suspect a different or even diametrically opposite intention, the intellectual arbitrariness of artistic originality, the uncertainty resulting from the lack of a common artistic language (i.e., an uncertainty in the independent interpretation and evaluation of certain works as opposed to an interpretation that places the works in the entirety of the artist's oeuvre, reconstructing its context), or the symptoms suggesting the depletion of form possibilities, can all be the causes of such a reception. Only very rarely do we fall under the spell of modern art with the same intensity that characterizes the reception of old artists' works; the last time the author of this book had similar experience in connection with contemporary art was occasioned by Francis Bacon's works and, on my home ground, by the art of György Jovánovics and Dezsö Váli. This cannot be induced by conservative epigones, not to mention the circumstance that now the conservative epigones can be placed in a postmodern context—perhaps even using the same formula of forgery as original.

Naturally, there is the possibility that what we are witnessing now is not the inevitable weariness following the great artistic accomplishments of this century (a weariness that has, by the way, often been observed in the history of art), but rather its new form of existence—for example, placed in the perspective of the *post-histoire*—for which our earlier concepts of art, and especially the classical concept, are inadequate. However, we do not have to here concern ourselves with this aspect of the problem. The purpose of the above contemplation has merely been to decide whether the viewpoint of "forgery as original" can really offer those perspectives that János György Szilágyi has attributed to it.

Undoubtedly, the suspicions that arose in the second half of the 1970s originated in part from the experiences that the art movements intending to relativize or eliminate originality, above all the Multiple movement, had been accumulating ever since the early 1960s,[90] and in part were justified by subsequent developments, insofar as forgery, copy, and quotation as original became one of the leading paradigms of postmodern art. However, in the process of becoming a style and model, postmodernism lost the very same energies of which Szilágyi had such high expectations. And strange as it may seem, this development can be deduced from his reasoning. Although it is true that the provocations of the traditional concepts of art might have called attention to the point that the lines of division in culture are not drawn between the original and the genuine, or the forgery and the nongenuine (pseudo-art, kitsch, etc.). "The copies made with reverence for the old masters' works"[91] can be genuine. The original can be impossible to forge, since imitation of it is itself original. Forgery too can be original, for example in the case of ironic copies or such old forgeries that have become independent precisely by revealing the differences. All these examples refer to artistic practice. The question is: Can a forgery be genuine? My answer is: As a gesture, yes—as an established mode of artistic practice, no.

"Forgery is one of the classical possibilities of antiart—why couldn't we grab it as a form of expression to demonstrate that we live in a perpetually forged world?" is the way Szilágyi posed the question.[92] The danger of putting forward such an extreme generalization of critical content, with its tendency to mirror reality, is that it might turn into its affirmative negation. According to a commonly accepted interpretation, the false becomes true in Andy Warhol's works—the artist appropriates the attitude and techniques of the industry of cultural consumption in order to demonstrate what a fake world we live in. I see no compelling arguments, however, against a diametrically opposed and equally satisfactory interpretation, according to which Warhol in fact converted to this attitude, rather than appropriating it, and became one of its most effective propagators insofar as he made high culture from part of mass culture, turning it into commodity fetishism.

As to forgery, looking on it by itself, we cannot tell whether it is a critic or an upholder of the fake world. The former alternative is more likely to be true in the case of a philosophically profound dramatic gesture, and the later is more probable in the case of the constant repetition of this gesture: In its *forgery* and establishment as a trend. In the 1960s and early 1970s, Elaine Sturtevant copied the works of pop artists and the installations of Beuys; then in 1973 she created her work entitled *Duchamp's Fontaine* (to replace the lost original, Duchamp himself had produced a new version in 1964). At the time Sturtevant's experiments were not among the "established" and accepted trends; the ensuing polemics induced her to abandon these experiments. But then in 1985, 11 years later, she resumed these experiments and instantly became one of the forerunners of Appropriation Art, a group first appearing on the art scene with an exhibition and growing into a well-established formation.[93]

"'Appropriation Art' should be considered the successor of Concept Art: The art-work character is manifested in the idea and in the method of execution, in Bidlo's case in the imitative copying. The result is immanent and, when viewed by itself, has no meaning. The original and the copy are treated as equals, with their mutual relationship characterized by arbitrariness. Bidlo paints 'after Picasso' and signs it as 'Bidlo.' Lichtenstein is said to have copied a Bidlo made 'after Lichtenstein,' to which he gave the title 'After Bidlo.'"[94] Incidentally, Lichtenstein's gesture, again, is more like criticism via witticism than an effort to sustain the established trend of "forgery"-copy art.

For here the hermeneutic dialogue between the originals and the "perfect" copies/forgeries striving for indistinguishability is suspended (at least at the level of intention), rather than being continued. The dialogue still has some excellent adherents. Instead, the principle of computability is recommended. Naturally, this too can be interpreted as a criticism of modern culture; for example, in the following way: "How ironic, then, that almost nobody is shocked by the sexuality of *Olympia,* the violence of Caravaggio's *Judith and Holofernes,* or even by the drama of *Crows Over the Wheat Field,* but that everyone would be shocked to discover that museum-goers had not been viewing the originals by Manet, Caravaggio, and van Gogh but near-perfect copies. However earlier generations perceived the content of these pictures, for us they are just artworks. Learning that these three paintings had been replaced by visually indistinguishable copies would be disturbing."[95] And forgery would be the artistic form of this disturbance and annoyance: "disturbatory art."

But the question can once again be asked: What are the arguments to suggest that this confusion would turn the viewers back to the appreciation of artworks with a richness of meaning, rather than sustaining the present situation, or that it would not *convince* the viewers that there is justification for arbitrary computability, thus undermining the historical concept of art? Because the recognition of the compensatory nature of the neurotic, empty, and self-seeking preoccupation with originality—at least with regard to historical works of art—cannot lead to the surrender of the concept and the positive values of originality.

In my opinion, the critical examination of János György Szilágyi's essay points to the conclusion that the gap between the concepts of certain representative movements on the one hand and the classical European art of continuous tradition on the other *cannot* be bridged. One alternative is that, preserving our confidence in the maintainability of tradition through all reforms, we uphold a critical position with regard to the paradigm of forgery as original. The other alternative is that, having confidence in the potency of this paradigm, we radically reevaluate the entire tradition, without regard to its original interpretative context.

But there is still a third alternative: Not having confidence in the viability of a new, unified, and universal concept of art, we accept that the various paradigms and concepts of art have a parallel existence in modern culture in the form of separate stories. Some of these stories are shorter, some longer; some of the actors are claimed by more than one story, and some of them do in fact feature in several of the stories. Instead of being independent of each other, these stories are in dialogue, debating and even fighting with one another. There are stories that split into several smaller stories, and there are stories that swallow up other stories. This is not the prestabilized harmony of the postmodern, which knows no debate and therefore knows no accommodation either (or to be more precise, it forms but one of the many stories). A great many things might happen in the stories, as well as between the stories, and there is only one thing that gets lost in this concept: The inevitability of the requirement that these stories *must* unite in one great story, in the great narrative rightly criticized by Lyotard.

There are several arguments and observations to support the latter alternative. One such observation is that most of the things I have discussed in this chapter apply solely to the fine arts. Could it be that the great edifice of the eighteenth century—the consolidation of the various branches of art in the concept of unified art, with its great narrative put forward in the nineteenth century—will again fall into separate stories in the twentieth century?

――――――――――――――――――――― **Notes** ―――――――――――――――――――――

1. M[eyer] H[oward] Abrams, *The Mirror and the Lamp: Romantic Theory and the Critical Tradition.* Oxford, UK: Oxford University Press, 1971 [1953], 32f.

2. I use the word "probably" because, as far as I know, in the Magritte literature there is no information to support such an "iconographical" identification. The painting belongs to a six-piece series made in 1928–1929, the common feature of which, according to David Sylvester, is that they represent words written in flat frames. (Cf. Sylvester, *Magritte.* London: Thames & Hudson, 1992, 174.) In any case, I asked several of my friends to name the

object depicted in the painting, and nearly all of them went for the bedpan. Even if it was not according to Magritte's intentions, this response goes to show Duchamp's cultural influence.

3. The Magritte drawing from 1929 see, for example, in Suzi Gablik, *Magritte* Greenwich, CT: New York Graphic Society, 1970, 139.

4. Michel Foucault: "Ceci n'est pas une pipe," in *Fata morgana* (Montpelier, 1973).

5. Max Imdahl: "Überlegungen zur Identität des Bildes," in *Identität (Poetik und Hermeneutik, VIII)* (Munich: Wilhelm Fink, 1979), 187–211.

6. Quoted by Werner Hofmann, *Grundlagen der modernen Kunst. Eine Einführung in ihre symbolischen Formen.* (Stuttgart: Alfred Kröner, 1978), 329.

7. Cf. Arthur C. Danto, *The Transfiguration of the Commonplace* (Cambridge, MA: Harvard University Press, 1981), 201.

8. Quoted by Michael Wreen: "Is, Madam? Nay, It Seems!" in ed. Denis Dutton, *The Forger's Art* (Berkeley: University of California Press, 1983, 199, note 57, chapter 1. On the same issue see the symposium on plagiarism, "Plagiarism—A symposium," in *Times Literary Supplement*, April 9, 1982. "Should anyone be allowed to put his own words into someone else's mouth; should anyone be permitted to publish someone else's wisdom as his own? Both imply a certain mimicry. In the modern age this was pejoratively referred to as forgery and plagiarism, and in the medieval as lying and stealing. While hardly any terms with a positive sense exist in the modern vocabulary (except for the theory of literary narration), in the medieval they frequently occurred; these were all based on the priority of the material related over the person relating it (whether it was the author or the writer quoted), on the priority of the reader's 'support' over the writer's self-portrayal, as well as on other similar ethical viewpoints, which were accepted as valid in every field of literature (*scriptio, tractatio, stilus* . . .), not just in those of fiction and poetry: speaking through the mouth of a different person meant self-denial in the service of representing 'truth' or a 'cause.' Appropriating somebody else's lines *in bonam partem* meant the promotion and continuation of tradition on one's own responsibility. In a moral and in a literary sense alike it is called *imitatio,* even in the case when other authors are quoted verbatim under one's own name." Peter von Moos, "Fictio auctoris. Eine theoriegeschichtliche Miniatur am Rande der Institutio Traiani," in *Fälschungen im Mittelalter: Internat. Kongreß d. Monumenta Germaniae Historica, München, 16–19. September 1986. Teil 1. Kongreßdaten und Festvorträge; Literatur und Fälschung* (Hannover: Hahn, 1988), 740.

9. In addition to certain pragmatic limits, the accuracy of repetitions as quotes has some cultural historical variations. "In Antiquity the inaccuracy of quotes showed the sovereign and spontaneous presence of the entire literary culture." Ibid., 758.

10. St. Bonaventura's distinction is quoted by Giles Constable: "Forgery and Plagiarism in the Middle Age," in *Archiv für Diplomatik, Schriftgeschichte, Siegel- und Wappenkunde* 29 (1983): 28.

11. Péter Esterházy, *Bevezetés a szépirodalomba* ("An Introduction to Literature") (Budapest: Magvetö, 1986), 645.

12. Hans Robert Jauß, "Italo Calvino: 'Wenn ein Reisender in einer Winternacht.' Plädoyer für eine postmoderne Ästhetik," in *Studien zum Epochenwandel der ästhetischen Moderne* (Frankfurt: Suhrkamp, 1990), 274.

13. Cf. Nelson Goodman, *Languages of Art—An Approach to a Theory of Symbols* (Indianapolis: Bobbs-Merrill, 1968), the first section ("The Perfect Fake") of the third chapter ("Art and Authenticity"), 99ff. Goodman's problem—and solution!—has even made it to being mentioned in such a general summary of philosophy as Nigel Warburton's work, *Philosophy. The Basics* (London: Routledge, 1992). A similar case is related, obviously quite independently from Goodman, by the writer Thomas Bernhard in his "comedy" entitled *Alte Meister.* The hero meets a Welshman in the Kunsthistorisches Museum, Vienna, who is shocked to discover that the Viennese *The Man with a White Beard* is not just perfectly similar, but in fact entirely *identical* to the Tintoretto in his possession, hanging on the wall of his bedroom. One of the two must obviously be a forgery (Frankfurt: Suhrkamp, 1988), 150ff.

14. Cf. Jerry A. Fodor, "*Déja vu* All Over Again: How Danto's Aesthetics Recapitulates the Philosophy of Mind," in ed. Mark Rollins, *Danto and His Critics* (Oxford, UK: Blackwell, 1993), 42. The Wittgenstein quote comes from *Philosophical Investigations* (Oxford, UK: Blackwell, 1952), 621§.

15. Goodman, op. cit., 101.

16. This is not a fictitious example. Among the copies made after Pieter Lastman's *Suzanne and the Elders* (1614), there exists a version by Rembrandt (executed in the mid-1630s in red crayon); also, Rembrandt's identically entitled large canvass in Berlin (1647) repeats Lastman's compositional arrangement. Cf. Egbert Haverkamp-Begemann, with Carolyn Logan, *Creative Copies: Interpretative Drawings from Michelangelo to Picasso* (New York: The Drawing Center, 9 April–23 July 1988), 111ff.

17. David Hume, "Of the Standard of Taste," in *Essays* (Oxford, UK: Oxford University Press, 1963), 242.

18. Goodman, op. cit., 122. Umberto Eco varies the same idea in the following sentence: "To prove the originality of an object is the same as to regard it *to be the token of its own origin.*" Umberto Eco, *I limiti dell' interpretazione* (Milano: Bompiani, 1990), 184.

19. As William Kennick in his essay entitled "Art and Inauthenticity," in *The Journal of Aesthetics and Art Criticism* 44, no. 1 (1985), 5. Also see page 12, note 17.

20. Those latest trends in fine art, which emphatically turn their back on the traditional notion of originality, and which no longer assign any value to "the physical touch of the artist's hand" (such as the *multiple-ars multiplicata* movements, for example), regard their own experiments as an attempt to break away from the autographic nature of fine art. "Sol Le Witt compared his mural paintings to musical score sheets, from which he or any other person can perform the opus." Claus Pias, "Abschied vom Original? Original, Multiple und kompatible Produktion," in *Das Jahrhundert des Multiple. Von Duchamp bis Gegenwart*, ed. Zdenek Felix, Ausstellung, Deichtorhallen Hamburg, 2. September bis 30. October, 1994 (Hamburg: Oktagon, 1994), 78. The

ideologists of "digital art" anticipate the disappearance of artworks. Cf. Daniel Pinchbeck, "The Second Renaissance," in *Wired* (December 1994): 158.

21. Jorge Luis Borges, "Pierre Ménard, Author of the *Quixote*," in *Labyrinths: Selected Stories & Other Writings*, ed. Donald A. Yates and James E. Irby (New York: New Directions, 1964), 42.

22. Eco, op. cit., 175f.

23. Goodman, op. cit., 108.

24. Mark Sagoff, "The Aesthetic Status of Forgeries," in The Forger's Art (Dutton, op. cit.), 133f. (The study was originally published in *The Journal of Aesthetics and Art Criticism* 25 [1976].)

25. Ibid., 152f.

26. Ibid., 145.

27. This is Goodman's concept of style, the stylistic relevance of the questions of who/when/where. Cf. Goodman, "The Status of Style," in *Critical Inquiry* 1, no. 4 (1975): 799. In one of his discourses, Goodman himself rejects the argument that distances in time and space would necessarily eliminate any stylistic bonds. "Clearly, although the original and an almost indistinguishable copy made far away from it in time and place differ in some stylistic property and are even in some two different styles, they are in a more usual and important sense very much in the same style." Nelson Goodman, "On Being in Style," in *Of Mind and Other Matters* (Cambridge, MA: Harvard University Press, 1984), 134. Monroe C. Beardley polemicizes with Sagoff along very similar lines. Cf. Beardsley, "Notes on Forgery," in *The Forger's Art* (Dutton, op. cit.), 230. Anthony Ralls, who refutes the supposition concealed in the original example (i.e., the claim that one of the two paintings should be unique on the basis of its quality, as he believes that the essential features of all works of art can be reproduced), arrives at an even more radical and more debatable conclusion, suggesting that the uniqueness of a work of art is solely based on its location in space and time. (This is the concept I referred to in chapter 2 as "material identity.") Cf. Anthony Ralls, "The Uniqueness and Reproducibility of a Work of Art: A Critique of Goodman's Theory," in *Philosophical Quarterly* 22 (1972): 18.

28. William Kennick has quite rightly called attention not only to the untenability of identifying forgery with copying, but also to the point that copying is not necessarily accompanied by similarity: copies achieved by changing the proportions, sizes, and rules of projection, and thus eliminating similarity, are also possible, for example in the case of anamorphic copies. For the sake of the argument, he probably aims for too much sharpness in trying to separate the various types of forgeries, or nonoriginals, of which fakes form but one group. He distinguishes between forged works of art, copies, reproductions, works made "after" somebody, works by an artist belonging to another artist's school, works by the follower of an artist, works from a workshop, works falsely attributed. Cf. Kennick, op. cit., 8 and 4. The clear distinction between fakes and forgeries is also recommended by Hunter Steele in the debate: "Fakes and Forgeries," in *British Journal of Aesthetics* 17 (1977): 254ff. These distinctions, which are perfectly justified from the view-

point of art-historical classification and to which I myself have added a few earlier on in the book (see chapter 3, note 21), are perhaps far too minute and static from a philosophical point of view. Forgeries can thus be set apart from the rest only on a moral or legal basis, although from the point of view of cultural practice, it is precisely the continuous metamorphoses and decomposition of these categories that are relevant. "We may, if we like, distinguish forgeries from other copies by the intention of the makers, or better, I think, by the way the copies function at a given time," Goodman replies. (Goodman, "A Note on Copies," in *Journal of Aesthetics and Art Criticism* 44, no. 3 [1986]: 291.)

29. Sagoff, op. cit., 148.

30. Quoted by Mariann Gergely, Péter György, and Gábor Pataki, "Megjegynzések Kassák Lajos korai müveinek sorsához" ("Notes on the Fate of Lajos Kassák's Early Works"), in *Kassák: A Magyar Nemzeti Múzeum és a Petőfi Irodalmi Múzeum emlékkiállítása* ("Kassák. A Memorial Exhibition Organized Jointly by the Hungarian National Museum and the Petifi Literary Museum"), Catalog, n.d. [1987], 143. "Can anyone be quite certain that none of the innumerable fake Utrillos at present on the market was painted by Utrillo?" Gilbert Bagnani poses the question in his essay entitled "On Fakes and Forgeries," in *The Phoenix* 14 (1960): 229.

31. Cf. William H. Honan, "Diary Excerpts Said to Be Mussolini," in *New York Times*, June 27, 1994, A6.

32. Sagoff, op. cit., 147.

33. See *Fake? The Art of Deception*, ed. Mark Jones (Berkeley: University of California Press, 1990), 53ff.

34. Rosalind E. Krauss, "The Originality of the Avant-Garde," in *The Originality of the Avant-Garde and Other Modernist Myths* (Cambridge, MA: MIT Press, 1993 [1985]), 193.

35. Mark Sagoff, "Historical Authenticity," in *Erkenntnis: An International Journal of Analytical Philosophy* 12, no. 1 (1978): 91.

36. Quoted by E. H. Gombrich, *Art and Illusion* (Princeton, NJ: Princeton University Press, 1962), 367. Cf. Sagoff, "The Aesthetic Status of Forgery," in *Erkenntnis: An International Journal of Analytical Philosophy* 12, no. 1 (1978): 146.

37. Mark Sagoff, "The Aesthetic Status of Forgery," in *Erkenntnis: An International Journal of Analytical Philosophy* 12, no. 1 (1978): 149.

38. Cf. Kennick, op. cit., 4f. The work in question, *St. John the Baptist*, is displayed in the gallery Doria-Pamphilj in Rome. The original can be found in the Capitolium Museum of Rome.

37. One of the traditional concepts of originality as an aesthetic value was defended in the debate by John Hoaglund, who considered the three components of originality: authenticity, uniqueness, and creativity ("Originality and Aesthetic Value," in *British Journal of Aesthetics* 16, no. 1 [1976]: 46ff.) Nevertheless, Hoaglund himself is aware of the point that this is actually the tradition of the Greek-inspired Western concept of art—and even in that regard forms only one part of it. As for the archaic, the non-European, the late-antique, the medieval, or most modern European series of works, or a new school of reception, it is possible to develop and practice a concept of origi-

nality that is in direct opposition to that other concept, either equating originality with authenticity or experiencing the creativity component of originality (among other places) in the nonunique, or even in the nonauthentic.

40. Mark Sagoff, "On Restoring and Reproducing Art," in *Journal of Philosophy* 75 (1978): 453.

41. I have already quoted Danto's remark: "Objects do not wear their histories on their surfaces." Danto, op. cit., 44.

42. Let me remind the readers of that "tiny yellow surface of the wall" in
Vermeer's painting *The View of Delft*, as Marcel Proust has captured it: "Enfin
il fut devant le Ver Meer, qu'il se rappelait plus éclatant, plus différent de tout
ce qu'il connaissait, mais où, grâce à l'article du critique, il remarqua pour la
premiùre fois des petits personnages en bleu, que le sable était rose, et enfin
le précieuse matière du tout petit pan de mur jaune. Ses étourdissements aug-
mentaient; il attachait son regard, comme un enfant à un papillon jaune qu'il
veut saisir, au précieux petit pan de mur. 'C'est ainsi que j'aurais dû écrire,
disait-il. Mes derniers livres sont trop secs, il aurait fallu passer plusieurs
couches de couleur, rendre ma phrase en elle-même précieuse, comme ce
petit pan de mur jaune.'" Proust, *La prisonnière. A la recherche du temps perdu*
V (Paris: Gallimard, Bibiliothèque de la Pléiade, 1954), vol. III, 187.

43. Arthur C. Danto, *Beyond the Brillo Box: The Visual Arts in Post-Historical
Perspective. Introduction* (New York: Farrar, Straus, Giroux, 1992), 44.

44. Noël Carroll's astute reconstruction and criticism has demonstrated
that these essentialist definitions are all linked to one particular historicist
precondition: The theory of the "end" of art—or more precisely, of art *history*
—as originally put forward by Hegel and revived by Danto. Cf. Carroll,
"Essence, Expression, and History: Arthur Danto's Philosophy of Art," in
Danto and His Critics (Rollins, op. cit.), 79ff.

45. Cf. William K. Wimsatt Jr. and Monroe Beardsley, "The Intentional
Fallacy." This famous and frequently published study originally appeared in
the *Sewanee Review* 54 (1946).

46. Cf. Fodor, op. cit., 41.

47. Danto, *The Transfiguration of the Commonplace*, op. cit., 124.

48. Richard Wollheim, "Danto's Gallery of Indiscernibles," in *Danto and
His Critics* (Rollins, op. cit.), 35.

49. Danto, *The Transfiguration of the Commonplace*, op. cit., 51.

50. Mike Bidlo did, indeed, exhibit 80 replicas of Picasso's works under his
own signature in 1988 in the Castelli Gallery, New York. One of the works,
which is now displayed in the Galerie Bischosfberger, Zurich, is the accurate,
full-scale replica of Picasso's *Algerian Women* (1955), which is itself a variation
of Delacroix's similarly entitled work. The title: *Not Picasso* (1987). Cf. Jörg
Huber, "Imitative Strategien in der bildenden Kunst," in *Imitationen—Nachahmung und Modell. Von Der Lust am Falschen*, ed. Jörg Huber, Martin Heller, and
Hans Ulrich Reck (Basel: Stroemfeld/Roter Stern, 1989. Museum für Gestaltung, Zürich. Ausstellungskatalog), 143f.

51. Danto, *The Transfiguration of the Commonplace*, op. cit., 36f.

52. Ibid., 146f.

53. Carroll, op. cit., 101.

54. Danto, "Responses and Replies," in *Danto and His Critics* (Rollins, op. cit.), 211.

55. In Danto's view this is an example of the transfiguration of the commonplace. Cf. *The Transfiguration of the Commonplace*, op. cit., 46.

56. Cf. Richard Wollheim, *Painting as an Art* (London: Thames & Hudson, 1987), 243ff.; also cf. György Somlyó, *Picasso* (Budapest: Magyar Helikon, 1981), 68ff.

57. Richard Wollheim, *Arts and its Objects: With Six Supplementary Essays* (Cambridge, UK: Cambridge University Press, 1980), 195ff.

58. Ibid., 198.

59. Ibid., 198f.

60. Ibid., 199.

61. Cf. Hans-Georg Gadamer, *Wahrheit und Methode* (Tübingen: J.C.B. Mohr [Paul Siebeck], 1975), 284ff.

62. Ian Mackenzie, "Gadamer's Hermeneutics and the Uses of Forgery," in *The Journal of Aesthetics and Art Criticism* 45, no. 1 (1986): 45.

63. Cf. Ernst Hans Gombrich, "Style," in *International Encyclopedia of the Social Sciences*, ed. David L. Sills (London: Macmillan, 1968), 361.

64. Cf. Eric Donald Hirsch, *Validity in Interpretation* (New Haven, CT: Yale University Press, 1967), 4. Quoted by Mackenzie, op. cit.

65. Cf. Sándor Radnóti, *"Tisztelt közönség, kulcsot te találj . . ."* ("Honored Public, Go on, Find your own Ending . . .") (Budapest: Gondolat, 1990), 56ff.

66. György Márkus studied the validity of the universality of Gadamer's hermeneutics using the example of the history of the interpretation of philosophical tradition. He writes the following: "Gadamer's philosophy at least on some points seems to posit a historically and culturally specific and limited model of interpretation as its valid form, while at the same time it seems to suppress the normative force of this claim through its ontologization as a happening of effective history." Márkus, "Diogenes Laertios *contra* Gadamer, Universal or Historical Hermeneutics?," in *Life After Postmodernism*, ed. John Fekete (New York: St. Martin's Press, 1987), 143.

67. János György Szilágyi, *Legbölcsebb az Idı. Antik vázák hamisítványai* ("Time: The Wisest of them All. The Forgeries of Antique Vases") (Budapest: Corvina, 1987), 47.

68. Danto, "Responses and Replies," in *Danto and His Critics* (Rollins, op. cit.), 198.

69. Following the Croatian art historian Ljubo Karaman, Bialostocki distinguishes provinces that are subordinated to one centrum from peripheries that receive stimuli from several regions and are in the position to choose, in which case the latter might have a culture both autonomous and original. Cf. Jan Bialostocki, "Some Values of Artistic Periphery," in *World Art: Themes of Unity and Diversity. Acts of the XXVIth International Congress of the History of Art*, vol. I, ed. Irving Lavin (University Park: Pennsylvania State University Press, 1986), 49ff. These are obviously relative notions, which the radical development of world communication in the twentieth century might easily modify. Nevertheless, the distinction between the unproductive provincial culture and the fertile peripheral culture is far from being irrelevant in the

case of a small culture such as the Hungarian, which is situated far from the cultural centers, or has been kept apart from them for historical reasons.

70. Gadamer, *Wahrheit und Methode*, op. cit., 356.

71. Szilágyi, op. cit., 13.

72. Szilágyi, op. cit., 17.

73. "Christian Zervos's illustrated book entitled *L'art en Grèce* provides one of the most interesting documents of this renaissance, as well as also serving as a kind of canonic reference for the location of the whiteround vases in the accepted artistic taste of the period. It was published in 1935, three years after the first volume of his great Picasso monograph came out." Szilágyi, op. cit., 21.

74. Arthur Koestler, "The Aesthetics of Snobbery," *Anchor Review* 1 (1955).

75. Cf. chapter 3, notes 5 and 26.

76. Quoted by David Sox, *Unmasking the Forger: The Dossena Deception* (New York: Universe, 1987), 59.

77. Cf. chapter 2, note 1.

78. Szilágyi, op. cit., 38.

79. John Pope-Hennessy, *The Study and Criticism of Italian Sculpture* (New York: Metropolitan Museum of Art/Princeton, NJ: Princeton University Press, 1980), 266.

80. "In order to be able to prove that F_b is a forgery, first a judge must be able to prove that F_a is original. Therefore, he must examine the supposedly original picture *as if it was a document.* . . ." Eco, op. cit., 183. And the moralizing viewpoint survives parallel with this documentarist–historicist approach. Even behind such major academic accomplishments as those summed up by Bernard Ashmole in his lecture, "Forgeries in Ancient Sculpture in Marble: Creation and Detection," the main purpose is the *exclusion* of forgery, with its scholarly *understanding* being confined to its moral rejection: "A modern forgery, however talented its author, however much pleasure he may gain from the creative effort that it involves, is made for one main purpose, to gain money by fraud." The First J. L. Myres Memorial Lecture (Oxford, 1961), 15.

81. Szilágyi, op. cit., 40f.

82. Gadamer, op. cit., 80.

83. Szilágyi, op. cit., 47f.

84. Szilágyi defines the way in which a modern researcher of antique art should approach forgeries as follows: "He must be able to tell apart antique from nonantique, otherwise he will not be able to understand the antique world; he must know that modern forgeries represent a certain value, not in the sense that they allow the archaeologist or the expert to show off his professional aptitude by unmasking them, but in that it reflects our relationship to the antique period, it shows one course of antiquity. As far as the researcher is concerned, however, should there be something important about the actuality of antique art that he would like to express with the help of his discipline, then he should *personally* view and enjoy the antique works of art, as if they had been created today." Szilágyi, "Antikenfälschung und Antikenrezeption," *Acta Antiqua Akademiae Scientiarum Hungaricae*, T. XXX. fasc. 1–4 (1988).

85. Szilágyi's essay was first published in the 1978/2 issue of the magazine *Antik tanulmányok* ("Antique Studies") under the title, "Antik vázák hamisítványai" ("The Forgeries of Antique Vases"). The present title—a quote from Thales of Miletus—was inserted there as a motto.

86. "The two painters who probably had the greatest effect on our century were Pablo Picasso and Marcel Duchamp. The first through his works, the second through one work, which was the direct negation of the concept of works of art." Octavio Paz, "Apariencia desnuda. La obra de Marcel Duchamp," in *Obras completas VI* (Barcelona: Circuló de Lectores, 1992).

87. Danto, "Responses and Replies," in *Danto and His Critics* (Rollins, op. cit.), 198.; also, Danto, "Appreciation and Interpretation," in *The Philosophical Disenfranchisement of Art* (New York: Columbia University Press, 1986), 35.

88. Szilágyi, *Legbölcsebb az Idö*, op. cit., 47.

89. Cf. Edgar Wind, *Art and Anarchy* (London: Duckworth, 1985), 2 and passim.

90. The latest summary of this can be found in *Das Jahrhundert des Multiple. Von Duchamp bis Gegenwart,* ed. Zdenek Felix, Ausstellung, Deichtorhallen Hamburg, 2 September bis 30 October 1994 (Hamburg: Oktagon, 1994).

91. Szilágyi, op. cit., 45.

92. Szilágyi, op. cit.

93. Cf. Huber, "Imitative Strategien in der bildenden Kunst," op. cit., 141. Also cf. Ulli Moser, "Originalitätsdokumente. Die Künstlerin Elaine Sturtevant malt Kopien grosser Zeitgenossen," in *Original Kopie. Parnass.* Sonderheft 7, 92ff. Also cf. Doris von Drateln: "Der Dialog mit dem Gleichen," in *Kunstforum* 111 (January/February 1991), 180ff.

94. Huber, op. cit., 145.

95. David Carrier, "The Fake Artwork," in *The Aesthete in the City: The Philosophy and Practice of American Abstract Painting in the 1980s* (University Park: Pennsylvania State University Press, 1994), 123.

5

LITERARY MYSTIFICATION

Ut pictura poesis?

As in painting, so in poetry. This line from Horace (*Epistulae* V, 361), admittedly taken out of context, was used—backed up by Simonides of Ceos's saying, handed down by Plutarch, to the effect that painting is mute poetry and poetry is talking painting—from the sixteenth to the eighteenth centuries to lend support (with the authority of the humanist quote) to painting's demand for equality, for its final liberation from its lowly position as a craft and a guild. "With justified lamentation painting complains, that she has been driven of the liberal arts, although she is a true daughter of nature and appeals to [the] noblest of senses. Hence, writers, it is wrong to have left her outside . . .," Matthias Corvinus, king of Hungary declares in the first part of Leonardo's tract on painting, "The Contest of the Arts."[1]

Although the dispute over the priority of the various branches of art did have certain medieval antecedents, and similar comparisons could even be found in antiquity, it was in the Renaissance that the birth process began with the systematic comparison of the arts, with the discovery of their respective affinities and boundaries, with the formulation of shared principles, with the splintering off of certain forms of human activity (crafts, sciences), and with the gradual suppression of the practical, moral, religious, and political functions of artworks, eventually leading, after three centuries of theoretical labor terminating in the classic century of aesthetics, to the creation—the *construction*, really—of the concept of art. It unites the five major

155

branches of art—painting, sculpture, architecture, music, and poetry—in the *modern system of art,* to which the various authors occasionally added art forms of less solid and continuous traditional background or shorter historical lifespan. (It was Paul Oskar Kristeller who pointed this out in his classic study relating the story of the above birth process.[2]) The humanist teaching of *ut pictura poesis* in this system ends its career, and the three-century-long effort to demonstrate the similarity of the two art forms is concluded with Lessing's *Laocoön.*[3] They are dissimilar, but there exists a level of conceptual generalization—and this is *the* concept of art—at which the same categories apply to both of them.

Moses Mendelssohn, for example, defined the task of aesthetics as follows: "In fact, aesthetics should in general cover the scholarship of the discovery of beauty, the theories of every aesthetics and art; therefore, each explanation and theory should be general enough to be applicable, without constraint, to every form of the beaux arts. If, for example, an explanation for the sublime is given in aesthetics, then we should be able to apply it to a sublime style of writing, the same way as to the sublime contours of painting and sculpture, to the sublime passages in music or to sublime architecture. . . ."[4]

"The unification of the beaux arts into a single principle, which would thereby be capable of expressing the aesthetic ideas"[5] has been achieved by one great school of philosophical aesthetics after another. Kristeller's account, which started out from Kant's appraisal, can be continued and expanded. Art criticism, along with the nineteenth-century development of the *aestheticizing* type of art history, and even including the early twentieth-century efforts by the rigorous art theories, the program of which was summed up in the title of Oskar Walzel's famous book, *Wechselseitige Erhellung der Künste* ("The Mutual Illumination of the Arts"),[6] all emphasized the sisterhood of the muses. The difference between the current notion of the muses and their mythical origins also testifies to the modern revolution, since originally the fine arts were not included in the disciplines presided over by the muses, whereas astronomy, historiography, philosophy, and oration were.

Upon examining the components of this sisterhood, we realize that, following the demand for *autonomy* that works of art as well as the various art forms developed in the Renaissance, the sum total of artworks and art forms, or art as a whole, also presented its demand for autonomy, developing its own independent sphere, with its independent categories and above all else with the capacity for productive genius, which Kant reserved exclusively for the arts. (On the other hand, to the same extent that the art sphere has become autonomous, the arts have lost the diverse roles they used to play in everyday life.) Sociologically, the various types of artistic activity—the social status of which varied to an extraordinary degree, from the very top of the hierarchies right down to the bottom—have grown together to form a continuum; the sociological category of the artist, whether a poet, painter, or musician, became firmly established in the nineteenth century. By contrast, the sociological definition of the audience became less clear: The openness of the work of art and the indeterminacy of the audience are interconnected. In a world that was becoming ever more profane, the recognition, unification, and partition of productive genius and original creation in the various fields also served to satisfy transcendent demands; the Romantic artistic creed became a characteristic variation in the new system of art.

However, it was above all else the new artistic practices that breathed life into the conceptual construct of art, providing it with a true existence, as shown by so much evidence in the panoramic view of nineteenth-century art, from the shortest of short stories to the utopia of *Gesamtkunstwerk,* from the poetry related to sounds and colors to the endeavors to achieve pure painterliness and pure poetry, etc.

In addition to the above-mentioned group of the great five, other art forms have always been around, requesting permission to join in the attempts to unify art: peripheral art forms of a decorative or casual character (garden landscaping, for example); complex art forms, in which the classical catalogers recognize the presence of several "basic" art forms (theatre, opera, dance); and art forms that are, successfully or not, based on some new innovation (color organ, photography, cinema). The greatest theoretical difficulty seems to have arisen in connection with literature—the relationship between poetry and literature, and between literature and art. This is indicated by the difficulties connected with the canonization of prosaic genres. The conflict between epos and novel in Goethe's age provides evidence not only for the continuously recurring quarrel between the old and new, but also for the concern with which those involved in art have always looked upon the prosaic forms. "As with all forms of the novel, the form of *Meister* is not at all poetic," Schiller wrote to Goethe in 1797[7]; but the works of other novelists too were characterized by the attempt to compensate for the prose of the novel with its paradoxical *poesis.* One is haunted by the suspicion that *prosaic* is the opposite of *poetic* and, by implication, of artistic as well.

Being used as a collective term for all literary works, literature cannot offer a well-defined division between artistic and nonartistic writing. This is why, in the fight for priority among the art forms, music and painting have so often become paradigmatic. This is also connected with Nietzsche's view that tragedy originated from the spirit of music. But as for the struggle for priority among the arts that went on in the Renaissance (the one that involved Leonardo), here the point was made that, of all the subjects of poetry, "nothing belongs exclusively to its own profession; because when it wants to make a speech it can be sure to be defeated by the orators; when it talks about astrology, it relates what it has stolen from the astrologists; when it talks about philosophy, it relates what it has stolen from the philosophers; and indeed, poetry has no well-deserved place of its own; it is like a street vendor who retails the goods made by the various craftsmen."[8] What is expressed in this criticism is the point that the medium of literature—i.e., language—is the most general medium of human communication—and more specifically, of intellectual communication—and that the boundaries between the artistic and nonartistic ways of molding it, of shaping it into writing, are fluid. The artistic character of the other art forms, those not mediated by language, stands out much more clearly against the nonartistic forms of human activity.

Furthermore, the universal and homogenized concept of art had to create its own conceptual counterparts, such as the *prose* of everyday life. And not only this: It also had to distinguish, within the activities of artistic character, between *low* art on the one hand and *high* art or *art proper* on the other. This was carried out by both the Schellingian division of artistic products into aesthetic and ordinary, and by the Schlegelian division into free arts and useful or pleasant mechanical arts based on demand, regardless of the deep-rooted difference between the two concepts in other respects.[9] When these distinctions became theoretically established at the end of the eighteenth century, literature once again provided more examples of low art than any other area of contemporary culture. (Only in the mass culture of the twentieth century, swollen to a size hitherto unseen, did the priority of the *picture* replace that of music and writing.) In formulating his radical cultural criticism, the young Friedrich Schlegel was able to recognize the indifference to form and the huge demand for thematic curiosity in countless areas of *poesis*: "As in an aesthetic flea market, *Volkspoesie* and *Bontonpoesie* are offered side by side, and even a metaphysician will not seek in vain for something to suit his mood. There are Nordic or Christian epopees for lovers of the North and Christianity, lovers of mystical tremble find their mystical ghost stories, cannibalistic odes for poetry lovers thus inclined, Greek costume for lovers of antiquity, tales of knights for heroic tongues, and yes, even ancient German *Nationalpoesie* for the dilettantes of Germanity."[10] The abundance of literary material and the wealth of disguises, along with the possibility that this critical sternness, besides censuring the worthless hacks, might also inadvertently fall on some of the significant tendencies and major works of art of the period—well, all this brings into relief the other aspect of distinguishing between high and low art: Namely, that it is literature, again, where this boundary is the most fluid.

Therefore there might be serious doubts concerning the principle of *ut pictura poesis*; from the moment that the equality, not necessarily of value but at least of right, of these two art forms became apparent, these doubts became just as legitimate as the conviction that the arts could mutually illuminate one another.

In this book I have presented forgery as an aesthetic problem, but up till now artistic forgery has been limited to the forgery of works of fine art. The reader might have already begun to wonder whether everything that has been said about painting would also apply to poetry. My answer, for the moment paradoxical, is that although my conclusions claim an aesthetic validity that extends beyond the realm of fine arts, the forgery of works of fine art is not identical, and indeed not even similar, to the forgery of literary works.

Tracing the evidence of forged works of art back to the period before the Renaissance in Europe is both difficult and inconclusive. There is essentially only one period in which the emergence of faked works of art can be suspected: the age of the Roman Empire. The forgery of valuable objects was, of course, common in the Middle Ages. Coins were also forged—in selecting the case of the provostship of Itebö (Hungary) from the numerous examples available on the subject, the author admits to indulging in national pride. The monks of this provostship, who were engaged in the forgery of coins, even managed to enrage Pope Honorius III in 1221.[11] Although aesthetic considerations are pertinent to coins, it was hardly the issue in this particular instance. Seals were also forged: A whole collection of them was found in 1391 in the house of the literate master named János of the village of Madácsháza—the seals of the former kings of Hungary.[12] Then there was the forgery of religious relics, although in this case they were either not manmade (that is, natural objects such as the earthly remains of saints, etc.[13]), or were made not with an artistic purpose (other relics, like the instruments of torture used on martyrs, the nails and splinters of the holy cross, the graves of bishops), or, although created with an artistic purpose, were revered not for their artistic value or the artist's person but—similarly to the previous alternatives—for cultic reasons.[14] In any case, painting and sculpture formed a characteristic "alliance" with the relics in Western Christianity.[15] The forgery of paintings qualified as the forgery of relics rather than of art. Although perhaps not exactly qualifying as a fully developed criticism of forgery, the thousand-year war waged for the authenticity of the relics, officially declared at the IVth Council of Lateran, nonetheless demonstrates the large number of forgeries as well as the sensitivity associated with them. The notion of originality was applied to relics long before it was mentioned in connection with paintings. Before 1200 the cult of paintings independent of relics, or of paintings that themselves became relics, appeared only rarely in the West.[16]

There are forged objects such as maps or armorial bearings whereby the pictorial nature is of primary importance. But even in this case it is quite apparent that these either have no aesthetic function or that their aesthetic function is of secondary importance. In these instances too the unity of *pictura* and *scriptura* is indispensable.

Therefore the forgery of objects was much more closely related to the forgery of text than was the case with the modern forgery of art. Still, it is not uncommon even in the latter case that the "authenticity" of a forged work of art is supported by forged documents concerning the alleged provenance, and the legends of origin—through the imitation of oral or written traditions—do have their own significance. But the subordinate role of these follows from the entire modern approach to art. From the aesthetic point of view, a work of art is identical with its own history only insofar as it "wears its history on its surface," that is, to such an extent that the historical knowledge has become part of the aesthetic experience. The unstable unity of the forgery of art and the forgery of history points precisely to the same thing. In the modern practice of forgery such unity is not indispensable: Once he has done everything to turn his painting into a historicizing pastiche, the forger leaves the historical placement—the task of attributing and dating—to the expert viewers, as described by Eric Hebborn in his autobiography,[17] in the hope that the work will be taken for what it appears to be. In the unmasking of forgeries too, the viewpoints of an aesthetic, historical (and technical) nature become separated. It is quite often the case that the story itself still holds out firmly, but the work of art proves to be a forgery on other grounds.

By contrast, in the case of hagiographic forgeries, the fakes and their forged legends are in perfect unity. Without both the history relating the life and the suffering of a particular saint and the story of the relic itself, the relic is incomplete. The skepticism and suspicion, which could be evidenced beginning in the early fifth century and which was revealed, among others, by St. Augustine, St. Gregory the Great, and later by Erasmus of Rotterdam, made the written record of the relic's history, along with the *vita*-s and the *passions,* a prerequisite, thus rendering these items open to skepticism.[18] Forging written material often meant the forging of objects too, since the old documents had to be presented. "If literary and religious forgery and their counterpart modes of criticism survived the fall of the ancient world, however, forgery and criticism of legal authorities became the dominant new forms in the Middle Ages. Most practitioners of forgery and criticism were clerics and lawyers. Their methods usually centered not on the production of literary texts—though these were written, especially when a religious order needed to justify its possession of the wonder-working bones of a saint by providing a narrative of their passage from their original home—but on the devising of faked documents, documents apparently legitimate in *physical form, color, seals,* and wording. As in antiquity, so in the Middle Ages, techniques of authentication could infiltrate literature"[19] (my emphasis).

Regardless of the point that both the calligraphy and seals had aesthetic relevance, the material aesthetic appeal of forged documents was perhaps related to the aesthetic qualities of artworks even more remotely than was the case with coins or relics. The forgery of artworks—in other words, of artistic creations appreciated for their aesthetic values as well as for the artistic importance of their creator (or style)—formed not just another step in the history of forging objects, but a new era, a new world. And since the most resolute advances with regard to the new concept of art were made in the fine arts, and the rules of the game in art were changed in the Renaissance, it is understandable that in his *Paragone,* Leonardo, rather than settling for equality, already demanded seniority for his field.

By contrast, the modern forgery of literature has premodern analogies as well as specific tricks, all of which can look back on a tradition of more than 2,000 years—not to mention the point that the greatest accomplishments of this type of forgery originated from antiquity and the Middle Ages. Writing, scholarship, and literature formed a continuum at that time, much more than did objects and works of art. Obviously, there are sociocultural reasons such as the permanent privileges of literacy over the handicrafts to explain why the object was forged in the case of works of art, however valuable they may have been from an aesthetic point of view, while in the case of a forged document, be it as dry as dust, stylistic and aesthetic considerations played a significant part in the wording. The elements of forging documents and fiction (document narration), storytelling, and documentary were mixed.

Donatio Constantini, that document of world-historical importance, which was forged in the eighth century to establish the temporal powers of the Papacy and according to which Constantine the
Great, having been cured of leprosy by drinking holy water, is supposed to have handed primacy over the Western world to Pope
Sylvester, is simultaneously a legend and a (forged) deed of con-
veyance. It has been suggested that the pious story, which originally
meant to serve the edification of the pilgrims of Lateran, became a
pseudolegal document only in later times.[20] As to the forgeries of historical works, such as *Historia Augusta,* a collection of biographies of
Roman emperors, written in the fourth century by six alleged
authors, or *Historia Regum Britanniæ* by Geoffrey of Monmouth from
the twelfth century, or the works written by the humanist Annius
Viterbensis (1432–1502) and attributed to various antique authors, it
is difficult to decide whether we should regard them as "fictional history" or "historical fiction."[21]

Documentary and fiction were mixed together in other genres
also. "The Hellenistic age indulged in a proliferation of fabrication.
Thus imaginative biography, letters written by statesmen or sages,
exotic and Utopian romance, erudite mystifications."[22] From the
fourth century B.C. on, "rhetorical and tragic historiography," in competition with poetry, in a way relativized Aristotle's famous distinction between the two: ". . . the rhetors rendered the distinction
between original and fabricated documents very difficult to make. In
order to demonstrate their own stylistic aptitude, they concocted
speeches and letters by famous historical figures, both men and
women. A new literary genre emerged in the first century B.C.: the
epistolary novel. . . . As a form of stylistic exercise, the rhetors' students composed the appropriate letters and speeches."[23] Sample collections of letters are also known from the Middle Ages, comprised of
parodistic and fictitious letters; in subsequent periods, and most
notably in the late Middle Ages, letters came to form one of the most
entertaining literary genres.[24]

Abelard's famous *Historia calamitatum* ("The History of My Calam-
ity," 1133–1134?) is also a (probably fictitious) letter written to a trou-
bled friend, whom Abelard hoped to be able to console by relating his
own, and even greater, misfortune. It includes Abelard's and Heloise's
correspondence of seven letters; Heloise, by then the Abbess of the
convent Paraclitus, reflects on *Historia calamitatum,* which tells the
story of their common tribulation. (The girl's uncle avenged the couple's secret marriage by hiring men "to cut off that part of my body,
with which I brought disgrace on them," in Abelard's words.[25]) Ever
since the late eighteenth century, these documents (and especially the

letters), having acquired a mythical significance in the history of emotional and amorous culture, have been surrounded by a cloud of suspicion.[26] The great Munich conference on medieval forgery in 1986 saw the dramatic clash between the respective views of John F. Benton and Hubert Silvestre. Although it was Benton who more recently (in 1972) revived the suspicion that the letters were actually forgeries made in the thirteenth century, later he revised his view, using stylistic arguments (based on the selection and frequency of words) to show that the work had indeed been written by Abelard. Heloise's letters were also written by Abelard, which would mean that, to a considerable extent, the original author rendered the recollection into a fiction, a work of fine literature. In fact, many would say that he created the first modern autobiography. This would apply even more so, if Silvestre was right; he has been led by historical arguments to the conclusion that the work in question is a forgery, which was made a 150 years after the events; he even has an idea for the motive behind the forgery.[27] It is perhaps needless to say that, regardless of the future course of this debate—in which the past 200 years have not been enough to resolve the fundamental issues—the outcome not only will leave unaffected the evaluation of Abelard's and Heloise's historical personalities, neither will it reduce the significance of their fictitious–mythological personality, their literary figures.

One of the recurring conclusions drawn by the authorities on antique and medieval literary forgery is that in this field the disentanglement of fiction and nonfiction, of the literary and documentary elements, is either impossible or at least very difficult. This is further complicated by the fact that experts very often face considerable difficulties in determining whether the work in question is a forgery at all. Wolfgang Speyer has repeatedly emphasized that not all pseudepigrapha—i.e., literary works that have an author different from that which is implied by the title, content, and tradition—are forgeries. And we are not talking only about works that for various reasons—confusion due to similarities regarding the titles or the authors' names, mistaken attribution, works produced either by members of a school under the name of the master or by the staff of a chancellery under the name of the chancellor—*became* forgeries: "On the basis of the research carried out so far, it is impossible to decide in every single instance about religious pseudepigrapha whether they are original in a mythical sense, or freely treated, or forged."[28]

The designation of a separate category for "true religious pseudepigrapha," the first member of this three-fold division, obviously serves the justifiable aim of preventing the often inadequate charge of forgery, as formulated by the followers of the Enlightenment, in con-

nection with the apocryphal writings within a certain religious movement. Nevertheless, it is not always possible to distinguish the decla-
rations attributed to the divine, angelical, and apostolic heroes of
either the Old Testament or the myths, as well as those attributed to
the saints of the Church, from the products of free artistic fantasy or
forgery.

Fully appreciating the point that in this instance I present a historical area in connection with which I cannot claim to possess any
expertise at all, I venture to suggest that the difficulties lying in the
separation of fake from nonfake, of fiction from reality, are connected
not only to the difficulties associated with the reconstructibility of
ancient history and not only to the present state of research, but also
to the protean nature of literature itself. The forgery of works of fine
art—I hope I put across my case convincingly—is deeply interconnected with the autonomy of works of art, with the cognizance of artistic individuality and originality, with the historical reflection of art—
in short, with the modern system of art. It appears, however, that there
is an even deeper connection between literature and forgery, one that
is related to the fictitious nature of storytelling and poetic speech in
general. The *recognition* of the fictitious, nonmimetic, and consensual
elements of the painterly or sculptural vision is an extremely late
development, while literary narration has, from the start, distinguished itself from all other forms of literature and speech by its
markedly fictitious character. The reason why the recognizability of literary forgeries is hindered is that the means of literary forgery closely
fit into the accepted means of poetic speech. The mystification concerning both the history of the origin of the work and its authorship,
as well the person of the story's central character or the person of the
narrator, the intention to have the fiction, whereby the product of fantasy is reality, accepted, etc.—all these offer no definite clues, from the
viewpoint of literature, for making this distinction. On the contrary,
when we recognize them in the textual context of literature, the *aesthetic* experience of this recognition itself often moves us to interpret
the material differently, or at least to accept a possible poetic reading
of it. In making the distinction between forgeries and originals in fine
art, I started out from the premise that the existence of forgeries is at
the same time the criticism and parasite of the modern concept of art;
it was for this reason that the forger's *intention* could be disregarded in
the definition. If, on the other hand, a great many of the experts on
premodern literary forgeries start out from the pragmatic and, if you
will, sensible point of view that only those instances qualify as forgery
in which the fraudulent intention of either the author or the later user
can be recognized—or with regard to texts of fine literature, in which

the nonliterary purpose can be identified—then it is most likely the extreme proximity of forgeries to several literary genres that necessitates the representation of this unimaginative, nonliterary viewpoint.

And indeed, who would not be able to see the parallels between the mystifications of Hellenistic prose, including the forgeries, on the one hand, and the fictitious documentarism of the triumphant beginnings of modern prose—the maritime novels, travel diaries, biographies, epistolary novels, etc., on the other? Even to link Abelard's "epistolary novel," whether forged or original, to the first "true" epistolary novel, Richardson's *Pamela* (1740), would not seem too absurd.[29] Not to mention the point that the pseudoepigraphic mask—the pseudo, the fake—often becomes a literary *genre*: "It can generally be observed that unsigned works are usually attributed to the first and greatest representative of the same literary genre: the hexametric eposes were ascribed to Homer, the hexametric didactic poems to Hesiod, the gnomes to Theognis, the drinking songs and love poems to Anacreon, the fables to Aesop, etc. The pseudo-Menanderian, the pseudo-Catoian, the pseudo-Varroian, and the pseudo-Senecaian maxims also belong to this category. This might have served the purpose of lending greater weight to the work or the maxim in question."[30] The same "magnet effect" can be seen in the Middle Ages—be this authority a pagan classic or a Christian saint or patriarch. Even those authors whose names were known signed their works using Classical pseudonyms, proving that the pseudo-Martials and, even more to the point, the popular pseudo-Ovids were less forgeries than *genres*. Presenting Ovid as a hedonist, or even as a Christian, was also an accepted practice.[31]

My message, whereby it was the proximity of the forged and *fictitious* that prevented the productive separation of literature and literary forgery (at the same time allowing us to catch a glimpse of the nature of literature), is incisively expressed by an important medieval author, John of Salisbury, himself possibly guilty of forging a pseudo-Plutarchian work, *Institutio Traiani*: "Since he identifies, following Augustinus, the notion of 'falsification' or *'falsitas'* with the notion of 'vanity, emptiness' or *'vanitas,'* and sums all these up in the comprehensive category of *nugae* (uselessness, frivolousness, idle talk), he sees the artistic truth of comedy in its fictitiousness and apparentness, in the representation of the 'life comedy,' with all its pretentiousness, duplicity, deception and illusion."[32]

Premodern Forgery?

Dante throws the forgers into the tenth stage of his eighth circle of hell. These sinners were, of course, guilty of forging money, official documents, and wills rather than works of art. I choose not to discuss the separate historical problem of forging money, since before the arrival of banknotes the counterfeit coins were illegal not because they were not worth their face value, but because they were issued unlawfully. (The black monks of Itebö, Hungary used the monastic order's treasures to forge coins, and then ran off with them.) The major types of premodern forgery are of a literary character in the broader sense of the word: Forgeries of religious, philosophical, scholarly, political as well as esoteric writings, historiographical works, deeds, letters, and fine literature. These types were constantly mixing with one another and it often proves difficult to confirm the act of forgery, as seen from the above. Nevertheless, the scholarly effort to clarify the situation is far from being a recent development; one of the classic and recurring, albeit not always prominent, tasks of criticism, and most notably of philological criticism, has been the demonstration of false authorship and the interpretation of its intentions. The practicing of both elements of this task could be observed already in the Neoplatonic commentaries of Aristotle's works.[33]

In searching for the motives of *mala fide* fakes (i.e., of deliberate forgeries), we should feel confident about generalizing Speyer's typology (with additional considerations borrowed from elsewhere). Such a motive could be constituted by the intention to increase the importance of the writing (or the other way around—to increase the cult of the person named as author); the striving for effect (or the other way around—the manifestation of a significant personality's influence); financial gain (incidentally, this is rarely observed in connection with Jewish or Christian forgeries); personal rivalry and conflict; the humiliation or the ridiculing of an opponent or colleague (this type includes several cases from fine art, which I earlier described as being "picaresque"); pure entertainment; the augmentation of tradition; the defense of philosophical positions; and the furthering of political, local-patriotic, religious–political, or religious aims.[34]

When, in his monograph on feudal society, Marc Bloch inquires about the reasons why forgery, although regularly practiced in every age, was particularly flourishing in the eighth and ninth centuries, he comes to the paradoxical conclusion that it was precisely a peculiar respect for the past, a powerful kind of conservatism or traditionalism, that made people try to reconstruct the past in the way that it *must have been*. This was a homogenizing adjustment of the past to the present, its rehabilitation following its physical destruction and the chaotic entanglement of its strands.[35]

According to Horst Fuhrmann, a major expert on medieval forgery, this rehabilitation was directed less at the past than at the world order itself, so as to correct its chaotic condition. It strove to realize the divine plan for the world; therefore it is its validity rather than its formal authenticity that should be the focus of our attention[36]: "From time to time it is precisely the forger who, acting on a certain religious feeling of responsibility, rids tradition of some of its off-shoots. . . . From this perspective, the spirit of the period has no better advocate than the forger: what has been thought necessary but found wanting by many, he provides. It was for this reason that those forgeries which were in harmony with some general desire were able to penetrate life so deeply. What would the medieval conception of heaven be like without the fake *Dionysius,* for example, or what would the pictures of the *Ecclesia primitiva* and the *Vita apostolica* be like without the pseudo-Isidorian collection?"[37] Then, almost a quarter-of-a-century later, in the concluding lecture of the conference on medieval forgeries, he associates this idea with the genre of the *fiction* presenting a better world, of the *utopia*: "Several forgeries transferred to earlier periods should be regarded as sketches representing the Christian ways of life from closeness to grace . . .; the forgeries which depict an earlier period themselves have an already simulated reality. To put it bluntly: in the past, the function of utopia was partly fulfilled by forgery, by fiction."[38]

The history of antique Greek and Latin, Jewish, early Christian, and medieval forgeries can be found among the various historical disciplines, divided according to subject and period (history of religion, literature, law, diplomatic relations, etc.), as well as in source criticism. It might even involve historical psychology and historical sociology. Nevertheless, all these studies, whether actually performed or existing only potentially, tend to dismember the phenomenon rather than unite it. A considerable part of the material might require a theological interpretation in addition to a treatment in religious history, Bible criticism, etc.; but this has very little to do with the fact that 130 comedies were attributed to Plautus, when only 24 were definitely written by him (according to Varro).[39] Galen once told how he had discovered in a Roman bookshop a book unknown to him yet published under his name, which led him to distinguish, in a separate book, his original works from the forgeries broadly circulated. It would be difficult to associate this typically urbanistic anecdote not only with the pious practices of the Frankish monks compiling the pseudo-Isidorian decrees, but also with Nicolaus Cusanus's discovery of the forged nature of one or two among them. In view of the fact that the global approach to it is characterized more by practical exclusions than by a definition, I am of the opinion that premodern forgery cannot have a general theory. Granted, some conclusions can be drawn; for example, one could infer a relatively low level of individualism from the anonymity, or pseudo-anonymity, of a large number of works requiring considerable intellectual capacities. But this phenomenon is not completely identical with forgery, and it is contradicted by the very specific instances that periodically revealed the strong criticism of false authorship, along with the delicate matters of copyright and authors' sensitivities.

What all this implies is that, although there is such a thing as premodern forgery, it has no separate history: Its strict isolation can only be based on the often ambiguous or artificial, or impossible, or more often simply unhistorical—reconstruction of fraudulent intentions.

I would like to call attention to one particular feature of this extremely variegated picture, a feature that remains functional even in modern *literary* forgeries. (My suspicion is, by the way, that writing a separate history of modern literary forgeries would be an equally spurious undertaking.) All those motives I bear in mind, which I have just now listed among the incentives of forgery; modern examples could also be brought, but the analogies in most of the cases would remain formal, since notions such as authority or fame (which forgery either is based on or wishes to strengthen), for example, always require historical foundations. Menander's or Plautus's fame is different from St.Paul's, and the fame of all of them is different from Shakespeare's, or to refer to a notorious (diary) forgery from the 1980s, all these are very different from the fame of Adolf Hitler. Nevertheless, literary forgery does have a characteristic feature, which matches in importance the connection between forgery and story-telling/poetic fiction discussed in the previous section.

Every forgery includes its own myth or legend of origin. Sometimes this myth consists of nothing more than the association with either a false author or a faked date of origin. As Don Juan's archaic myth has, in Kierkegaard's opinion, been preserved merely by a number, the number 1003, so can the mysterious story of origin be captured solely in a name, escaping further investigation altogether. Still, with all fake or forged writings, the feigned origin forms such an essential feature that quite often the theme or spirit of the respective writings is also related to it in the closest possible way. One of the most important functions of literary forgeries is the reconstruction of one particular origin (religious, ecclesiastic, national, tribal, familial, philosophical, literary, etc.). The most important institutions of the medieval period—states, bishoprics, universities, etc.—were legitimized by false histories of origins. *Constitutum Constantini*, too, is a legend of origin. The author of *Corpus Areopagiticum* created a myth of origin for his work by choosing the appropriate name for himself:

according to this myth, the Greek convert who listened to the Apostle Paul's speech about the unknown God and witnessed the encounter between Jewish–Christian theology and Greek philosophy at the Areopagus (Acts 17:16–34) was the same person who relaid the foundations of Christian theology in a neo-Platonic manner.[40]

It was the famous humanist and critic Laurentius Valla (1407–1457) who first used philological arguments to prove the fictitious nature of both Constantine's donation and the author's name, Dionysios the Areopagite. One of the inquiries of philology addresses the authenticity of literary works. The relative tolerance shown towards forgeries in the Middle Ages was based on the concept that *falsum* was potentially true; therefore, as long as they did not contradict Catholic dogma, reading works of unauthenticated origin could also be edifying.[41] Nevertheless, even for Renaissance philologists, the problem of distinguishing between authentic and nonauthentic was not a major issue. Forgery often found itself at war with its criticism, and it seems that the suspicion that the history of philology felt towards forgeries reached its peak in the nineteenth century.

"I believe both Macpherson & Chatterton, that what they say is ancient is so" ——————— (William Blake) ———————

When David Hume first laid his hands on fragments of the poetry from the Scottish Highlands—still in manuscript form, in James Macpherson's (1736–1796) translation—he had his doubts about them. Later, however, he came to be convinced of the authenticity of the works, if not perhaps of the ancient origin ascribed to them by the translator: "In the family of every Highland chieftain, there was anciently retained a bard, whose office was the same with that of the Greek rhapsodists; and the general subject of the poems which they recited was the wars of Fingal; an epoch no less celebrated among them, than the wars of Troy among the Greek poets."[42] Three years later—by which time Macpherson's fragments (1760), which he attributed to anonymous bards, had been followed by the publication of two eposes, *Fingal* (1762) and *Tempora* (1763), both ascribed to Fingal's son, the third-century bard Ossian—Hume reported that, according to the prevalent view of the literary circles of London, these works were regarded as "palpable and most impudent forgery." "It is in vain to say, that their beauty [i.e., of the poems] will support them, independent of their authenticity: No; that beauty is not so much to the general taste as to ensure you of this event; and if people be once disgusted with the idea of a forgery, they are thence apt to entertain a more disadvantageous notion of the excellency of the production itself. . . . I must own, for my own part, that, though I have had many particular reasons to believe these poems genuine, more than it is possible for any Englishman of letters to have, yet I am not entirely without my scruples on that head."[43]

It was with a touch of desperate pathos that, on behalf of the literary circles as well in the name of "all the centuries," he publicly called upon Mr. Blair, the famous vicar who supported Macpherson and studied Ossian, to find evidence to prove that the poems had originated, if not in the age of Severus (the Roman emperor who had sent his army against the Scottish tribes in 208), then at least not within the previous five years. Hume asked Macpherson to locate the old manuscript containing a section of *Fingal,* which was claimed by the translator to be in the possession of a Scottish family, and demanded that he be allowed to compare the original and the translation. Macpherson was also asked to find evidence not only to show that poems such as these were still regularly sung in the Highlands, but also to verify that these resembled the translation. "You have a just and laudable zeal for the credit of these poems; they are, if genuine, one of the greatest curiosities in all respects, that ever was discovered in the commonwealth of letters. . . ."[44]

Nevertheless, he found Blair's results less than convincing, which led him to describe the poems, in a short (and from considerations of friendship, unpublished) essay as discreditable.[45] Through sound reasoning and some very clever arguments, he eliminated the possibility of the poems' authenticity. He demonstrated that the heroes of Ossian were knights-errant who displayed a chivalry more irrational than that of Amadis de Gaula or Lancelot de Lake. Considering the barbaric circumstances, he could accept neither the heroes' atheism nor their apparent gallantry towards women, etc. He unequivocally declared Macpherson to be a forger, drawing parallels between his translation and other literary works regarded as famous forgeries in that age: The letters of Phalaris, the tyrant of Acragas, Cicero's consolatio (self-consolation following the death of his daughter), or Petronius's *Satyricon* fragments (with regard to the latter, the parallel was quite unjustified).

Later, repeating sometimes verbatim arguments already expounded in the essay, he assured Gibbon, who had politely voiced his doubts about the poems of Ossian in his *Decline and Fall,* of his complete agreement: "It is, indeed, strange, that any men of Sense coud [sic] have imagin'd it possible, that above twenty thousand Verses, along with numberless historical Facts, sould have been preservd [sic] by oral Tradition during fifty Generations, by the rudest, perhaps, of all European Nations; the most necessitous, the most turbulent, and the most unsettled."[46] Hume even spelled out what it was that could muddle common sense: Passion and national prejudice. And although he did not as much as admit it, this national prejudice contributed to his initial enthusiasm, as well as it did to that of other great Scots (Robert Ferguson, Adam Smith, etc.).

The crucial motif of Ossian's history of origin was the national strife between the English and Scots. "A Scotchman must be a very sturdy moralist, who does not love Scotland better than truth: he will always love it better than inquiry; and if falsehood flatters his vanity, will not be very diligent to detect it," Doctor Johnson wrote in a shrewd and malignant note.[47] Nevertheless, the fabrication of ancient Scottish glory, of the history and cultural traditions of a nation, of its national hero (Fingal), along with the projection of the relations between modern Britannia and Scotland onto the relationship between the Roman conquerors and the Celts, together would not have been sufficient to explain the poem's fantastic international success, which fundamentally influenced the culture of several generations. The anti-Classical trend that aimed to relativize the Classical canon topographically, so to speak, was also necessary. And thus, the "Nordic epopee" became the equal counterpart of the southern—of Homer and Virgil—with the blind bard, Ossian, pairing off with the blind Homer (accompanied, in the cultural imagination of the British reader, by the figure of another great, blind epic poet, Milton).

This fitted-in well with the various "revival" movements, such as the Celtic revival. It was furthermore required that the oral tradition, having been excluded from elite culture, be revaluated at a higher rating, its capacity and memory potential be overvalued, and the "people," and especially the artistic genius of the people, be discovered. The fact that tradition in this case was created from almost nothing, from complete obscurity, paralleled this discovery, confirming the hypothesis of the oppressive nature of the Classical canon. Of course, anti-Classicism also meant neo-Classicism, in the form of primitivism. All this was then complemented with a touch of exoticism, reinforcing the image of the noble and sublime savage or barbarian, which had by then been well established in public opinion, and leading up to the anticivilizatory cultural criticism of which Rousseau was the most important representative. On top of all this, what was also needed was the majestic, strange and mysterious, dark, sentimental, and melancholic tone, which was alien to the Enlightenment and which foreshadowed and even set the pattern for Romanticism.

All this, however, only outlined a possibility. Without meaning to provide an exhaustive list, we name a few of those who were influenced by Ossian—Klopstock, Lessing, Herder, Bürger, Schiller, Goethe, Hölderlin, Novalis, Lenz, Tieck, Voss, Jean Paul, Mendelssohn, Diderot, Madame de Staël, Chateaubriand, Napoleon, Coleridge, Byron, Blake, and (despite his criticism) Wordsworth—and if I may remind the readers of the role Ossian played in Hungarian poetry,[48] then the kind of evolutional superiority that we find amusing in connection with Hölderlin, for example, who placed Ossian next to Orpheus, Homer, and Pindar,[49] and also in connection with the Hungarian Sándor Petöfi and János Arany, who compared "Homer and Ossian," will obviously prove to be unfounded. In addition to influencing poetic and artistic imagination, its effect also filtered through everyday culture. Anyone who was able to meet all the above-listed requirements of an age, and do so at a standard high enough to captivate the greatest intellects of that period, well earned the label "genius."

Nor can it be claimed that we, who were born much later, possess information that was not available to contemporaries and the generations immediately following. Unlike a typical case of fine-art forgery, here the turning point did not come with the "unmasking," since Macpherson's endeavor was accompanied by doubts and suspicions from the outset. His conduct was at the same time that of a free reconstructor and forger. As to the former, the introduction of *Tempora* clearly states: "The story of the poem, with which I had long been acquainted, enabled me to reduce the broken members of the piece in the order in which they now appear."[50] The phrasing explicitly refers to the practice of fine-art restorers, whose occupation was generally established as being freely inventive and complementary in character. Thus in addition to the *restorer*, the role of *translator* and *collector* also allowed one to take liberties in the middle of the eighteenth century.[51] Nevertheless, in *changing the genre* and in stringing the ballads together to create an epic poem in the manner of Homer, Virgil, and Milton, Macpherson clearly transgressed the limits of inventiveness that these roles permitted and that only appear as forgery when seen through modern eyes. Nor can his fraudulent intentions be questioned, as he intended to fabricate a manuscript and embarked on the translation of *Tempora* back into Gaelic. Nevertheless, it appears that the efforts to authenticate his work did not fill up his entire life, which was at the same time hinged on an *idea* closely related to Ossian (translating the *Iliad*, writing a history of Britain, assuming a role in politics by acting as a Scottish MP). It was precisely the pride and capriciousness with which Macpherson neglected the fate of his own work that Hume complained about in his letter written to Blair. James Boswell simply called him the "sublime savage," and Hume, upon learning in 1763 that Macpherson was about to leave for Florida to work as secretary to the Governor, thought to recommend that he visit the Chickisaws or the Cherokees: They might be able to tame and civilize him.[52]

The character of Thomas Chatterton (1752–1770), the other most influential forger of the period, indeed of English literature and perhaps of the entire modern age, was much more in harmony with his work. His contemporaries, as well as the following generation, were faced with the dilemma of having either to accept that this 16-year-old-boy had indeed stumbled on important documents of fifteen-century poetry, or to assume that he had created them himself, in which case he had to be the greatest genius in English literature since Shakespeare.

One of the main motives of Chatterton derived from his local patriotism: He wanted to boost the historical importance of his home town, Bristol, to compare with London. In his fantasy, he built up a complete historical world by presenting the fictitious chronicle of his town from pre-Roman times right up to the fifteenth century, with Thomas Rowley and his patron, Sir William Canynge, at the center. He also devised a special, archaic language for this world; fabricated its documents—letters, genealogies, and maps as well as historical, topographical, architectural, heraldic, numismatic, art-historical, and antiquarian studies and catalogs; and created its visual representation by producing roughly 300 "contemporary" drawings depicting heraldic and historical objects, including Bristol's imaginary castle. On top of all that, probably within the brief year, from summer 1768 to spring 1769, at the age of 16 or 17 he created Rowley's complete poetic oeuvre. It included a ballad consisting of 92 four-line stanzas entitled *Bristowe Tragedie or the Dethe of Syr Charles Baldwin,* as well as epic fragments, heroic odes, five theatrical plays (with a tragedy influenced by *Othello* and entitled *Aella* among them), minstrel songs, and other poetic works.[53] And he did all this with a display of such poetic power, and in such an original way, that it enraptured the greatest figures in English literature. Keats dedicated his *Endymion* to Chatterton's memory and also wrote a sonnet to him in 1815, declaring that Chatterton wrote in the purest English. The young poet exerted a remarkable influence on Blake and Wordsworth, Dante Gabriel Rossetti, Coleridge, and Walter Scott. His figure inspired Alfred de Vigny to write a play about him. (It was first performed in 1835, and then in 1876 Leoncavallo used it as the libretto for an opera.)

Admittedly, his figure also contributed to his Romantic influence: The "marvellous Boy" (Wordsworth) who took his own life at the age of eighteen, the "dear child of sorrow—son of misery" (Keats), the child prodigy flaring up and burning out.

In Chatterton's case too the fraudulent intention can be verified. Although hardly any of the pieces of Rowley's legend were published in Chatterton's lifetime, his letters to Horace Walpole substantiate his intention to deceive. At the beginning of their correspondence Chatterton offered Walpole, the person he had singled out to be the patron of his literary career, such an excellent lure (fifteenth-century evidence to verify and complement one of Walpole's art historical theories[54]) that it would have been very peculiar indeed if Walpole, in his initial delight over the confirmation of his theory and the discovery of the *missing link*—that all-important element in the history of forgeries—had not swallowed it.

Nevertheless, as with Macpherson so in this case, the fact that it was a forgery was not sufficient to explain the staggering effect. Incidentally, Macpherson exerted an influence on Chatterton too, whose seven Ossianic prose verses, largely written after the completion of the Rowley theme, served the purpose of carrying the Celtic/Scottish/Irish tradition over to the Saxon territory (as well as to Wales and the Isle of Man)—again, in order to support the central position of the Bristol region.[55]

I do not regard it to be my task to explain this extraordinary impact. I take it as a fact and use it as my point of departure in trying to explain why we should *feel* intuitively that the strikingly similar instances of forgery in fine arts and literature are in fact fundamentally different. Chatterton's example admirably suits this purpose. As we have seen, Macpherson's activities were, at least partly, analogous to that of a libertine restorer. By contrast, Rowley's oeuvre was entirely the result of Chatterton's creative, *ex nihilo* forgery. For the sake of the analogy we might for a moment regard the documents that Chatterton used for the creation of his poet's historical world to be the kind of *secondary documents* that frequently accompany fine art forgeries and that serve to prove the work's authenticity from a historical point of view (the letters and certificates of previous owners, the documents of contracting the artist, evidence of the contemporary reception of the work, etc.).

Naturally, the differences are equally conspicuous: For a start, the forger of a work of fine art would be reluctant to use such a mass of evidence in support of the legend of his work. This also goes to show that the legend of a work of art—the legend itself being a literary genre—is linked to literary mystification much more closely than to fine-art forgery. Secondly, in its *physical reality,* the work that Chatterton produced on artificially matured paper, using stylized, archaic calligraphy, drawings and spelling, itself forms a secondary document, since although one can of course use the autographic copy for the authentication of a literary work, this fact is irrelevant from the point of view of its reception. Unlike in fine art, the autographic copies are independent from the actual work of art. The literary practice, whereby Chatterton's works were admitted to the treasure house of English poetry after stripping them of their archaic stylization, even goes one step further, somewhat relativizing Goodman's rule on the "sameness of spelling," which set the precondition of an allographic literary work's self-identity (as opposed to the physical self-identity of an autograph work of fine art).[56]

Chatterton's example (and in a different respect Macpherson's too) can demonstrate that, along with the work itself, the legend of a work forms a primary component of literary mystification, while an autograph manuscript only forms a secondary accessory. It is precisely the other way around in the forgery of fine art, since in the latter case the autograph artwork obviously forms a primary element, while its legend is only secondary. It follows from the above that all those technical (i.e., physical and chemical) aspects of falsification, which have far-reaching theoretical consequences in the production of the fake fine-art object, have only secondary importance in literature, or frequently none at all. It is not an indispensable precondition in literary mystification to know the work in its "original" physical form, in its material reality; quite often the legend can substitute for this precondition.

By contrast, the creation of legends is a task of typically literary character, where the considerations concerning the *intention* to deceive have very little aesthetic significance. In his book published early in this century on literary forgeries, which incidentally received a great deal of criticism for its inaccuracies but is nevertheless invaluable to us on account of the substance of its arguments, J. A. Farrer points out that the reason why Chatterton singled out Horace Walpole (1717–1797) was that the latter's "Gothic novel," *The Castle of Otranto* (1764), may very well have provided him with a precedent. The foreword to the first edition recounts the legend of the novel, according to which the book was discovered in the library of a Catholic family in North England and printed in Naples in 1529, and had presumably been written sometime between 1025 and 1243. The author, who pretended to be the translator under an assumed name, only revealed his true identity two years later in the foreword to the second edition of the book.[57]

Chatterton's monographer poses the following question: "Would it not be as delicate a task to draw a precise line of demarcation between Chatterton's Rowley and Sterne's Tristram as between Sterne's Tristram and the narrator of *The History of Tom Jones*? We would not willingly limit ourselves to studying either Tristram or the narrating 'Fielding' as exercises in deception. With Chatterton, as with Fielding and Sterne, we must address ourselves to the function of the imagined narrator, to the quality of the imagined world, and to the special language with which he brings that world to life in our minds. Yet must also remember that, presumably unlike Fielding and Sterne, Chatterton was quite unwilling to view his imagined author as a fiction."[58] This latter difference is of a psychological or moral nature, besides being connected to the question of correspondence with the facts, and would be of secondary importance from the aesthetic point of view in the case of a major work of art. We must not forget that Walpole's omitted foreword, along with Chatterton's fiction (not to mention Richardson's *Pamela,* written earlier still) heralded the arrival of a new literary genre (or more precisely, its modern-day revival): A genre that concealed the author by relegating him to the role of "publisher" or "editor," while placing the narration in a historical setting and presenting it as an objet trouvé. This device, which was generally used in Romanticism, determined the structure even of the—from a stylistic viewpoint—Late Romantic philosophical prose of Kierkegaard's *Either–Or.* Moreover, it was admitted to the arsenal of modern prose. If, some 200 years ago, Walpole still felt obliged to make excuses for the deceit, then by doing so he provided evidence for the novelty of his device—which, for today's readers, is an all-too-familiar ploy.

To illuminate the same problem with the help of a different example, let us consider the literary genre of fantastic travel diaries, which draw on imagination to build up or forge an entirely new world, one that is distant in the spatial dimension rather than in the temporal one. But what is the difference between the two from a literary point of view? Swift's meticulous care in emphasizing that Gulliver's travels were based on actual facts is matched by George Psalmanazar's in his famous forgery, *Historical and Geographical Description of Formosa* (1704). And even when Swift's nonfictional documentarism turns out to be a parodic device, phantasmagoria and authentic reality—especially with regard to travel diaries guiding the readers through far-away lands—broadly overlapped and were difficult to separate, except in the realms of midgets, giants, and horses. No one mistook Gulliver's travels for a real-life adventure, while many believed that Robinson Crusoe's story was real. Defoe's *Robin-*

son Crusoe (a fictitious adventure based on a true story) and Chateaubriand's *Voyage en Amerique* (a nonfictional but—from the point of view of correspondence to the truth in the everyday sense of the word—deceitful travel book) both use the literary device of feigned authenticity.[59] Since the difference between the stories of travelers and those of travel liars[60] is not poetical in character, journey descriptions that for some reason lose credibility, from a literary point of view might still become *fantastic*—as happened with a description of Formosa turning into the description of an imaginary Formosa. The aesthetic value is not necessarily affected by false pretenses. Still, we must not forget that in the figure of the narrator, Psalmanazar even forged his own person in the sense that he—a European of mysterious (perhaps French) origin—pretended to be a proselytical Formosan.[61]

And as to the above-mentioned Chatterton monograph and the examples of Sterne and Fielding, they lend to the problem an even more general dimension, drawing attention to the poetic need to establish the point of view as well as the position and personal identity of the narrator. This is inevitably—and, in the modern literary practice, increasingly more deliberately—fictitious, with one of the attractive possibilities of fiction lying precisely in the denial of its fictitiousness, in the emphasis on its nonfictional, real character. This device of modern prose, which was born in the eighteenth century, becomes easily recognizable for every reader in a cultural learning process. For the same reason, the fact that "forgery," "lying," and false pretenses are all part and parcel of a literary work and thus are thrown into sharpest relief at the *beginning* of this process, as indeed it has been shown in Defoe's case or in the earlier mentioned foreword by Walpole. We might even say that it is this closeness, this mystifying character of literature, that precludes the differentiation of literary mystifications on principle.

Being the *travesty of originality,* fine-art forgery offers a clear-cut theoretical basis for such differentiation; therefore the forgery stories in fine art, which assume the characteristic literary form of picaresque stories, simultaneously question the modern value of originality (thus ridiculing the experts), the unmasked nonoriginal, the forger, and the forgery. By contrast, the literary forger, in other words the literary mystifier, is a remarkable character: Unmasking him will only help increase his originality. Chatterton has come to embody the originality concept that is associated with Young's name in English literary mythology. And this is not contradicted by the type of literary forgery that, unlike Chatterton's (who created his forgery *ex nihilo*), hides behind the disguise of existing authors, since in literature this requires more than mere craftsmanship: It is obviously linked to an eminent type of literary talent. But more on that later.

Chatterton's "historical novel" on Rowley has a definite ideological background, and a very interesting one too: On the one hand it can be identified with historicism, and on the other, as Donald S. Taylor has demonstrated, with the discovery of archaic and modern— bourgeois if you like—heroism. (Rowley's chief patron, the merchant grand seigneur, is the embodiment of this latter type.) This in itself is not, however, directly connected with mystification. By contrast, Macpherson's ideology is *identical* with the legend of forgery. The legend of an ancient work of art surviving orally through an outrageously long period, which was precisely what aroused Hume's suspicions from the start, kindled the awareness of many in the Romantic generation, and some of its vulgar remnants are still present in our culture. This had a twofold consequence: A number of nineteenth-century writers attempted to create the missing epic poem in popular poetry, occasionally even undertaking mystifications similar in character to Macpherson's; secondly, an aura of suspicion surrounded some genuinely archaic works. As to the latter, such suspicion was evidenced, for example, in connection with the *Edda Songs* and the *Igor Song*. As to the former, an entire industry emerged at the turn of the eighteenth and beginning of the nineteenth centuries, specializing in the forgery of Scottish ballads. Then there was the Czech Václav Hanka, who published his forged manuscripts of *Dvůr Králové* and *Zelená Hora* in 1817; in 1872 the Hungarian Kálmán Thaly published ten of his stylistic imitations of Kuruts' (Hungarian insurrectionists at the turn of the seventeenth century) poetry, mixed with some genuine material. The Estonian national epos, the *Kalevipoeg*, is actually the work of Friedrich Reinhold Kreutzwald (1803–1882), who reconstructed certain fragments, gave them a metric form, and composed a homogeneous epic story on an academic commission and out of Herderian enthusiasm, without any intention to forge.

The third famous case of late-eighteenth-century English literary forgery can be compared to Macpherson's and Chatterton's deceptions neither on the merits of its success nor on that of its quality; I have only chosen to mention it because the story itself typifies a third version of modern literary forgery. In contrast to Macpherson's national patriotism and Chatterton's local patriotism, the personal motivation of William Henry Ireland (1777–1835) was of a familial nature: The seventeen-year-old boy, actually a great admirer of Chatterton's, wanted to delight his father, who was a collector of antiques and a fan of Shakespeare's, with an unknown Shakespeare manuscript, which was then followed by several other Shakespeare documents and "works." In one particular letter Shakespeare assured one of the ancestors of the Ireland family of his everlasting friendship for rescuing him from the river Thames(!); another letter, in a way testifying to the young forger's ideological motives in addition to his familial impulse, reveals the poet's Anglican confession. With its omissions, the "discovered" manuscript of *Lear*—and in parts of *Hamlet* as well—provides evidence for the criticism of taste of eighteenth-century proprieties. However, the two most ambitious of all his undertakings were *Vortigern* and *Henry II*.[62] In 1795, following the publication of the collection, the academic world almost immediately unmasked the greatly publicized forgery, while the impostor admitted his act in an "authentic account" in 1796. Obviously, the mischief was preserved in cultural memory only on account of Shakespeare's name, as well as for the famous incidents of credulity and the extent of the outrage felt over such blasphemy.[63]

As for us, we have a different reason to bring up the incident. The earlier examples already meant to prove that literary forgery can only be distinguished from literature on the basis of subjective malice and fraudulent intentions; therefore, with regard to the literary product, the two *cannot* in fact be separated. If, in Macpherson's case, the main literary motive was the reconstruction of a *myth* (i), and in Chatterton's case, the construction of a free fantasy world viewed from a historical distance (the other subdivision of this type, illustrated by George Psalmanazar's example, is the construction of a free fantasy world viewed from a *spatial* distance) (ii), then the third type should be the (possibly fraudulent) reworking of the *literary influence,* the variation, the paraphrase, or pastiche of another writer's work, presented as original (iii). The work done on a myth, the free modification and renarration of the mythical treasures of human race (i), the free flight of fantasy in a story or description and its extension in space and time (ii), the ability to evoke and imitate or to experiment with literary material bequested with or without the name of an author, the free selection between literary styles and presentations (iii)—all these form an inherent part of the art of literature, the degree of freedom of which increases in modernity. Probably also related to the increase of this degree of freedom is the fact that, following the decline of the ideological stakes of populism and historicism, and after the epochs of credulity, enthusiastic acceptance, and critical rejection, the last few decades have increasingly come to be characterized by the tendencies of revising and rehabilitating Macpherson and Chatterton.

"In the history of literature, the question of the authenticity of forgeries or pious frauds has played an important role and has given valuable impetus to further investigations. Thus the controversy about Macpherson's *Ossian* stimulated the study of Gaelic folk poetry, the controversy around Chatterton led to an intensified study of English medieval history and literature, and the Ireland forgeries of Shakespeare plays and documents led to debates about Shakespeare and the history of the Elizabethan stage."[64] I have selected these three cases from the viewpoint of the typology of literature rather than from that of the history of literature or the history of criticism. One can justifiably pose the question as to why the basic examples of these three modern types of literary forgery emerged almost simultaneously and almost in the same place.

The cases of Macpherson, Chatterton, and Ireland are far from being unique. The eighteenth-century history of the British Isles is at the same time the great history of literary forgery. In addition to Psalmanazar's story, I should also mention the extraordinary case of William Lauder, who tried to resort to forgery in an attempt to prove that Milton's *Paradise Lost* actually plagiarized Latin authors; then there was the Scottish forger of ballads, John Pinkerton, or the fantast Iolo Morganwg. But these are only the most famous cases, the tip of the iceberg, concealing the masses of forgers beneath. And although the criticism of literary forgery, along with often-exaggerated suspiciousness regarding it, reached its climax in the nineteenth century, the practice of forgery has not abated, and there are several examples to demonstrate a certain tolerance towards it. Traces of it can be found in the literary works on the subject: Oscar Wilde's delicate short story about a Shakespeare forgery, entitled "The Portrait of Mr. W. H.,"[65] or Rudyard Kipling's "Dayspring Mishandled" (1928), which tells the story of a Chaucer forgery.

The sociocultural pattern, manifested in our examples almost in the form of a lineal descent (since Chatterton was encouraged not only by Walpole's precedent, but by Macpherson's case also, while Ireland received inspiration from Chatterton), was obviously connected to the emerging characteristics of British civilization in the eighteenth century, which—with regard to the upper classes—made England the home of eccentrics. Displaying practical sense and fantasticality, extravagance and composure, playfulness and eccentricity; having a mind for curiosities and practical jokes as well as for fair play, for idiosyncrasies and obsessions as well as for adventurism: Here is a short list of those—often caricatured—national characteristics that could all have contributed to the fact that forgers were so easily forgiven; that their deeds, in addition to provoking some self-gratifying outrage, were looked upon with amusement and acknowledgment; that their crime, if it was crime at all, was seen as a gentlemanly crime. Samuel Johnson, who harbored a spite for Macpherson, felt a restrained admiration for Chatterton and agreed to write a foreword to Lauder's book; as to his attitude towards Psalmanazar (admittedly only when the old man had mended his ways), Johnson looked up to him with a religious reverence.

At the same time, however, any attempt to make a rigorous distinction between original and forgery was quite simply lacking in a very broad section of literature. In the eighteenth century, England witnessed its first period of literary mass production, when the proliferation of news magazines, book publishers, book shops, and public libraries demanded a similarly substantial increase in the output of new literature. "There were five thousand people subsisting by writing, printing, publishing, and marketing papers in London of 1722, and those who earned a living in the literary market by the middle of the century would probably have to be reckoned in the tens of thousands. It was no longer necessary to be a 'man of letters' or a university graduate to be a professional writer. Housewives and bookkeepers who wanted to make a few extra pounds now wrote novels, as did country clergymen who had formerly dabbled in botany or archeology. Few of these writers felt any need to defend either their works or their profits, and few apparently were concerned about literary standards."

The Sylph, a short-lived, single-essay periodical published late in the century, devoted an issue to a lively parody of the way in which the popular novels were being slapped together: The trick is to spread the words mechanically across the page, shuffle them about to form sentences, and ". . . according to the arrangement and collection of them [they] become *narrations, speeches, sentiments, descriptions, etc.,* and when *a very great quantity of them* . . . are wedged together after a particular form and manner, they are denominated a NOVEL. . . ." Another magazine writer recommended, in the manner of Swift, that engines be adopted to make the novel-writing process easier, and contributors to several other respected journals of the latter half of the century made frequent quips about the plagiarisms, repetitions, and patchwork that often went into what was released as a novel.[66]

On top of all the plagiaries, clippings, and other piratical acts, this popular section of literary culture—consisting of various documents and pseudodocuments; for example, genuine or forged romantic travel books or novels disguised as travel books as well as genuine novels—also abounded in proper forgeries. Or, to be more precise, in literary manipulations classified as forgeries according to our current notions. Although copyright protection had existed ever since 1709, and "the Act was based on the modern notion of the individualized, inimitable act of literary creation: The birth of the author-owned text,"[67] the *commercialization* of literature only increased the inclination to violate the law, in practice primarily protecting the employer (the publisher), and not the employee (the writer).[68] Also related to this phenomenon was the growing custom of publishing anonymous works. Of the two major sources of forgery I have already mentioned the first: The fraudulent mixing of fiction and nonfiction. The second is a consequence of literary success, in the sense that the audience demands the continuation. The genre of continuation, the *sequel*, provides a large scope for forgery, especially under the circumstances of anonymity. In eighteenth-century England, a large number of sequels was published, including several forged ones. (Admittedly, the most famous forged sequel in world literature had been published a good hundred years earlier, when the author publishing the second part of *Don Quixote* in 1614 under the assumed name of Alonso Fernández de Avellanedas was made the butt of several jokes in the *genuine* second part.)

In the higher strata of literary culture, the sensitivity shown towards forgeries never waned: This is evidenced in William Lauder's false charges (supported by forgeries) against Milton on the one hand, as well as in the scandal concerning the originality of Alexander Pope's Homer translation[69] in the 1720s, and on the other hand in Edward Young's theories on the notion of originality. Nevertheless, the various literary segments were not separated by a fixed demarcation. Great masterpieces were born in the lower segments (for example, Defoe's), while the works produced in the higher segments were also exposed to the market. (Macpherson's books brought him considerable financial profit, and Ireland's forgeries were reprinted even after the unmasking.) The patterns of literary methods could filter *upward*.

In any case, the above brief survey of the literary forgery scene of eighteenth-century England points to a fourth type of forgery in addition to the three listed earlier, one that perhaps might not be of central importance to our case but nevertheless forms the most general type of the forgery industry in literature. As with any other "good," the literary work as a commodity forms the subject of forgery, provided it is marketable, profitable, and forgable. And not only can a literary creation be plagiarized, but its "trademark" can be forged altogether. This trademark can be the name of the author, the hero, the legend of origin, the publisher, or the series of publication. The forgeries of myth, fantasy, and effects can mix with the forgeries of commodities, and might even *become* forged commodities themselves.

Poor Chatterton did not live to see his forgeries become commodities; and as for Macpherson, he certainly did not regard his native land's poetry, genuine and forged alike, as commodities. Wilhelm Hauff (1802–1827), who in his novel *Der Mann im Mond oder der Zug des Herzens ist des Schicksals Stimme* (1826) imitated and parodied the manners of a contemporary producer of bestsellers, H. Clauren, definitely entered into the territory of forgery when he decided to publish his work under the name of H. Clauren. After his unmasking (which incidentally showed H. Clauren up for a fool), Hauff claimed in his sermon "Kontrovers-Predigt über H. Clauren und den Mann im Monde" that by writing the book he only intended to reveal the immoral tendencies in H. Clauren's novels; this was, in all probability, meant to be but a dream of the caliph Stork. In fact, he (or his publisher) must have been lured into using the false name by the record-breaking circulation of H. Clauren's books. Perhaps he even anticipated what in fact turned out to be true: That the scandal would instantly make the Hauff name famous. *Der Mann im Mond* forged author and commodity at the same time.[70]

——————— Literary Forgery and Fictitiousness ———————

Using the example of eighteenth-century England, a country abounding in literary mystifications, forgeries, and borderline cases between the two, I have isolated three poetically relevant types of mystification. The first one was based on the construction of myths, the second on fantasy work, and the third on stylistic imitation. These three types (which at the same time mean the three fundamental outlets both of artistic ability and of communication with the audience) generally appear separately, but allow me to mention a unique twentieth-century example, one in which all three types are present simultaneously and yet the result is an infinitely rich and original poetic oeuvre rather than forgery in any sense. The Hungarian Sándor Weöres's (1913–1989) poetry contributed to the continuation of various myths, but also, and without any exaggeration, to the treasure house of Hungarian folk songs. Not only did he create the entire poetic oeuvre of *Psyche,* the nineteenth-century poetess, but he even arranged the meticulously dated poems, the fictitious letters, and the contemporary recollections in such an order (occasionally even mixing them with a few genuine nineteenth-century works, the poems of László Ungvár-németi Tóth) that the audience fell under the spell of reading an authentic chronicle, and indeed the entire material was presented in the form of a novel. The collection comes complete with a scholarly postscript as well as with a philological appendix and character description of the poetess. I know from personal communication that the poet showed the first pieces of *Psyche* to his wife, not as his own work but as his "finding." In another of his works he even drew the map of the imaginary empire Mahruh (the remote influence of Ossian is evidenced here in a bard's lamenting the "ancient star" during the time of final destruction; his fairy play *Holdbéli csónakos* ["Moon Boatman"] features, along with Hungarians, Greeks, Celts, and Saracens, the Celtic queen Tempora). And finally, to give an idea of what great art he was able to develop from the method of pastiche, I would like to draw attention to Negyedik szimfónia (Fourth Symphony), otherwise known as "Hódolat Arany Jánosnak" ("Homage to János Arany"), in which he was not only able to recall Arany's poetic language, but he even managed to sound the separate registers of this language, thus revealing the various layers of this poetic bequest.

The other major recent example of modern mystification belonging to the Chatterton class, albeit without the intent to deceive, is provided by a contemporary, Sir Andrew Marbot. Weöres's *Psyche* was published in 1972; Wolfgang Hildesheimer's *Marbot* came out in 1981.[71] Like Weöres, Hildesheimer too liberally quotes from the letters and notes of his hero, the melancholic connoisseur and genius; nevertheless, with Hildesheimer, it is the nonfictional genre of the *biography*, rather than of the work, that is developed into a novel. The same way that now, with the existing new advances in technology, it is possible to mix fiction and nonfiction, the real-life figures of documentaries with the fictional characters of cinematographic history (Woody Allen's *Zelig*; Robert Zemeckis's *Forrest Gump*), so do both authors "weave their heroes into the cultural history of early nineteenth century," as revealed in *Marbot*'s inside cover. The number of real-life characters that Psyche becomes associated with includes famous Hungarian men of letters, as well as Beethoven, Goethe, Eichendorff, and Hölderlin, while in his own country, then during his "grand tour," and finally in his self-imposed Italian exile, Marbot makes the acquaintance of Blake, Turner, Byron, Delacroix, Corot, Goethe, Schopenhauer, Leopardi, Rumohr, and August von Platen. The inside cover unmasked Psyche; Hildesheimer's book didn't unmask Marbot, the only reference is the one on the cover given in the earlier quote. The deception is made even more extensive by the fact that the latter author even forged pictures: He borrowed and reproduced in his book portraits by Delacroix and others, claiming that they depicted Marbot and his relatives. To enhance the documentary character, the author smuggled his hero's name into the letters, memoirs, etc., of several well-known figures, besides often publishing the English "original" of Marbot's own works. Only the list of names at the end of the book gives the game away: It contains *no* fictitious characters. At the time of its publication, the more credulous readers were genuinely deceived by the Marbot biography.[72] "For those who followed my work from the start, this theme could not have come as a complete surprise. I have generally been interested in forgers and fallen people. In Marbot's case both types are present: The forger as a grammatical subject—this is, naturally, I, the biographer—and the fallen as a grammatical object: Sir Andrew Marbot, who is occasionally also me."[73]

Mystification and fiction *coincide* in the cases of Chatterton's Rowley, Karl Emerich Krämer's George Forestier,[74] Weöres's Psyche, Hildesheimer's Marbot, and Pessoa's poets. The only difference is perhaps that the path on which they arrived at their fictitious heroes leads through mystification to fiction in the first two cases, and the other way around in the latter cases. The fiction *realizes* the imagination, the myth, the tradition (in the realm of literary creations) and *mystifies* the reality outside the work.[75] Mystification—fraud—creates the appearance of reality, while poetic fiction lends the effect of unreality. Whenever the latter is preserved in the coincidence of the two, the way of achieving it becomes aesthetically irrelevant. This is analogous to the possibility of basing the (unreal) poetic fiction on positively real and psychologically well-defined dreams, visions, and hallucinations; indeed, the possibility cannot be discarded that a work of art is really the accurate recording of these dreams, visions, and hallucinations, at the level of the author's intentions. This is in fact one of the possible interpretations of the visionary artist William Blake's remark on Chatterton's authenticity (captured in the heading of the previous section).

For the modern audience, the poetic authenticity of mystification is based on the disclosed unreality (or development into unreality) of fiction. This is why an *unmasked* mystification does not lose its poetic magic, as the disclosure of the fictitiousness of the author, etc., might even increase the poetic quality of unreality.

The poetic inauthenticity of a fiction is quite simply connected to its defective quality. In Gottfried Keller's masterly short story, "Die mißbrauchten Liebesbriefen," there is obviously no aesthetic difference between the letters of the husband and the wife, although the husband's letters—whose aspirations for literary fame explain his imposition of this lofty-toned love correspondence to his wife—are original (in the personal/historical sense of the world), albeit insincere; by contrast, his wife's letters—who in her desperation copies her husband's letters and sends them to the school teacher next

door, whose replies she then forwards to her husband as her own—
are forgeries. And although Keller wisely refrains from including
specimens of the replies, it is quite possible that these are the more
valuable, considering that the husband was merely completing an
exercise in copying mannered and shallow examples, while the
school teacher, who believed that he was involved in a genuine love
correspondence, on realizing the affectation and stupidity of the
language, accepted it as a sacrifice of love, enriching it with intellect
and feeling. The relationship between fiction and reality is a very
complex one in this facetious triangle, which is in fact formed by
two men writing letters to each other and a woman anxiously copying and dispatching them in both directions. The husband's emotional outpourings are fictitious, insofar as they are merely the
reflections of a literary tradition and fashion as well as the travesties
of a profoundly feigned emotional attitude. He writes his ordinary
letters on a different kind of stationary, so as to make his literary correspondence stand out all the more clearly. For the teacher, it is the
language and style that are fictitious, behind which he hopes to discover, and does in fact awaken, the reality of love. For the woman,
the letters of both the husband and teacher are unreal and fictitious.
It is only her determination to save her marriage by satisfying the
caprices of her husband that has any reality at all; that and the growing confusion she feels towards the teacher on seeing the dangerous
passion which her innocent joke stirs up within him. And finally
there is of course the satirical fiction of Keller, the writer of the short
stories of Seldwyla: The unfolding of an anecdote, in the background
of which the movements and the airs of the self-conceited and pre-
tentious literati are contrasted with the worldview and *poesis* of
level-headed bourgeois uprightness. This nontextual reality, which is
meant to be a concrete criticism as well as a normative lifestyle-offer-
ing for the contemporary audience, itself becomes a meditative fiction and the artistic agent of the short story for later readers, whose
life experiences are different from the writer's.

The manifold relationship to reality of the *same* fictitious text
(i.e., the love correspondence of Keller's characters) can serve to illustrate the point that the contrast between fiction and reality cannot be
captured in a dogmatic manner. In discussing literary mystification I
have all along been confronted with the following dilemma: The fact
that a story is not true (because it never happened, or it happened
with somebody else, or it was written by a person different from the
one who claims to have written it or who is said to have written it)
can be equally either a device of literary fiction or an act of fraud, or
in fact both of these simultaneously.

Forgery is a borderline case of fiction. This is an area where we do not regard, nor does anyone force us to regard, the fiction to be a world that is not true in comparison to the everyday world; we look at it as *another* world, the references of which apply only to itself, not to this world. Nevertheless its truth and its reality can be reconstructed within its own realm. In literature, forgery is a fiction that wants to achieve success in the real world. For this reason, in some sense it can be used to test that particular theory of fiction, which wants to replace the *ontological* antagonism of fiction and reality with the *functional* difference between them.

Wolfgang Iser regards the relationship of fiction and reality to be one of a communicational, rather than an ontological, character; furthermore, he views fiction as a communicative structure, and the creation of fictitious texts as an intentional act. In this way he has managed to resolve the old antagonism between the two, along with relieving literary creations of the burden of *either* having to represent reality—in fact, an ordered model of reality—or having to deviate from it, as described in the theory of representation and in deviation stylistics.[76] Instead of representing reality, or deliberately deviating from it, the text enters into an interaction with it. In his later writing he changed the duality of fiction and reality into a trio by way of introducing the imaginary, with fiction presented as some kind of mediator between the other two. It is in fiction that the imaginary is realized and reality is irrealized. The product of free fantasy assumes a form and becomes a definite and solid conception, while even the most ordinary piece of reality, instead of being manifested in its familiar context, appears to be floating in thin air so to speak.

Iser's idea reflects on the notion of the literary (and aesthetic) *modern*. I would like to draw attention to a particular aspect of it, one that has perhaps received less attention so far, namely, that Iser's idea separates the aesthetic attitude both from the *ordinary*, natural attitude and from the imaginary attitude that refers to "pure" irreality, at least one of the possible interpretations of which regards irreality as a higher, or a *religious*, reality. Rather surprisingly, the structure of this separation bears resemblance to the basic idea of Lukács's late aesthetics, while the idea that separation is at the same time mediation carries within it the communicative potential.

This separation outlines the boundaries of the sphere of modern aesthetics, while the mediation allocates the reality of the creation of fictitious texts in the space of "border crossings" in both directions (i.e., from the direction of both everyday reality and imaginary nonreality). This largely holds true for modernity, despite being a reduction, which, in order to abolish the logocentric dichotomy of reality and fiction, sacrifices the traditional bonus of it: a still-functioning aesthetic potential that might be called the border-crossing of fiction into "reality"—and pure imagination.

As far as the latter is concerned, suffice it to quote one of Hans Robert Jauß's remarks: "If the awareness of fiction, in other words the awareness of the 'As-if,' always accompanies our experiences associated with aesthetic functions, the imaginary—in the sense of an irreality more powerful and more authentic than reality—can obviously still be experienced as something which eliminates this 'As-if.'"[77]

Iser describes the relationship between the aesthetic 'As-if' and the *everyday* attitude as follows:

> A fictitious text contains a large number of identifiable reality-fragments, gained either from the sociocultural textual world or from earlier literary texts. To this extent, a wholly recognizable world returns to the fictitious text, which is nevertheless invented. As a result, we place this world between brackets so as to indicate: The world represented here is not given, but it should be seen as if it was given. This has the very important consequence that, with the recognition of invented-ness, everything, the entire world constructed in the literary text, becomes *As-if (Als-Ob)*. The bracketing thus achieved makes it obvious that all natural attitudes towards this representational world should be suspended. . . . Here we can evidence the first major difference from the fiction which disguises its character, since the natural attitudes continue to function there. The very function of unmasking might be that the natural attitudes remain unaffected and the fiction is comprehended as reality, which is capable of explaining realities.[78]

Forgery, for example, conceals its fictitious character and wants to sustain those natural attitudes by which its references are embedded in everyday life. Instead of a fictitious Formosa, it insists on representing the real thing; instead of a Shakespearian pastiche, it comes up with a "genuine" Shakespearian drama; rather than producing a mythicizing/historicizing pseudo-epos, in which to exhibit the free play of fantasy, it sticks to its colors, maintaining that what we have in front of us is actually the translation of a genuinely ancient epos. But when a literary forgery is organized into a work of art, then—whether or not we accept the concealed fiction—we come face to face with the fiction of the poetic creation, which certainly cannot be reduced to the question of whether it was written by Rowley or Chatterton and that for this reason does have fictitious aspects, masked and unmasked, as well as self-unmasking. Furthermore, the Rowley of natural attitudes cannot be separated from the "Rowley" of fiction with anything resembling the precision of laboratory methods.

A known *topos* restores poetry to its natural attitude, making it plain that poetic expression itself (or poetic expression in everyday life) is in fact lying and deceit. If then anyone still wants to defend the dignity of art—either by attributing reality to artistic deception and wisdom to the act of falling for it (as did Gorgias at the beginning of the tradition), or by esteeming artistic semblance, illusion, and delusion more highly than truth, reality, or life (as did Nietzsche at the end of the tradition)—then in the process of doing so they achieve the distinction between the everyday (or the natural) and the artistic, which Iser referred to as bracketing the natural attitude (and which is incidentally not very different from the homogeneous medium of aesthetics suspending all directly practical goals, as formulated in Lukács's late aesthetic theory).

Let me remind the reader here of the analysis I put forward in chapter 3 (under the section heading, "The Tradition of Art"), in which I proposed that it is reality (the reality of life-world) that a work of art distinguishes itself from, at the same time as it defines reality by virtue of this distinction. Since fiction is in a constant dialogue with the life-world, its transformation into a world has its limits: The reality outside the artwork cannot be closed off; we can disappear neither in the maze of the Chinese painter nor in the forest of the Ardennes. It is not by coincidence that the generalization of the above-mentioned topos—poetry as lying—had its classic origin in the theatrical illusion of drama.[79] This is the one genre in which it is the easiest to conclude that anyone who cannot distinguish between a theatrical act and reality, whether because he thinks that the former forms part of his own real world or because he is so much engrossed in the latter, is incapable of perceiving art. A silent cognizance, the evidence of discernment must be present. Nevertheless, it would be unreasonably dogmatic to demand this cognizance continuously from the audience. In fact, what we are talking about is more like a tendency, in which the moments of complete discernment and complete lack of discernment alternate, with the extreme cases of identification with everyday life and engrossment in the world of the play also included in the latter.

It should be apparent that the above-mentioned problem of theatrical illusion can be translated into the seemingly simpler but in fact more complex problematics of the relationship between invented and true stories. The first is unreal and fictional, the second is real and nonfictional (within certain limits); the first unmasks its fictionality, the second conceals its fictionality (outside the above-mentioned limits). With regard to the first one, even accepting that "the already bracketed world is still not a subject for its own sake, but the subject of some kind of an arrangement or concept,"[80] the question still remains as to whether it is not part of the freedom of conception, of artistic perception, that as in one direction we enjoy (among others) the infiniteness and irreality of fantasy, so in the other direction we attempt to relapse momentarily into the natural attitude, viewing fiction as a true story and real-life subject. If it is true that, in fiction, fantasy is realized and reality is unrealized, in a way suspending the irreality of the one and the reality of the other, then should not the reverse process also have a place in the dialectics of reception? Could not the artworks temporarily suspend *fiction*, their "As-if" character itself? Just as a true story can gradually become unreal, whether because it assumes the form of an anecdote or because its documentary value erodes with the passing of time, so can reality itself become fabulous.

Historiography, this classic opposite of poetry (the contrast between *res fictae* and *res factae* has one of the greatest traditions in formulating the relationship between invented and true stories), can provide numerous examples to this effect. "We can read *Quentin Durward* (Walter Scott's novel) as a piece of medieval history (if we extract the fiction from it, we shall be left with a picture of the past, featuring several authentic details), Ranke's *French History*, on the other hand, can readily be regarded as a 'work of art in historiography,' and then, similarly to Scott's novels, it can be enjoyed aesthetically."[81]

The idea that the borderline between the masking and unmasking of fiction should be seen as the watershed between artistic and nonartistic fiction does not seem convincing to me. In fact, what we are witnessing here is the constant interplay of masking and unmasking, in which our *modern* perception gives priority to the latter. This is related to the next problem: The history of the origin of the suppression of natural attitudes on the one hand, and of the transcendent fantasy-world on the other: In other words, the history of the origin of the *awareness of fictionality*.

The intermediate position of fiction between the irreality of religiously inspired fantasy—in other words, higher reality—and the reality of everyday life is manifested, as it is elsewhere, in the fact that it appeared on the scene precisely at the time when the divinely inspired character of poetry was called into question; but when it emerged, it did so in the form of an accusation typically formulated by natural attitude: That it is all lies. "Apparently, as long as the poet's words were perceived as divine inspiration, the fictitious character of poetic creation was not acknowledged by the men of antiquity. Initially, the idea of fiction emerged as a tool of criticism. So, when Xenophanes points out that the poets' visions about the gods derive from their assigning to the gods a voice and a figure similar to that of the mortals, as well as from their believing that, like ordinary people, the gods, too, are born (Fragment no. 14), the fiction here is explained as psychological projection, and wherever this explanation is accepted, the poetic word loses its claim for truth and inspirational origin. It was roughly at the same time that the second Isaiah scorned the cultic gods of the various peoples in a similar fashion for being the products of human hand (Isaiah 40:19f.; 41:6f.; and especially 44:9–20). . . ."[82]

At the beginning of European tradition and at the beginning of modernity some of the poetic creations—themselves qualifying as fiction—criticized other poetic creation(s) for being fictional. Stesikhoros's palinode, with its lines being quoted in the following in Plato's *Phaedrus*, "recants" Homer's lies. In addressing Helen, Stesikhoros asserts that "this story is not true, you did not board the well-benched ships, you did not reach the Citadel of Troy."[83] He contests Homer's fiction with another variant of the myth. With regard to the theme of *Don Quixote's* fiction, it is based on the conflict of fiction and reality: The hero confuses his books with reality, interpreting reality according to the patterns of chivalrous novels:

> . . . never before did worldly reality, with all its contingencies and multiplicity of meanings, come to light so vividly, and become relatable so readily as it did here, against the horizon of fiction. But nor did the ideal nature of poetic fiction, as the product of human creativity, ever become so readily recognizable as it did here, against the horizon of the nonideal, everyday world.[84]

Although the creation of fiction has, *from the very beginning*, formed an organic part of poetic creation, fictionality's coming to awareness, its self-reflection and retrospective reflection, has been different in the various genres, and their geneses (in plural) have continuously been present throughout the entire history of literature. While quite obviously being present already in Homer's case, the awareness of fiction was still the subject of the eighteenth- and nineteenth-centuries' debate on the genre of novel, arguing the pros and cons of prosaism versus poeticism, which I have already mentioned at the beginning of this chapter: What was at stake here was whether to integrate novels into high art as poetic fiction, or to regard them as being the imprint of the prose of everyday life and, as such, part of mass culture and low art.

The often-retrospective poetical quality of literary mystifications, and the features of mystification that sometimes tend to become dominant in poetic works, are all connected to this rather complex state of affairs. It is the constant contact of fictitious as forged and fictitious as poetic that establishes the poetry of literary forgeries.

Notes

1. Leonardo da Vinci, *Treatise on Painting*, trans. A. P. McMahon (Princeton, NJ: Princeton University Press, 1956). In fact, Leonardo wanted more than equality; he wanted painting to be recognized as the first among the arts, and in order to achieve this he gave a stinging/parodic twist to Simonides's saying: Painting is mute poetry, poetry is blind painting. It is well known that, of all the forms of fine art, he only referred to painting. Sculpture (following antique tradition) was placed at the bottom—since it was closer to craftsmanship, to the mechanical arts; it was not science but a common trade, and from the greater physical exertion associated with it Leonardo inferred a lesser intellectual effort.

2. Paul O. Kristeller, "The Modern System of the Arts: A Study in the History of Aesthetics," *Journal of the History of Ideas* XII (1951): 496–527; XIII (1952): 17–47.

3. The best introduction of this theme is still found in Rensselaer W. Lee, "*Ut pictura poesis*: The Humanistic Theory of Painting," *Art Bulletin* 22 (1940): 197–269.

4. Moses Mendelssohn, "G. F. Meyer: Auszug aus den Anfangsgründen aller schönen Künste und Wissenschaften. Recension," in *Gesammelte Schriften II* (Leipzig: Brockhaus, 1844), 314. Quoted by Kristeller, op. cit., part II, 37.

5. Immanuel Kant, *Kritik der Urteilskraft. Werkausgabe* Bd X (Frankfurt: Suhrkamp, 1989), 51§.

6. Oskar Walzel, *Wechselseitige Erhellung der Künste. Ein Beitrag zur Würdigung kunstgeschichtlicher Begriffe* (Berlin: Kant-Gesellschaft, 1917), 56. "Could these categories (Wöfflin's basic art historical concepts) be applied to poetry?" he asks.

7. *Briefwechsel zwischen Goethe und Schiller in den Jahren 1794 bis 1805* (Stuttgart: Union Deutsche Verlaggesellschaft, n.d.), 321f.

8. Leonardo, op. cit., 28. "Fictitious speech, most notably of literary prose, resembles in its verbal structure the everyday, utilitarian use of speech so closely that they are difficult to tell apart. This is why it was classified as a parasite by Austin and Searle," Wolfgang Iser, *Der Akt des Lesens. Theorie ästhetischer Wirkung* (Munich: Fink, 1976), 102.

9. Cf. Friedrich Wilhelm Joseph von Schelling, "System des transzendentalen Idealismus," in *Ausgewählte Schriften*, vol. I (Frankfurt: Suhrkamp, 1985), 690; Friedrich Schlegel, "Über das Studium der griechischen Poesie," in *Kritische Schriften und Fragmente (1794–1797)*, Bd. 1, ed. Ernst Behler and Hans Eichner. Studienausgabe (Paderborn: Ferdinand Schöningh, 1988), 62–137. Also see my study entitled "Mass Culture" in *Reconstructing Aesthetics*, ed. Agnes Heller and Ferenc Fehér (Oxford, UK: Basil Blackwell, 1986), 77–103.

10. Schlegel, op. cit.

11. Cf. Frigyes Pesty, "Az iteböi prépostság" ("The Provostship of Itebö"), *Századok* (Budapest, 1875): 679.

12. Cf. Erik Fügedi, "Ein berufsmäßiger Fälscher, Der Fall Johann von Madácsháza, 1391," in *Fälschungen im Mittelalter, internat. Kongreß d. Monumenta*

Germaniae Historica, München, 16–19. September 1986. Part IV. Diplomatische Fälschungen (II) (Hannover: Hahn, 1988), 639ff.

13. "Thanne shewe I forth my longe cristal stones / Y crammed ful of cloutes and of bones / Relikes been they as wenen they echon less . . ."—the Pardoner says in Chaucer's *The Canterbury Tales. The Pardoner's Prologue. The Text of the Canterbury Tales,* vol. IV, ed. John A. Manly and Edith Rickert. (Chicago: University of Chicago, 1940), 85. In Boccaccio's *Decameron,* the tenth story of the sixth day goes as follows: "Brother Cipolla promises to show some peasants the feathers of Archangel Gabriel's wing; but since he only finds pieces of charcoal in their place, he tells them that these are the remains of the charcoal which was used for the burning of St. Lawrence."

14. ". . . there were important differences between the nature and types of forgery and plagiarism in the Middle Ages and today. Perhaps the most characteristic form of modern forgery, that of works of art, was unknown at that time. . . . The closest medieval parallel to modern forgery of art was the flourishing manufacture and trade in false relics, which were esteemed then much as works of art are now." Giles Constable, "Forgery and Plagiarism in the Middle Age," *Archiv für Diplomatik, Schriftgeschichte, Siegel- und Wappenkunde* 29 (1983): 6f.

15. Cf. Hans Belting, *Bild und Kult. Eine Geschichte des Bildes vor dem Zeitalter der Kunst* (Munich: Beck, 1990), 336ff.

16. Ibid., 342.

17. Cf. chapter 1, note 54.

18. Cf. Klaus Schreiner, "'Discrimini veri ac falsi.' Ansätze und Formen der Kritik in der Heiligen- und Reliquienverehrung des Mittelalters," *Archiv für Kulturgeschichte* XLVIII (1966): 1.

19. Anthony Grafton, *Forgers and Critics: Creativity and Duplicity in Western Scholarship* (Princeton, NJ: Princeton University Press, 1990), 24.

20. N. Huyghebaert's hypothesis is referred to by Grafton, op. cit., 134, and also by Constable, op. cit., 7f.

21. Ronald Syme, *Emperors and Biography: Studies in the Historia Augusta* (Oxford, UK: Clarendon Press, 1971), 263. Professor Constable is of a similar opinion: "Whether such works [apocryphal writings published either anonymously or under a false name, and imitating other works] are called frauds or fictions depends to some extent on the views and causes they promoted, some of which were less innocent and disinterested than others." Constable, op. cit., 20.

22. Syme, op. cit., 264.

23. Wolfgang Speyer, *Die literarische Fälschung im heidnischen und christlichen Altertum* (Munich: Beck, 1971), 22.

24. Cf. Hans Martin Schaller, "Scherz und Ernst in erfundenen Briefen des Mittelalters," in *Fälschungen im Mittelalter . . .,* Part V, op. cit., 79ff.

25. Pierre Abelard, *Historia calamitatum* (Toronto, ON: Pontifical Institute of Medieval Studies, 1954).

26. All the views concerning the letters put forward before the 1970s are described in detail in Peter von Moos's book, *Mittelalterforschung und Ideologiekritik. Der Gelehrtenstreit um Héloise* (Munich: Fink, 1974). It reveals that

they essentially boil down to five hypotheses. Every single logical possibility has been represented: The letters are either the documents of an actual correspondence, or were written by Abélard in the form of an epistolary dialogue, or they are the works of Héloise, written perhaps after Abelard's death, or the grieving couple came together and created their correspondence, or they were written by a third, or possibly more, person(s). These are the main hypotheses, complemented by further sub- or supplementary hypotheses (later redactions, interpolations, etc.) See page 121. Cf. Peter von Moos, "Heloise und Abaelard," in *Gefälscht! Betrug in Literatur, Kunst, Musik, Wissenschaft und Politik*, ed. Karl Corino (Nördlingen: Greno, 1988), 150ff.

27. Cf. John F. Benton, "The Correspondence of Abelard and Heloise" and Hubert Silvestre, "Die Liebesgeschichte zwischen Abaelard und Heloise: der Anteil des Romans," in *Fälschungen im Mittelalter . . .*, Part V, op. cit., 95ff. and 121ff. In Silvestre's view, the forgery is a propagandistic writing, which proposes a compromise in the question of celibacy forced on secular priests: It wished to replace the institution of celibacy with that of concubinage; in other words, priests should not marry but should be able to keep lovers. The fictional Héloise's stern opposition to marriage meant to get this message through, according to this view. See pages 155ff.

28. Wolfgang Speyer, "Religiöse Pseudepigraphie und literarische Fälschung," in *Pseudepigraphie in der heidnischen und jüdisch-christlichen Antike*, ed. Norbert Brox (Darmstadt: Wissenschaftliche Buchgesellschaft, 1977), 244.

29. The way Giles Constable does it in his study entitled "Forged Letters in the Middle Ages," op. cit., 25. The British cult of the "first modern woman," Héloise, was founded by Pope's "heroic letter," *Eloisa to Abelard* (1717). Her European popularity in the eighteenth century is evidenced in Rousseau's epistolary novel, *Julie, ou la Nouvelle Héloise* (1761).

30. Speyer, "Religiöse Pseudepigraphie und literarische Fälschung," op. cit., 217.

31. Cf. Paul Lehmann, *Pseudo-antike Literatur des Mittelalters* (Darmstadt: Wissenschaftliche Buchgesellschaft, 1964 [1927]).

32. Peter von Moos, "*Fictio auctoris*. Eine theoriegeschichtliche Miniatur am Rande der Institutio Traiani," in *Fälschungen im Mittelalter: internat. Kongreß d. Monumenta Germaniae Historica, Munich, 16–19. September 1986. Part I. Kongreßdaten und Festvorträge; Literatur und Fälschung* (Hannover: Hahn, 1988), 770. For the current evaluation of the pseudo-Plutarch work preserved in *Policraticus* by John of Salisbury alias Johannes Saresberiensis (1159) also see Max Kerner, "Die Institutio Traiani—spätantike Lehrschrift oder hochmittelalterliche Fiktion?," in *Fälschungen im Mittelalter . . . (I)*, op. cit., 715ff. The idea cited about the lies of poets (often complemented by the comment that this is precisely how they reveal the truth) itself forms a topos of antique origin. Preceded only by the respective observations of Xenophanes, Solon and Pindar, the criticism of the epic poets' deceptions makes one of its earliest appearances in Gorgias's saying: "Tragedy, by means of legends and emotions, creates a deception in which the deceiver is more honest than the non-deceiver, and the deceived is wiser than the non-deceived." Plutarch, *De glor.*

Ath. 5, 348 c: frg. B 23 Diels, in Wladislav Tatarkiewicz, *History of Aesthetics I. Ancient Aesthetics* (The Hague: PWN-Polish Scientific Publishers, 1970), 107.

33. Cf. Carl Werner Müller, "Die neuplatonische Aristoteleskommenta-toren über die Ursache der Pseudepigraphie," in *Pseudepigraphie in der heidnischen und jüdisch–christlichen Antike,* op. cit., 264–71.

34. Cf. Speyer, *Die literarische Fälschung im heidnischen und christlichen Altertum,* op. cit., 131ff.

35. Cf. Marc Bloch, *Feudal Society,* vol. I (Chicago: University of Chicago Press/ Phoenix Books, 1964), 92f.

36. Cf. Horst Fuhrmann, "Die Fälschungen im Mittelalter. Überlegungen zum mittelalterlichen Wahrheitsbegriff," *Historische Zeitschrift* 197 (1963). Also see Constable, "Forgery and Plagiarism in the Middle Age," op. cit., 20f.

37. Ibid., 540. Denis the Pseudo-Areopagite is the name given to the unknown author of the teological and philosophical works that emerged around the sixth century and were published under the assumed name of St. Paul's Athenian converter. *Decretales Pseudo-Isidorianae* is a collection of writings attributed to St. Isidore of Seville (c.556–636) but in fact compiled of forged papal letters and other documents originating from around 850; it exerted an apparent influence on canonic law from the eleventh to the twentieth centuries. Cf. Horst Fuhrmann, *Einfluß und Verbreitung der pseudoisidorischen Fälschungen, I–III* (Stuttgart: Anton Hiersemann, 1972). A documented version of the quoted study by Fuhrmann (*Über Fälschungen im Mittelalter*) is published in this book: Vol. I, 64ff.

38. Horst Fuhrmann, "Von der Wahrheit der Fälscher," in *Fälschungen im Mittelalter . . . (I),* op. cit., 94. In opposition to the views held by Fuhrmann (and Constable [see note 14]), which emphasize the difference between premodern and modern forgeries as well as the medieval tolerance shown towards forgeries, Elisabeth A. R. Brown is of the opinion that forgeries were condemned in the medieval era just as firmly as they were in later times, only the necessary critical distance had not yet been formed towards the demand for documentary evidence rising steadily later—and especially so in the twelfth and thirteenth centuries. Cf. *"Falsitas pia sive reprehensibilis.* Medieval Forgers and Their Intentions," in *Fälschungen im Mittelalter . . . (I),* op. cit., 101ff.

39. Cf. for example, János György Szilágyi, "Plautus," in Szilágyi, *Paradigmák* (Budapest: Magvető, 1982), 60f.

40. Initially, Denis the Pseudo-Areopagite's work was regarded to be a monophysitic forgery, the authenticity of which was called into question on the basis of the quite-justified argument that his name had not been mentioned as an author in the works of the earlier fathers. However, his apostolic authority was accepted from the seventh century onward. Beginning with the ninth century, the Athenian convert and philosopher came to be identified—on the basis of another forged legend—with a third Denis, the Apostle of the Gauls and the patron saint of the French kings. According to this, after he had followed Paul to Rome, Denis the Areopagite was sent on a mission to Gallia by Pope Clement, where he became the first bishop of Paris and later suffered martyrdom. Cf. David Luscombe, "Denis the Pseudo-Areopagite in the Middle Ages," in *Fälschungen im Mittelalter . . . (I),* op. cit., 133ff.

Regarding the identity of the great philosopher, Ronald F. Hathaway lists the 22 main hypotheses in his work, *Hierarchy and the Definition of Order in the Letters of Pseudo-Dionysius* (The Hague: Martinus Nijhoff, 1969), 33ff. In his study entitled "Az areopagoszi beszéd" ("The Areopagitic Sermon"), Gyula Rugási writes the following: "The Apostle Paul . . . left the main square of Athens not entirely without accomplishing anything. Some people, including the city councilor who was referred to in the text as Denis the Areopagite, had been converted. It cannot have been a coincidence that this name emerged centuries later not among the representatives of the Stoic or Epicurean schools but among those of Neo-Platonism, the movement so crucially important to the foundation of Christian philosophy and theology. The greatest representative of the so-called Christian Neo-Platonism—his true identity is unknown to us—tried to bridge the chasm that was (always) yawning between the word of the annunciation and the logos of Greek philosophy. The anonymous fifth-century philosopher, to whom we are indebted for the topography of heavenly and worldly hierarchy, was not and could not have been present, yet he should be regarded as the principal witness of the events taking place at the Areopagite!" in *Majdnem nem lehet másként. Vajda Mihály 60. születésnapjára,* ed. Ferenc Fehér, András Kardos, and Sándor Radnóti (Budapest: Cserépfalvi, 1995), 342.

41. Cf. Paul Gerhard Schmidt, "Kritische Philologie und pseudoantike Literatur," in *Die Antike-Rezeption in den Wissenschaften während der Renaissance,* ed. August Buck and Klaus Heitmann (Weinheim: Acta Humaniora, 1983), 121.

42. David Hume's letter dated from August 16, 1760, in *Letters,* vol. I, ed. J. Y. T. Greig (Oxford, UK: Clarendon Press, 1969 [1932]), 329.

43. David Hume's letter to Hugh Blair, dated September 19, 1763, ibid., 399.

44. Ibid., 400.

45. Cf. David Hume, "Essay on the Genuineness of the Poems," in J. H. Burton, *The Life and Correspondence of David Hume.* 2 vols. (Edinburgh: N. Tait, 1846), vol. I, 471–80. This early edition also contains Blair's replies. Also cf. Fiona J. Stafford, *The Sublime Savage. A Study of James Macpherson and the Poems of Ossian* (Edinburgh: Edinburgh University Press, 1988), 170 and 179, note 22, as well as the relevant section of Ernest Campbell Mossner's monograph on Hume, *The Life of David Hume* (Oxford, UK: Clarendon Press, 1980), 414–20.

46. David Hume's letter to Edward Gibbon, dated March 18, 1776, op, cit., vol. II, 309. Cf. Burton, op. cit., vol. I, 472.

47. Samuel Johnson, *A Journey to the Western Islands of Scotland* [1775] (New Haven, CT: Yale University Press, 1971), 119.

48. Cf. Sándor Maller, *Ossian Magyarországon 1788–1849* ("Ossian in Hungary") (Debrecen: N.p., 1940).

49. Cf. Howard Gaskill, "Hölderlin und Ossian," in *Hölderlin-Jahrbuch* (1990–1991): 112.

50. Quoted by Stufford, op. cit., 125.

51. The writer of an Oxford dissertation has good reasons to discuss Thomas Percy's (1729–1811) collection of Old English poetry (1756) in the

context of forgeries. Gwyneth Lewis, *Eighteenth-Century Literary Forgeries with Special Reference to the Work of Iolo Morganwg.* Unpublished Ph.D. dissertation, Oxford, 1991. Cf. also Ian Haywood, *Faking It: Art and the Politics of Forgery* (New York: St. Martin's Press, 1987), 46f.

52. David Hume's letter to Hugh Blair, dated October 6, 1763, op. cit., vol. I, 216.

53. Chatterton's lifework has a modern critical edition, with its editor even publishing a monograph on him. Cf. *The Complete Work of Thomas Chatterton I–II*, ed. Donald S. Taylor (Oxford, UK: Clarendon Press, 1971); also by Taylor: *Thomas Chatterton's Art: Experiments in Imagined History* (Princeton, NJ: Princeton University Press, 1978).

54. Rowley's documents seemed to corroborate Walpole's theory (expounded in his book, *Anecdotes of Painting in England*, published in 1765, and then again in 1767) about the English origin of the oil technique in painting (which would have implied in turn that Jan van Eyck had also learned it in Britain). Cf. Chatterton's letter to Walpole, dated March 25, 1769, with the enclosed document, "The Ryse of Peyncteynge, yn Englande, wroten bie T. Rowleie," along with Walpole's reply to Chatterton (dated March 28, 1769), fulfilling the expectations of the latter, in *The Complete Work of Thomas Chatterton I*, op. cit., 258ff. The rapid result was quickly followed by disappointment: Walpole's unmailed letter of uncertain date, which could not, however, have been written more than a few months later, shows that he was already perfectly cognizant of the trap and the mischief. See page 376f.

55. Cf. D. S. Taylor's notes to the Saxon poem "Ethelgar," in *The Complete Work of Thomas Chatterton II*, op. cit., 949f.

56. For example, in *The Oxford Book of English Verse* (the 1924 edition of which I hold in my hand), the beautiful refrain of one of the songs of *Aella* goes as follows: "My love is dead, / Gone to his death-bed / All under the willow-tree." The same according to Chatterton's spelling went as follows: "Mie love ys dedde, / Gon to hys deathe-[in two passages: death] bedde, / Al under the wyllowe tree" (page 210f.). The correction of a deliberate archaization forms but a special case of this practice. Outside of critical editions, taking into account considerations of linguistic development is quite a regular phenomenon. The sameness of spelling has its pragmatic limits.

57. Cf. J. A. Farrer, *Literarische Fälschungen* (Leipzig: Theod. Thomas, 1907), 109f. In his accusatory letter to Walpole, Chatterton explicitly refers to this connection: "thou mayst call me Cheat- / Say, didst thou ne'er indulge in such Deceit? / Who wrote *Otranto*?" in *The Complete Work of Thomas Chatterton I*, op. cit., 341. Cf. also Haywood, op. cit., 58f.; also Helmut Winter, "Thomas Chatterton—Fälscher oder Originalgenie?" in *Gefälscht!*, op. cit., 196ff.

58. Taylor, *Thomas Chatterton's Art*, op. cit., 48f.

59. Cf. Urs Bitterli, *Die "Wilden" und die Zivilisierten." Grundzüge einer Geistes- und Kulturgeschichte der europäisch-überseeischen Begegnung* (Munich: Beck, 1976). Although Chateaubriand did travel in America, he never set foot on those treacherous and partly unexplored frontiers he described in his book.

60. On the distinction, see Percy G. Adams, *Travellers and Travel Liars 1660–1800* (Berkeley: University of California Press, 1962). The origin of the

forged itineraries goes back deep into medieval times. Sir John Mandeville's compilation from 1356–1357 became the travel book of the pilgrims of the Holy Land, and also a bestseller in several countries of Europe.

61. For its history see, for example, Farrer, op. cit., 60ff.; *Fake? The Art of Deception*, ed. Mark Jones (Berkeley: University of California Press, 1990), 90f.; and Haywood, op. cit., 22ff.

62. W. H. Ireland, Vortigern, an Historical Tragedy in Five Acts *Represented at the Theatre Royal, Drury Lane and* Henry The Second, an Historical Drama *Supposed to be Written by the Author of* Vortigern *together with an Authentic Account of the Shaksperian Manuscripts, &c.* (New York: Augustus M. Kelley Publishers, 1971 [1799, 1796]). The Ireland story can be found, for example, in Lewis, op. cit., and Haywood, op. cit., 65ff.

63. James Boswell went down on his knees to kiss the manuscript. Having received confirmation of the fraud, a man called James Boaden, who had earlier stood up for the authenticity of the documents, announced that it was "precisely the same thing as taking the holy chalice from the altar, and . . . therein!!!!" Quoted from Ireland's detailed confession, published in 1805, by Lewis, op. cit.

64. René Wellek-Austin Warren, *Theory of Literature* (London: Penguin, 1963), 67.

65. ". . . we had a long discussion about Macpherson, Ireland, and Chatterton and that with regard to the last I insisted that his so-called forgeries were merely the result of an artistic desire for perfect representation; that we had no right to quarrel with an artist for the conditions under which he chose to present his work; and that all Art being to a certain degree a mode of acting, an attempt to realize one's own personality on some imaginative plane out of reach of the trammelling accidents and limitations of real life, to censure an artist for a forgery was to confuse an ethical with an aesthetical problem." Oscar Wilde, "The Portrait of Mr. W. H," in *The Work of Oscar Wilde 1856–1900*, ed. G. F. Maine (London: Collins, 1948), 1089.

66. Leo Lowenthal, "The Debate over Art and Popular Culture: English Eighteenth Century as a Case Study," in *Literature, Popular Culture and Society* (Palo Alto, CA: Pacific Books, 1961), 70 and 93f.

67. Haywood, op. cit., 21.

68. Cf. Haywood, op. cit., 29ff. Defoe wrote in 1725: "The Booksellers are the Master Manufacturers or Employers. The several Writers, Authors, Copyers, Sub-writers, and all other Operators with Pen and Ink are the workmen employed by the said Master Manufacturers" (page 30).

69. Cf. Haywood, op. cit., 31ff.

70. Cf. Sibylle Mulot, "Die Fälschung der Fälschung. Wilhelm Hauffs 'Mann im Mond,'" in *Gefälscht!*, op. cit., 251ff. The literary texts preceding literary texts, the "hypertext" preceding "hypotext" were examined, classified, and illustrated mostly on French material by Gerard Genette in his book *Palimpsestes. La littérature au second degré* (Paris: Éditions du Seuil, 1982).

71. Sándor Weöres, *Psyché. Egy hajdani költönö írásai* ("The Writings of a Poetess of Yore") (Budapest: Magvetö, 1972); Wolfgang Hildesheimer, *Marbot. Eine Biographie* (Frankfurt: Suhrkamp, 1981).

72. Cf. Wolfgang Hildesheimer, "Arbeitsprotokolle des Verfahrens 'Marbot,'" in *Das Ende der Fiktionen. Reden aus fünfundzwanzig Jahren* (Frankfurt: Suhrkamp, 1984), 145f.

73. Hildesheimer, op. cit., 140. In Hildesheimer's first book entitled *Lieblose Legenden*, the fictitious character of Gottlieb Theodor Pilz (1789– 1856) already made his appearance. His claim to fame was that he did not write a diary during his Italian travels, and that he saw the prime goal of his life in dissuading great men from creating (for example, we are indebted to him for Rossini's silence). As I have already mentioned, Hildesheimer's second book (1953) is about fine-art forgeries (*Paradies der falschen Vögel* [Frankfurt: Suhrkamp, 1975]).

74. The poetic oeuvre and biography of Forestier, a legionnaire of German/ French origin who was born in 1921 and disappeared in Indochina in 1951, was the creation of Krämer (1918–1987). His volume of poetry was welcomed even by Gottfried Benn. Cf. Benn, "Bemerkungen zu drei Gedichtbänden," in *Gesammelte Werke IV. Autobiographische und vermischte Schriften* (Stuttgart: Klett-Cotta, 1986), 314f. Also cf. Hans-Jürgen Schmitt, "Der Fall Georg Forestier," in *Gefälscht!*, op. cit., 317ff.

75. Cf. Wolfgang Iser, "Akte des Fingierens oder Was ist das Fiktive im fiktionalen Text?," in *Funktionen des Fiktiven. Poetik und Hermeneutik X*, ed. Dieter Henrich and Wolfgang Iser (Munich: Fink, 1983), 136.

76. Cf. Iser, *Der Akt des Lesens. Theorie ästhetischer Wirkung*, op. cit., 87ff., especially 103f., 120, and 145 ff. The deviatory model of the structuralist theory of text was created by Jan Mukařovský.

77. Hans Robert Jauß, *Ästhetische Erfahrung und literarische Hermeneutik* (Frankfurt: Suhrkamp, 1982), 304. Cf. "Das Vollkommene als Faszinosum des Imaginären," in *Funktionen des Fiktiven. Poetik und Hermeneutik X*, op. cit., 444.

78. Iser, "Akte des Fingierens oder Was ist das Fiktive im fiktionalen Text?," op. cit., 139.

79. As has been shown by B. Snell's work, *Die Entdeckung des Geistes*. Hans Blumenberg refers to him in "Wirklichkeitsbegriff und Möglichkeit des Romans," in *Nachahmung und Illusion: Poetik und Hermeneutik I*, ed. H. R. Jauß (Munich: Fink, 1969), 9. The examples we have brought up (Gorgias, John of Salisbury, cf. note 32 of this chapter) also refer to the dramatic genres, and Nietzsche too started out from the origin of tragedy.

80. Iser, "Akte des Fingierens oder Was ist das Fiktive im fiktionalen Text?," op. cit., 139.

81. Jauß, *Ästhetische Erfahrung und literarische Hermeneutik*, op. cit., 328.

82. Wolfhart Pannenberg, "Das Irreale des Glaubens," in *Funktionen des Fiktiven. Poetik und Hermeneutik X*, op. cit., 18.

83. Plato, *Phaidros* 243a–b. Cf. C. R. Ligota, "'This Story is Not True.' Fact and Fiction in Antiquity," *Journal of the Warburg and Courtauld Institutes* 45 (1982): 1ff.

84. Jauß, *Ästhetische Erfahrung und literarische Hermeneutik*, op. cit., 302. Cf. "Zur historischen Genese der Scheidung von Fiktion und Realität," in *Funktionen des Fiktiven. Poetik und Hermeneutik X*, op. cit., 430.

THE FAKE PARADIGM

— The Limits of Extending the Forgery Metaphor —

A couple of decades ago a philosophy professor offered two courses: "Totality" was the title of the first one, while the second was entitled something like "The Philosophical Climate in the Austro-Hungarian Monarchy." One particularly malicious student asked: If the professor offers the first one, what is the need for offering the second?

If "everything" is forgery, then a similar question could be asked in connection with our subject matter also. If the notion of *forged* has intelligible opposites (genuine, true, original), then it itself is intelligible; from the relationship of "this is false—this is not false," one can derive the logical, moral, or aesthetic meaning of "this is false" or "this is not false" by reflective investigation. However, if the statement "this is false" is a total one—if it applies to everything, to the *world*—then what possible meaning could any particular thing have? Furthermore, what possible meaning could be assigned to the notion of *forged*?

The old German maxim *Falschheit regiert die ganze Welt* ("Falseness rules the entire world") is a sententious moralization, which reserves the truth for at least the one person who proclaims the maxim. The possible theological interpretation of the falseness of the world is related to the eschatological negation of the world and refers to the divine truth. The verdict of the world's *becoming* totally false assumes the existence of its historically determined opposite: That there was a time when it was not like that. This apocalyptic or cynical vision requires a dimension of the philosophy of history. And even so, it is unable to escape the dilemma patterned on the old formula of "all Cretans are liers": The more closed and more holistic it renders its *truth*, that is, that everything is *false* (not real but hyper-real or simulated), the emptier its paradox becomes.

This simplified scheme parodies Jean Baudrillard's sociocultural theory on *simulacra*, his philosophical science fiction. Of the several closing scenarios of modern culture (and society), his version is based on the paradigm of copying–forging–simulation. The simulacra are reproductions, and his question addresses our relation to the objects and events that they reproduce. For Baudrillard, the method of reproduction is also the method of social relations and power. He starts his story in the Renaissance, describing the three phases in the "orders" of simulacra. The *ending* of his story—but also of history, of art, of the individual, as well as of many other things, including work, production, the "social" phenomenon, etc.—is that in the course of its generational self-evolution, the reproduction, or the simulacrum, cuts itself loose from its references in modern culture, becomes an independent world-creating force and swallows up reality.

Initially, there was the liberation of signs, their emancipation from feudal bondage, the breaking free of the copying and forging of originals (*contrefaçon* means both). *Natural* and *forged* were both born in the Renaissance. The plaster stucco was able to imitate the widest range of materials in a very democratic manner; fashion cut across the hierarchy and relativized it; the machinery of the baroque theatre modeled reality; the dickey only had a front piece; and the fork as an artificial prosthesis was introduced. These simulacra of the first order still do not corrode the difference between similarity and reality. The copying of the classical age was followed by the mechanical reproduction, or the mass production, of the industrial age. The identical objects originate from the world of technology. The referential character of the original was abolished, along with the imitational character of both the copy and forgery. "In a series, objects become undefined simulacra one of the other."[1] In other words, they became simulacra of the second order. Finally, the simulacra of the third order belong to the present, constituted by simulation itself, in which every form is designed from the viewpoint of reproducibility, with every area of human life—politics, economics, culture, everyday life, etc.—being organized and controlled by simulative models and codes. This is the world of determined indeterminacy, in which the rule of structural law is ascribed to values, as opposed to the rule of natural law in the case of the first-order simulacra, and the rule of commercial law in the case of the second-order simulacra, with no way to escape from this formation.

Instead of a referential character, our mode of existence has the character of a referendum, in which every sign, every message is presented to us in the form of a two-choice questionnaire, a test based on a binary system of predefined questions and answers. The difference between the available choices is a "tactical hallucination." These tests and referenda constitute the perfect forms of cybernetic modeling and simulation. "No more true or false, because no more distinguishable hiatus between question and response."[2]

Similarly, the real cannot be distinguished from the imaginary, nor existence from appearance, as reality fades into its own image and dissolves into "hyper-reality." In hyper-reality, representation is forever replaced by reproduction, which aestheticizes everything, turning everything into art and thus effectively abolishing art. The world turns into a Disneyland. Its inhabitants turn into biological, genetic, and cybernetic mutants.[3] Implicitly, the irresolute nature of true and false also leaves open the question as to whether it is true knowledge that Baudrillard metaphorically transfers to other areas by borrowing his most important images and analogies from the field of sciences, or whether the indeterminacy of the genetic code, of DNA, etc., is itself transmuted into the metaphysics of hyper-reality. Furthermore, it is easy to see that Baudrillard's style of mixing prophecy with phenomenology universalizes a skeptical version of the theory and experience of the media of visual information (in his own terminology, *telematics*), as well as presenting a caricature of the lifestyle of American suburbia. Not only does his cynical theory condemn the cognitive ability of the human race to endless circumrotation, but he does not even sense the *reality of suffering*. ". . . Baudrillard is less a philosopher who offers arguments than an *écrivain* who expresses feelings that are 'in the air,'" David Carrier writes.[4]

But what is in the air? There are dozens of notions floating and hovering around us, which are all connected to the late-modern acceleration of change, as well as to the inadequacy of direct experience when confronted with the new forms of knowledge, to the extraordinary increase and inflation of reproduced visual information and visual experience, and to the decreasing transparency of the world. The growing tension between visibility and transparency creates the feeling of unreality, as well as arousing suspicion about the existence of invisible and unrecognizable patterns. There are experts and administrators whose job it is to copy and forge these patterns as well as to produce "suggestive images and slogans." They are referred to by a true *écrivain* (a *romancier* really), Milan Kundera, as "imagolo-gists," who take over the role of ideologists:

> This word at last makes it possible to lump together people formerly referred to by various designations: The staff of advertising agencies; the so-called communication advisors of statesmen; the designers who dream up the shapes of cars and fitness equipment; the creators of the fashion industry; the hairdressers; the stars of the entertainment business who dictate the norms of physical beauty and to whom all the other branches of imagology turn to for ideas.
>
> Reality was stronger than ideology. And it was precisely in this respect that imagology has surpassed ideology; imagology is stronger than reality, which incidentally no longer means the same to people that it meant to my grandmother, who lived in a Moravian village and knew everything from her own experience. . . .[5]

If we were to read as a philosophical exposition the chapter "Imagology" in Kundera's novel *Immortality,* then we would be able to draw two different conclusions from the decisive edge "imagology" enjoys over reality: One conclusion would constitute the criticism of it by idealizing the grandmother, "who still practiced a personal super-vision over reality,"[6] or to quote the pagan "pretechnological" utopia of a great philosopher (Martin Heidegger) in Richard Rorty's moving interpretation: ". . . a sparsely populated valley in the mountains, a valley in which life is given shape by its relationship to the primordial Fourfold—earth, sky, man, and gods."[7] The other conclusion would be the radical, absolute, "positively modern" viewpoint, which would accept without any reservations the rapidly changing images as reality and which, "for the sake of the eternal *imperative* of modernity," would be capable of betraying "its changeable content."[8] The one dis-covers the patterns of the transparency of existence in the premodern past, while the other has a mode of existence based on an uncondi-tional adaptability to a changeable future.

But is one allowed to read a novel as if it was a philosophical exposition? For one thing, Kundera has protested against it in the strongest possible terms.[9] As for me, I find it not at all impossible that a novel be read not *just* as a novel, but also as many other things, even including philosophy; nevertheless, it must be pointed out that neither of the above-mentioned conclusions contains the philosophy of the novel. The ideas expressed in a novel, even when they come from the mouth of the author, do not seek the truth directly but have a stylized and relative character, while those ideas that do shape a novel are often left unstated. The novel based on an antimodern utopia is different from the one based on the absolute (or absolutized) modern; with pictures completely independent of reality, turning into their own simulacra in which the personality is dissolved, the latter type corresponds—according to Baudrillard, at any rate—to the *nouveau roman*. In Kundera's novel, it is the *person* (Paul) who wants to be absolutely modern, whose personality therefore lacks both constancy and certainty, and who—as he himself suspects—is allied to his own grave diggers. Being one of the major genres of the tradition of modernity, the novel is the art of individuality, and the existence of individuals—including such memorable ones as the heroine of the novel, Agnes—presents the greatest obstacle to the futurist absolutization of modernity, to the simulacra swallowing up reality, to the rule of images.

This is so because, after all, the first intuitive attribute of a personality is that it is *real*, and as to the case of a great personality—which of course should not be confused with a famous or successful personality, or not even with an original one for that matter—its most important attribute is that it is *authentic*. In contrasting Kundera with Baudrillard, I do not wish to bow before Kundera's (and Rorty's) theoretical offer of the philosophical content of novels as an *alternative* to philosophy itself. The philosopher Baudrillard does indeed strike one as a misguided writer, and I have contrasted him with a genuine writer. In the three orders of simulacra, man initially made unique automatons in his own theatrical and playful image; then went on to produce series of functionally equivalent, useful robots[10]; and finally, in today's civilization, the simulacra are turning into people, and people into simulacra.

Admittedly, a significant (albeit invariably overestimated) part of the patterns of human behavior is rooted in rapidly changing, indirect life experiences conveyed mostly by the media, and television in particular, which has the most profound influence on people's lifestyles. It would nevertheless be absurd to infer from this circumstance that the hyper-reality of the life-form of universal copying also abolishes, or fictionalizes, the existential stakes of life. While one is justified in assuming a connection between terrorism and the media, for example, it would be going too far perhaps to regard terrorist acts as the simulacra of the journalism of "terroristic" shock and sensationalism, as has been suggested by Baudrillard in his article, "Our Theatre of Cruelty"; and as to the idea of regarding the innocent hostages, along with the murderers and on-lookers, as part of the system that renders the events fictitious in the *implosion* (the "inward burst" of reality)—now that is outright preposterous![11]

What seems to be the problem with the idea of the fictionalization of reality, of the world, of life, and of people is not that modern life-forms do not increasingly require fictions (such as the unjustifi-able hypotheses of life strategies, constructions of reality, experiences, postulates, auxiliary constructions, "As-ifs,"[12] etc., accepted rather than acquired). Nor is it the case that the fictitious character of these do not frequently become obscure, thus contributing to the transfor-mation of the fictions into the naive evidences of natural attitude. Nor would anyone deny that fiction and reality do not inevitably form a distinct dichotomy in the processes of learning and action. But it can definitely be maintained that fictions are numerous; that they do not keep to the same direction; and that they assume differ-ent positions in the existential hierarchy.

Furthermore, certain fictions are real or unreal *in comparison to* other fictions, depending on their functions, etc. This is what pro-vides the maneuvering space for individuals, and this is what pre-vents the unification and homogenization of the various fictions, which could otherwise render the *relational* categories of fictitious and real, of true and false, unintelligible. It cannot be by mere coin-cidence that it is the utopia of modern, antitraditionalist dictator-ships—i.e., their total world dominion with a tendency to compress everything into a continuum—that comes closest to the transforma-tion of reality into fiction; also significant is the point that, for Baudrillard, modern democracy appears in the form of a total tyranny of determined indeterminacy, being both impersonal and unde-tectable (because internalized).

But am I consistent in contrasting the diagnosis of the abolish-ment of the difference between the real and imaginary, existence and appearance, false and true, with a novel that is fictitious by defini-tion? The notion of absolute fiction was applied to literature before it was applied to the world: First in a negative, critical form, as seduc-tive fraud and deception—this was called *apaté* in Greek—and then in a positive, affirmative form, as the self-defense of literature (and art)—this was called the *self-referentiality* of works of art. But if we remove self-referentiality, the property of referring to no other "real-ity" but itself, from the context of the polemics in which this notion was used to repudiate the requirement to have content, then this indeed will prove to be a myth. The individuals of the novel are, of course, fictional, and thus not real according to the natural attitude; yet this is precisely what makes their relevance to the reader's world all the more intensive, as they offer themselves for metaphoric iden-tification. As I happen to have studied Baudrillard and read *Immor-tality* at the same time, for me Paul will forever remain the personi-fied metaphor of Baudrillard's spirit.

The Fake Art-Paradigm

Will we see in our time the release of art forgery from its farcical role, that of art's servant rebelling against autonomous art? If forgery does become the possible paradigm of contemporary art—as has been suggested from several corners—then would this not mean the end of the centuries-old history of artistic autonomy? Would this not also lead to the dissolution of the notion of forgery, once the artistic gesture of "forging" loses some or all of its provocative coloring? For one thing, in contemporary artistic practice forgery is always metaphorical, and it is this metaphor that is intended to guarantee the judiciousness of its paradigmatic extension.

What is being forged? Two major groups are readily identifiable: I refer to the one as *tradition,* and to the other as *banality.* The one takes its material from the canonic tradition of art, the other from everyday life. That the two natural sources of artistic material are explicitly "forged," rather than simply borrowed from, suggests that the material has become problematic in art. As opposed to its surreptitious mode of existence in the past, forgery now has to be obvious, or even conspicuous, in order to be able to call attention to this. Any work of art selected from tradition must be extremely well known; any object chosen from everyday life must be extremely vulgar. Marcel Duchamp, who was the founder of both directions in art, picked his material with deadly infallibility: He chose *Mona Lisa* from tradition and a pissoir from everyday life (or to take another example, he combined the two in one of his early happenings—in a modern tableau vivant: From everyday life, he presented his own nude body, as well as that of his female associate, and from tradition he presented Lucas Cranach's *Adam and Eve).*

The extreme case of elevating banal objects, acts, or texts to the level of art is to present them in their original condition. In this case the artistic effect is expected to come from the change of function or context. Nevertheless, the process can just as easily be described the other way around: The aim of forging the original function or context is to test the full power of artistic effect, or even to examine its mode of operation. Art becomes an experiment in how far one can go in minimizing the difference that separates the artistic from the real. Or to further radicalize the issue, one can in fact question the need to stop at all. With this development, a host of well-known themes of great diversity emerge: The gesture of art's self-elimination; the gesture of reality's aestheticization; art's fading into its own ideology or counterideology; the cynical criticism of art and its transformation into an emphatic lifestyle; the proclamation of the banality of the world or of the arts; the radical democratization of art under the slogan "everybody is an artist" by refusing to draw a line between artists and ordinary people; and so forth.

There might be, however, a less radical interpretation, one that is formulated according to Kandinsky's description from 1912: "The forms of materialization selected from the stock of matter by the intellect can easily be arranged between two poles. These are: 1) the great abstraction, and 2) the great realism."[13] It was in the 1960s, following the close of the period of Abstract Expressionism, that the pendulum swung in the other direction (or earlier experiments came to the focus of attention), and the direct presentation of the various pieces of reality originated from the extreme versions of these movements.

What is the situation with regard to the forgery of tradition (or, as it is now often called, with regard to its appropriation)? One would suspect that in presenting works of tradition anew, whether in fragments or their entirety, whether retouched or unretouched, artists partly rely on the wear and tear, the erosion and banalization of the works occupying a central place in the canon, while partly contributing to this erosion themselves. Why do timeless art treasures corrode? Probably for the same reason that they became timeless. As a result of the imbalance that developed between the authoritative and the exemplary functions in the process of canonization, the works of the past were removed from the live, practical-creative side of artistic life: They came to be confined in museums. In saying this, I do not mean to chant the boring refrain that they have become dead. Anyone who has ever stood in long queues, waiting for hours to be admitted to the retrospective exhibition of a great artist of the past, would have something to say about the truth of this platitude.

On the *receptive* side of artistic life the past is very much alive, and its publicity is increasing. Today, when the demarcation between high culture and mass culture is extremely difficult to define in the case of contemporary works of art, the act of placing older works of art (those that comprise the major part of current reception) into museums is clearly designed to protect, segregate, and enrich high culture. This is a safe-guarded stock of increasing rather than decreasing volume, and any segment of it is there for us to turn to at any time—in correspondence with the growing freedom of individual reception. We as viewers can turn to them—this is what is meant by their being authoritative—and their effect can be movingly alive. Another contributor to this effect, however, is the silent (and not necessarily nostalgic) knowledge that it is no longer possible to create works of art "in this way" today—they can no longer be exemplary (or if somebody still chooses to work in this way today, as do for example the forgers of tradition, then he does not strive for, nor does he achieve, the same effect). Paradoxically, it is precisely the stars of old high art who pose the greatest danger to this dynamic function of museologization: A function that preserves but does not rigidify high art. It is they who become worn out by inordinate consumption. For the danger *does* exist that they might become exemplary—in *mass culture*. We cannot discover them, cannot study them, and cannot enjoy a first encounter with them, because we have always known them. What I am talking about here is known far too well: The unfair selectiveness of cultural tourism, the aggressive marketing of reproductions and copies and variations of inferior quality, making concessions to the various layers of modern taste.

In New York, in the window display of a souvenir shop on MacDougal Street, I saw a miniature version of Michelangelo's *David*, which differed from the original only in that the penis—in contrast with the antique models of the original—was greatly enlarged, in accordance with the expectations of modern-male nude photography that verges on pornography. If we place the *artistic* forgery of tradition in these kinds of trends (and, since the borderline between "low" and "high" is growing obscure in contemporary art, it is sometimes enough of a difference, in the spirit of the institutional theory of art, to exhibit the same *item* not in a souvenir shop but 54 blocks uptown, in the Museum of Modern Art), then this will become a special case of the forgery of banality. Accordingly, in modern reception the tradition, since it is symbolized by banalized works, has been forged from the start, and the artistic forgery of these sends out the cynical message to the old in the name of contemporary art that "you are no better than I." The *inimitable is imitable*; or alternatively, it whispers nostalgically that "mass culture has ruined me and I—through my art—record this ruination." The *inimitable is inimitable.* Having been copied (accurately or defaced), duplicated, multiplied, and serialized, the old, famous, and familiar works of art have become the metaphors of the contemporary fate of high art. Günter Brus's collage and drawing in pencil entitled *Hommage a Schiele* (in which the artist repeats one of Schiele's nude drawing by using an affixed copy, then destroying it by turning it into a faceless and unrecognizable state) sends out this message very plainly.

This gesture itself is, however, entirely laid open to banalization by virtue of the circumstance that the forgery of tradition itself becomes a tradition. Never before has the issue of whether a concept is itself a banality or merely an ironic criticism imitating banality been made to depend so much on its originality, novelty, or wittiness. The concept also implies extremity. In the case of forging tradition, this extremity can be described as follows: It is the "indiscernible" reproduction of either a part or whole of an artwork of tradition, so as to form a part or whole of a new artwork, which is nevertheless made discernible by the extraordinary familiarity of the original and also, in the overwhelming majority of the cases, by a certain amount of tampering with it.

Now then, it would be impossible to deny that ever since the "forgery" of the traditions of Leonardo and Cervantes, and following the inventions of Duchamp in fine art and of Borges in literature, this definition would fit several works of art,[14] besides having inspired quite a few art-philosophical meditations. Nevertheless, this metaphor would still provide scarcely enough material from which to derive the new artistic practice. This is so partly because the vitality of the practical experience of museum visitation has controverted the perspective of the art-philosophical gesture of this metaphor: Instead of dying out and vanishing, art traditions can still play a part in the lives of the viewers, readers, and listeners. Despite all the alienation, appropriation, and parody they have been subjected to, the major pieces of the art tradition cannot be excluded from the museological tradition entirely and for good—every single encounter with them poses the question of whether to perceive them in the context of tradition or of banality. Nor can the possibility be excluded that, after a while, the alienating destruction itself will reach a stage that will necessitate the reconstruction of the "original" in the reception; in other words, that "first" encounter, the discovery, will nevertheless take place. On the other hand, the forgery metaphor proves to be an unsatisfactory one with regard to the relationship between contemporary works of art and tradition as well.

The traditional forms of the debate and dialogue between tradition and innovation—by that I mean that the forms that disregard the extreme cases of provocative and open forgery—have survived. The reason why modern art is in a crisis is not that there are no great artists able to sustain the connection of high art with the past (although such is the nature of the situation that they not always are at the focus of attention), but that high art, or autonomous art, has been frustrated and can no longer play the part of *one of the poles* in the family of arts. It has been frustrated by everyday life, mass culture, the media, and multiculturalism. These are today the four apocalyptic riders of the *other pole,* of aesthetic heteronomy.

In my view, autonomy and heteronomy together have constituted the maneuvering space of aesthetics throughout the entire period of modernity, while the works and aesthetic theories organizing around the poles have been in dynamic motion all along, frequently rearranging themselves and sometimes even trading places. The emergence of the modern institute of art failed to bring about a stationary state, even with regard to the system as a whole; on the contrary, it appears that the attempts to rearrange this system over and over again, even to the extent of breaking it up, have constituted the dynamic mode of existence of modern art. The universal conceptual construct of art was open to criticism from the start for being aristocratic as well as for assisting in the alienation from both everyday life and religion. Although being itself a parasite of the new notion of art, art forgery joined the raiders from within the besieged fort—admittedly wearing nothing more than the light armor of revelry and profiteering.

Not only did the various art forms differ with regard to their respective traditions, but neither could their new phenomena necessarily be integrated into the construct of modern art. Still, what sustained the system was the fact that the question of the associated integrative and disintegrative processes remained at the center of attention. "The way the disintegration of a genre takes place is that it is forced to move from the center towards the periphery, while at the same time new phenomena emerge from the by-products of literature, from unknown corners, and from the deep, making their way to fill the place of the former at the center," Yuriy Tynyanov writes in his wonderful study, "The Literary Fact" (1924).[15] The fact that the strongest charges against the system—initially put forward by peripheral art movements, initiatives, and theories—chastising it for formalism as well as for eliminating the living bonds of the works of art to everyday life, for displaying a detached impartiality, etc., so often returned, or more precisely, were so often built into the moving center; wherefore this fact suggests that the modern concept and system of art has been firmly established in our culture, and that the artistic activities corresponding to this system have shown great resilience.

But this is in fact not just a conflict between periphery and center, because the dialectic of integration and disintegration itself came to be built into the system, simultaneously producing *two* centers. What seems peripheral from one of the centers could be the center itself from another perspective. And when we consider both, we observe *two poles*. If we consider the great dichotomies, which keep recurring throughout the entire history of aesthetics—old↔new; antique↔modern; "the world" (as the world of a work of art)↔the reception of the world; *pulchritudo vaga↔pulchritudo adhaerens*; pure aesthetic judgment↔applied aesthetic judgment; beautiful↔sublime; naive↔sentimental; objective↔interesting; classical↔romantic; symbolic↔allegorical; Apollonian↔Dionysian; form↔content; *l'art pour l'art*↔committed; text↔world; immanence↔transcensus of the works of art; idealism (abstraction)↔realism (naturalism); aural↔ nonaural; high art↔mass culture; pure sign↔secondary sign—then we come to realize that they either referred to the relationship of autonomy and heteronomy or attempted the problematization of it.[16] The two centers or poles also play the role of mutually correcting each other. The subject of my book, the original↔forgery, copy, variation, etc., should also be interpreted in this way.

The crisis of modern art, the origins of which I trace back (at least with regard to fine art) to the 1960s, means that the continuation of this bipolar, aesthetic-maneuvering space has become uncertain, since the pole of heteronomy has been gaining the upper hand, threatening the other with total elimination. The major proposals for the hermeneutical and socioanthropological elimination of aesthetics are the theoretical symptoms of this phenomenon, while in the practice of art the walls erected to fence-off everyday life and mass culture—which have always been decaying but so far have always been reconstructed—are crumbling so extensively that the possibility of their reconstruction seems remote. Our sensual world is influenced— "regulated" according to many—by the applied art of the media, which in turn is determined by technological development. The extremists of multiculturalism direct the destructive fanaticism of their moral intoxication at the traditions of European culture—the same traditions that were in fact responsible for the stimulation of the multiculturalism of historical consciousness by the musealization of traditions.

If forgery is indeed the metaphor of modern art, then the open proclamation of this secret, or its routine application in the practice of art, would lead to the expansion of the heteronomous art concept(s) and also to the elimination of the aesthetic-maneuvering space. There would be *many arts,* but there would be *no art.* With regard to the notion of forgery, this would create two alternatives: It could turn out to be a transient category and rapidly lose meaning, as the power of its counterparts—autonomous and original— declined (this applies to the forgery of tradition and, on a more general level, to our relation to tradition). The dirty word of forgery today can still be replaced with the open and aggressive term of appropriation.[17] Alternatively, the forgery of the banalities of everyday life could withdraw from art, turning into a depressing metaphor of the entire life experience, similar to the one that we saw in Baudrillard's case.

The Museum

Is it possible that autonomous art has withdrawn into the museums? Is it possible that, "for the artistic modes of the highest order, for the ways in which truth asserts itself,"[18] we now have to turn back to the past, the mementos of which are collected and arranged in museums?

In order to be able to answer this question, we first have to show that the institution of museums has itself played a part in that modern dynamism, which created and polarized the maneuvering space of aesthetics. Looking back to the beginnings, we find that the gradual development of the museums of fine art has in a way come to form the historical symbol of the genesis of autonomy, insofar as the works of art of several traditions are brought together there, mostly after being stripped of their respective functions. Museums decontextualize, in the sense that they abolish the sacrality of the space in which an altarpiece is in its natural environment, or the bourgeois interior in which a still life is in its natural environment. As a consequence of certain antimodern suggestions, such changes of context are often referred to either as lamentable developments or as critical arguments of crucial importance. The consistent critics are at the same time the opponents of autonomy also, since the adaptability of the artworks' reception to changing contexts, historically as well as individually, is the manifestation of aesthetic autonomy. The museums are not the original environment for works of art (except for the case of artworks designed specifically for museums); museums are the place for the permanence in change.

Alternatively (and the other pole within the museums is manifested in this possibility), museums can reconstruct the original environment, in which case the dominant feature will be the artworks' links to their own age, their original context, their heteronomous pole. There are objects, such as primitive artworks, for example, which are collected from the perspective of either "ethnographical culturalism" or "aesthetic formalism." In the words of James Clifford, "since the turn of the century objects collected from non-Western sources have been classified in two major categories: as (scientific) cultural artifacts or as (aesthetic) works of art."[19]

This distinction is not reserved for ethnographical objects alone. In every object—or at least every object worth collecting—there is an internal tension between the historical and cultural context of its origin on the one hand and its adaptability to changes of context—its ability to make an impression in another context, so to speak—on the other; and as to the ability to make an impression, the guarantees for this are primarily *aesthetic*. It is the *autonomous* work of art that has the best chance to be able to enter into a dialogue with the viewers in a new context.

Of course, a work of art is just as much an object, and the polarization between its "contextual object (and heteronomous artwork)" nature and its "autonomous work of art, capable of change of contexts" nature can always be seen in its museum display. Since the institution of museums itself forces most of the exhibits accumulated there to go through a change of context, at the one pole it tries to *reconstruct* the original context while at the other it communicates the impossibility, or at least limited scope, of such a reconstruction, basing the presentation on the work's *aesthetic freedom*.

In addition to this internal polarization however, the museum is also open to criticism coming from various sources outside its walls—criticism that I have mentioned earlier. The museum is a lifeless, dusty, unreal memorial tombstone. Everything that is put into a museum becomes rigid and loses its actuality. In this debate the museum can take the position of both the autonomous and heteronomous poles. For example, it is *either* the institution of *désengagement* against committed, living art, in which case it is its autonomy that becomes the subject of criticism, *or* it is the instrument of the dominant culture's oppressive self-aggrandizement and consensus enforcement, in which case it is its heteronomy that comes under fire. It stands accused of either universalism or particularism. Being one of the most philosophical institutions of Western culture, museums are apt to react to every dilemma of cultural identity, and so every form of cultural criticism has a direct bearing on museum life.

Of all these possibilities, the complete survey of which would be possible only in a historical theory of the institution, I would like to mention only the simplest one: The debate of *the old and the new*. Earlier, while running through the list of the great dichotomies in the history of aesthetics (the conflict and compensation of which creates the maneuvering space of aesthetics), this was the first debate I mentioned, which is natural enough considering that this debate, which in various forms has spanned the entire period of modernity, was historically the first. As shown by the designation, the movements of the avant-garde considered themselves to be the vanguards of progress, of the future, of the new. Their conflicts with museums focusing on the past could not have come as a surprise. This is not to say that they had nothing to do with tradition, but they deliberately took their tradition from noncanonized, nonmuseologized culture, from that of ancient history and the primitives. In the debate of the old and the new (from the point of view of emerging art), it was the new that came out on top.

My question is as follows: Isn't it possible that the pendulum of modernity is now swinging too far in the opposite direction?[20] Shouldn't we draw a new line between high art and low or applied art in such a way that while the latter is mainly inspired by futurology (in preparation for the future challenges of technology, science, communication, fashion, and advertising), the former surveys the past, receives its inspiration from the old (whether we are talking about form or attitude), and moves into the museums? Low and applied art is "positively modern" and avant-garde; high art is "modernity-traditionalist" and arrière-garde. Thirty years ago the conceptualists and minimalists wanted to make art indistinguishable from everyday life. Now they want to obliterate the borderline between artistic fantasy and everyday phantasmagoria. So now it is the individuality, the materiality, and the originality of the works of art that would be rendered archaic by the infinite possibilities of digital technology, computer science, and simulation and the creation of virtual reality, the apologists and prophets of which relentlessly claim that "digital technology is eroding . . . the foundation of the élite contemporary art world—the museum and gallery system."[21]

Strangely contrasted with this futurism is the hermeneutic character of our high culture; the point that our main *cultural* activity is characterized less by *scouting* the future than by *reading* the past. If modern art moves into museums today, then the forgery of tradition forms a philosophically radical gesture of this event rather than its paradigm. In that case it is not Duchamp's (and Warhol's) Leonardo what gives *example*, but Francis Bacon's Velázquez and Van Gogh what gives *measure*.

Notes

1. Jean Baudrillard, "The Orders of Simulacra," in *Simulations* (New York: Foreign Agents Series, Semiotext(e), 1983), 97.

2. Ibid., 123.

3. Cf. Jean Baudrillard, *L'autre par lui-même. Habilitation* (Paris: Galilée, 1987).

4. David Carrier, "Baudrillard as Philosopher," in *The Aesthete in the City* (University Park: Pennsylvania State University Press, 1994), 109.

5. Milan Kundera, *Immortality*, trans. Peter Kussi. New York: HarperPerennial, 1992.

6. Ibid.

7. Richard Rorty, "Heidegger, Kundera, and Dickens," in *Essays on Heidegger and Others* (Cambridge, UK: Cambridge University Press, 1991), 75.

8. Kundera, op. cit.

9. On the compensatory conflict of philosophy and the novel, see Kundera's essay entitled *The Art of the Novel* (New York: Grove Press, 1986). On the "art of the peculiarly novel-like essay," Kundera points out that "it does not claim that it comes up with an incontrovertible message, only with a hypothetical, playful or ironic one" (page 87); also see page 101ff.

10. Cf. Baudrillard, "The Orders of Simulacra," op. cit.

11. Cf. Jean Baudrillard, "Notre Théâtre de la cruauté," *Libération* 4 and 5–6 October 1977.

12. On fiction's philosophical coming-to-awareness, cf. Odo Marquard, "Kunst als Antifiktion—Versuch über den Weg der Wirklichkeit ins Fiktive," in *Aesthetica und Anaesthetica—Philosophische Überlegungen* (Paderborn: Schöningh, 1989). Also see the same in *Funktionen des Fiktiven. Poetik und Hermeneutik X*, ed. Dieter Henrich and Wolfgang Iser (Munich: Fink, 1983), 35ff.

13. Quoted by Werner Hofmann, *Grundlagen der modernen Kunst. Eine Einführung in ihre symbolischen Formen* (Stuttgart: Alfred Kröner, 1978), 153.

14. I discussed this in chapter 4 under its first heading, "The Dilemma of Indistinguishability."

15. Yuriy Tynyanov, "Literaturniy Fakt" ("The Literary Fact"), in *Poetika*. Moscow: Nauka, 1977.

16. In a series of essays I wrote between 1978 and 1988, I attempted to expound this bipolar structure of the discursive space of aesthetics. *Tisztelt közönség, kulcsot te találj . . .* ("Honored public, go on, find your own ending . . .") (Budapest: Gondolat, 1990). Also cf. Odo Marquard's study, "Kunst als Kompensation ihres Endes," in which the author explicitly states that "philosophical aesthetics is invariably a twofold aesthetics, in which art is always represented twice . . . respectively to aesthetics' success or failure in achieving aesthetical autonomy," in Marquard, op. cit., 118.

17. Cf. Péter György, "A kisajátítás esetei" ("The Cases of Appropriation"), in *Müvészet és média találkozása a boncasztalon* ("The Encounter of Art and Media on the Dissection Table") (Budapest: Kulturtrade, 1995), 45ff.

18. Georg Wilhelm Friedrich Hegel, *Vorlesungen über Aesthetik I*, ed. H. G. Hotho (Berlin: Duncker und Humblot, 1835), 134.

19. James Clifford, *The Predicament of Culture* (Cambridge, MA: Harvard University Press, 1988), 222.

20. I have borrowed the figurative expression used by Ágnes Heller and Ferenc Fehér in their study, "The Pendulum of Modernity." Cf. Heller–Fehér, *A modernitás ingája* ("The Pendulum of Modernity") (Budapest: T-Twins, 1993).

21. Daniel Pinchbeck, "The Second Renaissance," *Wired* (December 1994): 157.

BIBLIOGRAPHY

Abelard, Pierre. *Historia calamitatum*. Toronto: Pontifical Institute of Medieval Studies, 1954.

Abrams, M[eyer] H[oward]. *The Mirror and the Lamp: Romantic Theory and the Critical Tradition*. New York: Oxford University Press, 1971 [1953].

Adams, Percy G. *Travellers and Travel Liars 1660–1800*. Berkeley: University of California Press, 1962.

Adorno, Theodor Wiesengrund. *Ästhetische Theorie. Gesammelte Schriften VII*. Frankfurt: Suhrkamp, 1972.

Almerath, Thomas. *Kunst und Antiquitätenfälschungen*. Munich: Keyser, 1987.

Alpers, Svetlana [Leontief]. *"Ekphrasis and Aesthetic Attitudes in Vasari's Lives." Journal of the Warburg and Courtauld Institutes* 23 (1960).

Apollinaire, Guillaume. "Des Faux." In *Oeuvres en prose complètes II*. Paris: Gallimard, Pléiade, 1991, 74ff.

Arendt, Hannah. "Tradition and the Modern Age." In *Between Past and Future*. New York: Viking Press, 1968.

Arnau, Frank. *Kunst der Fälscher, Fälscher der Kunst*. Düsseldorf: Econ, 1960.

Ashmole, Bernard. "Forgeries of Ancient Sculpture: Creation and Detection." The First J. L. Myres Memorial Lecture, Oxford, 1961.

Ayrton, Michael. "Introduction." In K. E. Maison, *Themes and Variations*. London: Thames & Hudson, 1960.

Bagnani, Gilbert. "On Fakes and Forgeries." *Phoenix* 14 (1960).

Baudrillard, Jean. "Notre Théâtre de la cruauté." *Libération*, October 4 and 5–6, 1977.

———. "The Orders of Simulacra." In *Simulations*. New York: Foreign Agents Series, Semiotext(e), 1983.

———. *L'autre par lui-même. Habilitation*. Paris: Galilée, 1987.

217

Baumgart, Fritz. "Zu den Dossena-Fälschungen." In *Kunstchronik und Kunstliteratur. Beilage zur Zeitschrift für bildende Kunst* 1 (April 1929).

Beardsley, Monroe C. "Notes on Forgery." In *The Forger's Art*, ed. Denis Dutton. Berkeley: University of California Press, 1983, 225ff.

Bell, Clive. *Art*. London: Chatto & Windus, 1949.

Belting, Hans. "Vasari und die Folgen. Die Geschichte als Prozeß?" In *Das Ende der Kunstgeschichte?* Munich: Deutscher Kunstverlag, 1983.

———. *Bild und Kult. Eine Geschichte des Bildes vor dem Zeitalter der Kunst*. Munich: Beck, 1990.

Benjamin, Walter. "Geschichtsphilosophische Thesen." Thesis XIV. In *Schriften I*. Frankfurt: Suhrkamp, 1955.

———. "Das Kunstwerk im Zeitalter seiner technischen Reproduzierbarkeit" (Zweite Fassung). In *Gesammelte Schriften*, I/2. Frankfurt: Suhrkamp, 1974.

Benn, Gottfried. "Bemerkungen zu drei Gedichtbänden." In *Gesammelte Werke IV. Autobiographische und vermischte Schriften*. Stuttgart: Klett-Cotta, 1986, 314–19.

Benton, John F. "The Correspondence of Abelard and Héloise." In *Fälschungen im Mittelalter. Part V*. Hannover: Hahn, 1988, 95–120.

Bernhard, Thomas. *Alte Meister*. Frankfurt: Suhrkamp, 1988.

Bialostocki, Jan. "Some Values of Artistic Periphery." In *World Art: Themes of Unity and Diversity. Acts of the XXVIth International Congress of the History of Art*, ed. Irving Lavin. Vol. I. University Park: Pennsylvania State University Press, 1986, 49ff.

Bieber, Margarete. *Ancient Copies. Contributions to the History of Greek and Roman Art*. New York: New York University Press, 1977.

Bitterli, Urs. *Die "Wilden" und die "Zivilisierten." Grundzüge einer Geistes- und Kulturgeschichte der europäisch-überseeischen Begegnung*. Munich: Beck, 1976.

Blair, Claude, and Marian Campbell. "Le Mystère de Monsieur Marcy." *Connaisance des arts* 375 (1983).

Bloch, Marc. *Feudal Society*. Chicago: University of Chicago Press/Phoenix Books, 1964.

Bloch, Peter. "Fälschung." In *Reallexikon zur deutschen Kunstgeschichte*, ed. Otto Schmitt. Vol. VI. Munich: Alfred Druckenmüller Verlag, 1973.

———. "Gefälschte Kunst." *Zeitschrift für Ästhetik und allgemeine Kunstwissenschaft* 23/1 (1978).

Blumenberg, Hans. "Wirklichkeitsbegriff und Möglichkeit des Romans." In *Nachahmung und Illusion. Poetik und Hermeneutik I*, ed. H. R. Jauß. Munich: Fink, 1969.

Blunt, Anthony. *Artistic Theory In Italy 1450–1600*. Oxford, UK: Oxford University Press, 1978.

Bode, Wilhelm von. *Mein Leben. I–II*. Berlin: Hermann Reckendorf, 1930.

Boehm, Gottfried. "Kunst versus Geschichte: ein unerledigtes Problem." In G. Kubler, *Form der Zeit*. Frankfurt: Suhrkamp, 1982, 7–26.

Borges, Jorge Luis. "Pierre Ménard, Author of the *Quixote*." In *Labyrinths: Selected Stories & Other Writings*, ed. Donald A. Yates and James E. Irby. New York: New Directions, 1964.

Bredius, Abraham. "A New Vermeer." *Burlington Magazine* 71 (November 1937).

Brown, Beverly Louise. "Replication and the Art of Veronese." In *Retaining the Original*. Washington, DC: National Gallery of Art, 1989, 111ff.

Brown, Elisabeth A. R. *"Falsitas pia sive reprehensibilis*. Medieval Forgers and Their Intentions." In *Fälschungen im Mittelalter, Part I*. Hannover: Hahn, 1988, 101–19.

Brox, Norbert, ed. *Pseudepigrahie in der heidnischen und jüdisch–christlichen Antike*. Darmstadt: Wissenschaftliche Buchgesellschaft, 1977.

Burckhardt, Jakob. "Über die Echtheit alter Bilder." In *Die Kunst der Betrachtung. Aufsätze und Vorträge zur bildenden Kunst*. Cologne: DuMont, 1984.

Burnett, Andrew. "Coin faking in the Renaissance." In *Why Fakes Matter*, ed. Mark Jones. London: British Museum Press, 1992, 15ff.

———. "Renaissance Forgeries of Ancient Coins." In *Fake? The Art of Deception*, ed. Mark Jones. Berkeley: University of California Press, 1990, 136f.

Burton, J. H. *The Life and Correspondence of David Hume*. 2 vols. Edinburgh: N, Tait, 1846, vol. I, 471–80.

Campbell, Marian. "The Anarchist and Forger Louis Marcy." In *Fake? The Art of Deception*, ed. Mark Jones. Berkeley: University of California Press, 1990, 185.

Carey, Frances. "Tom Keating, *A Barn at Shoreham*." In *Fake? The Art of Deception*, ed. Mark Jones. Berkeley: University of California Press, 1990, 240ff.

Carrier, David. "Baudrillard as Philosopher." In *The Aesthete in the City. The Philosophy and Practice of American Abstract Painting in the 1980s*. University Park: Pennsylvania State University Press, 1994.

———. "The Fake Artwork." In *The Aesthete in the City. The Philosophy and Practice of American Abstract Painting in the 1980s*. University Park: Pennsylvania State University Press, 1994.

———. *The Aesthete in the City. The Philosophy and Practice of American Abstract Painting in the 1980s*. University Park: Pennsylvania State University Press, 1994.

Carroll, Noël. "Essence, Expression, and History: Arthur Danto's Philosophy of Art." In *Danto and His Critics*, ed. Mark Rollins. Oxford, UK: Blackwell, 1993, 79ff.

Cellini, Benvenuto. *Memoirs of a Florentine Artist; Written by Himself*, trans. Thomas Roscoe. London: Henry Colburn, 1823.

Chandler, Frank Wadleigh. *The Literature of Roguery*. New York: Burt Franklin, 1907.

Chaucer, Geoffrey. *The Canterbury Tales. The Pardoner's Prologue. The Text of the Canterbury Tales*, ed. John A. Manly and Edith Rickert. Vol. IV. Chicago: University of Chicago Press, 1940.

Clifford, James. *The Predicament of Culture*. Cambridge, MA: Harvard University Press, 1988.

Clunas, Craig. "Connoisseurs and aficionados: the real and the fake in Ming China (1368–1644)." In *Why Fakes Matter*, ed. Mark Jones. London: British Museum Press, 1992, 151ff.

Constable, Giles. "Forged Letters in the Middle Ages." In *Fälschungen im Mittelalter, Part V*. Hannover: Hahn, 1988, 9–36.

———. "Forgery and Plagiarism in the Middle Age." *Archiv für Diplomatik, Schriftgeschichte, Siegel- und Wappenkunde* 29 (1983).

Copier, Créer. *De Turner à Picasso: 300 oeuvres inspirées par les maîtres du Louvre.* Paris: Réunion des Musées Nationaux, 1993.

"Copies, répliques, faux." *Revue de l'art* 21 (1973).

Corino, Karl, ed. *Gefälscht! Betrug In Literatur, Kunst, Musik, Wissenschaft und Politik.* Nördlingen: Greno, 1988.

Creighton, Wilbur F[oster]. *The Parthenon in Nashville: From a Personal Viewpoint.* Rev. Ed. Nashville: N.p., 1991.

Csehi, Zoltán. *Albrecht Dürer és a szerzöi jog* ("Albrecht Dürer and the Copyright"). Unpublished dissertation. Budapest, 1992.

Dali, Salvador. *Le Mythe Tragique de l'Angelus de Millet.* Paris: Société Nouvelle des Éditions Jean-Jacques Pauvert, 1978.

Danto, Arthur C. "The Art World Revisited: Comedies of Similarity." In *Beyond the Brillo Box.* New York: Farrar, Strauss, Giroux, 1992, 33ff.

———. *The Transfiguration of the Commonplace.* Cambridge, MA: Harvard University Press, 1981.

———. "Appreciation and Interpretation." In *The Philosophical Disenfranchisement of Art.* New York: Columbia University Press, 1986.

———. "Art Works and Real Things." *Theoria* 39 (1973).

———. "Responses and Replies." In *Danto and his Critics,* ed. Marc Rollins. Oxford, UK: Blackwell, 1993, 193ff.

———. "The Artworld" (1964). In *Art and its Significance. An Anthology of Aesthetic Theory,* ed. Stephen David Ross. Albany: State University of New York Press, 1994, 470ff.

———. *Beyond the Brillo Box: The Visual Arts In Post-Historical Perspective.* New York: Farrar, Strauss, Giroux, 1992.

———. *The Philosophical Disenfranchisement of Art.* New York: Columbia University Press, 1986.

Dickie, George. *Art and Aesthetics: An Institutional Analysis.* Ithaca, NY: Cornell University Press, 1974.

Dilly, Heinrich. *Kunstgeschichte als Institution.* Frankfurt: Suhrkamp, 1979.

Döhmer, Klaus. "Zur Soziologie der Kunstfälschung." *Zeitschrift für Ästhetik und allgemeine Kunstwissenschaft* 23/1 (1978).

Drateln, Doris von. "Der Dialog mit dem Gleichen." *Kunstforum* 111 (January/February 1991).

Dutton, Denis, ed. *The Forger's Art. Forgery and the Philosophy of Art.* Berkeley: University of California Press, 1983.

Eco, Umberto. *I limiti dell' interpretatione.* Milano: Bompiani, 1990.

Einem, Herbert von. "Einleitung." In Anton Raphael Mengs, *Briefe an Raimondo Ghelli und Anton Marcon,* ed. H. von Einem. Göttingen: Vandenhoeck & Ruprecht, 1973.

[Elam, Caroline]. "The Rembrandt Retrial." Editorial. *Burlington Magazine* 84, no. 1070 (May 1992).

Esterházy, Péter. *Bevezetés a szépirodalomba* ("An Introduction to Literature"). Budapest: Magvetö, 1986.

Fakes and Forgeries. Catalog. Minneapolis Institute of Arts, 1973.

Falke, Otto von. "Die Marcy Fälschungen." *Belvedere* I (1922).

Fälschung und Forschung. Ausstellung. Museum Folkwang Essen, Oktober 1976–Januar 1977, Skulpturengalerie Staatliche Museen Preußischer Kulturbesitz Berlin, Januar–März 1977.

Fälschungen im Mittelalter: internat. Kongreß d. Monumenta Germaniae Historica, Munich, 16–19 September 1986. Part I: *Kongreßdaten und Festvorträge; Literatur und Fälschung*; Part II: *Gefälschte Rechtstexte; Der bestrafte Fälscher*; Parts III–IV: *Diplomatische Fälschungen*; Part V: *Fingierte Briefe; Frömmigkeit und Fälschung; Realienfälschungen*. Hannover: Hahn, 1988. (Part VI, *Register*, 1990.)

Farrer, J. A. *Literarische Fälschungen*. Leipzig: Theod. Thomas, 1907.

Felix, Zdenek, ed. *Das Jahrhundert des Multiple. Von Duchamp bis Gegenwart*. Ausstellung, Deichtorhallen Hamburg, 2 September bis 30 Oktober, 1994. Hamburg: Oktagon, 1994.

Fodor, Jerry A. "*Déjà vu* All Over Again: How Danto's Aesthetics Recapitulates the Philosophy of Mind." In *Danto and his Critics*, ed. Marc Rollins Oxford, UK: Blackwell, 1993.

Follett, Ken. *The Modigliani Scandal*. New York: Penguin, 1985 [1976].

Foucart, Jacques. "Rubens: copies, répliques, pastiches." In "Copies, répliques, faux." *Revue de l'art* 21 (1973): 48ff.

Foucault, Michel. "Ceci n'est pas une pipe." *Fata morgana*. Montpellier, 1973.

———. *L'ordre du discours*. Paris: Gallimard, 1971.

Freedberg, S[idney] J[oseph]. *Andrea del Sarto*. Cambridge, MA: Belknap/Harvard University Press, 1963.

Friedlaender, Ludwig. *Sittengeschichte Roms*, ed. Georg Wissowa [1919]. Stuttgart: Parkland, Ungekürzte Textausgabe, n.d.

Friedländer, Max J. "Die Madonna mit der Wickenblüte." *Zeitschrift für bildende Kunst* 45 (1909).

Fuhrmann, Horst. "Die Fälschungen im Mittelalter. Überlegungen zum mittelalterlichen Wahrheitsbegriff." *Historische Zeitschrift* 197 (1963).

———. "Von der Wahrheit der Fälscher." In *Fälschungen im Mittelalter*, Part l. Hannover: Hahn, 1988, 83–98.

———. *Einfluß und Verbreitung der pseudoisidorischen Fälschungen, I–III*. Stuttgart: Anton Hiersemann, 1972ff.

Furtwaengler, Adolf. *Neuere Fälschungen von Antiken*. Berlin: Giesecke & Devrient, 1899.

Fügedi, Erik. "Ein berufsmäßiger Fälscher: Der Fall Johann von Madácsháza, 1391." In *Fälschungen im Mittelalter*, Part IV. *Diplomatische Fälschungen (II)*. Hannover: Hahn, 1988, 639–51.

Gablik, Suzi. *Magritte*. Greenwich, CT: New York Graphic Society, 1970.

Gadamer, Hans-Georg. "Die Universalität des hermeneutischen Problems." In *Kleine Schriften I. Philosophie, Hermeneutik*. Tübingen: J.C.B. Mohr, 1976.

———. *Wahrheit und Methode*. Tübingen: J.C.B. Mohr (Paul Siebeck), 1975.

Gash, John. "Rembrandt or Not?" *Art in America* (January 1993).

Gaskill, Howard. "Hölderlin und Ossian." *Hölderlin-Jahrbuch* (1990–1991).

Genette, Gérard. *Palimpsestes. La littérature au second degré*. Paris: Seuil, 1982.

Gergely, Mariann, Péter György, and Gábor Pataki. "Megjegyzések Kassák Lajos korai müveinek sorsához" ("Notes on the Fate of Lajos Kassák's Early Works"). In *Kassák: A Magyar Nemzeti Múzeum és a Petöfi Irodalmi Múzeum emlékkiállítása* ("Kassák: A Memorial Exhibition Organized Jointly by the Hungarian National Museum and the Petöfi Literary Museum"). Catalog. Budapest: N.p., n.d. [1987].

Gerle, János, Attila Kovács, and Imre Makovecz. *A századforduló magyar épí-tészete* ("Hungarian Architecture at the Turn of the Century"). Budapest: Szépirodalmi–Bonex, 1990.

Glück, Gustav. "Fälschungen auf Dürers Namen aus der Sammlung Erzherzog Leopold Wilhelms." *Jahrbuch der kunsthistorischen Sammlungen des aller-höchsten Kaiserhauses* 28 (1909–1910).

———. "Original und Kopie. Ein Gespräch." In *Festschrift für Julius Schlosser zum 60. Geburtstag*, ed. Arpad Weixelgärtner and Leo Planiscig. Zurich: Amalther, 1927, 224ff.

Goethe & Schiller. Briefwechsel zwischen ~ und ~ In den Jahren 1794 bis 1805. Stuttgart: Union Deutsche Verlaggesellschaft, n.d.

Goethe, Johann Wolfgang. "Italienische Reise," part I. In *Goethes sämtliche Werke.* Jubiläums-Ausgabe. 26. Bd. Stuttgart: Cotta, n.d. [1882ff.].

Gombrich, Ernst Hans. "Style." In *International Encyclopedia of the Social Sciences*, ed. David L. Sills. London: Macmillan, 1968.

———. *Aby Warburg—An Intellectual Biography.* London: Warburg Institute, 1970.

———. *Art and Illusion.* Princeton, NJ: Princeton University Press, 1962.

———. "The Renaissance Conception of Artistic Progress and Its Consequen-ces." In *Norm and Form. Studies in the Art of the Renaissance.* London: Phai-don, 1971.

Goodman, Nelson. "A Note on Copies." *Journal of Aesthetics and Art Criticism* 44, no. 3 (1986).

———. "On Being In Style." In *Of Mind and Other Matters.* Cambridge, MA: Harvard University Press, 1984.

———. "The Status of Style." *Critical Inquiry* 1, no. 4 (1975).

———. *Languages of Art—An Approach to a Theory of Symbols.* Indianapolis: Bobbs-Merrill, 1968.

Grafton, Anthony. *Forgers and Critics. Creativity and Duplicity in Western Scholarship.* Princeton, NJ: Princeton University Press, 1990.

Grasskamp, Walter. *Die unästhetische Demokratie. Kunst in der Marktgesell-schaft.* Munich: Beck, 1992.

György, Péter. *Müvészet és média találkozása a boncasztalon* ("The Encounter of Art and Media on the Dissection Table"). Budapest: Kulturtrade, 1995.

Hartmann, Alfred Georg. *Das Künstlerwäldchen. Maler-, Bildhauer- und Archi-tekten-Anekdoten.* Berlin: Bruno Cassirer, 1917.

Haftmann, Werner. *Das italienische Säulenmonument.* Leipzig: N.p., 1939.

Haskell, Francis. "A Martyr of Attributionism. Morris Moore and the Louvre *Apollo and Marsyas.*" In *Past and Present in Art and Taste.* New Haven, CT: Yale University Press, 1987.

———. *The Painful Birth of the Art Book.* New York: Thames & Hudson, 1988.

Haskell, Francis, and Nicholas Penny. *Taste and the Antique. The Lure of Classical Sculpture 1500–1900*. New Haven, CT: Yale University Press, 1981.

Hathaway, Ronald F. *Hierarchy and the Definition of Order in the Letters of Pseudo-Donysius*. The Hague: Martinus Nijhoff, 1969.

Haverkamp-Begemann, Egbert, with Carolyn Logan. *Creative Copies: Interpretative Drawings from Michelangelo to Picasso*. New York: The Drawing Center, 9 April–23 July 1988.

Haworth-Booth, Mark. "Howard Grey and Graham Ovenden's Fake 'Victorian' Photos." In *Fake? The Art of Deception*, ed. Mark Jones. Berkeley: University of California Press, 1990, 244f.

Haywood, Ian. *Faking It: Art and the Politics of Forgery*. New York: St. Martin's Press, 1987.

Hebbel, Friedrich. "Michel Angelo." In *Werke*, Vol. III. Berlin: Weichert, n.d.

———. "Tagebücher Vol. III." *Sämtliche Werke* 2. Abt. Historisch-kritische Ausgabe. Berlin: Behr, 1905.

Hebborn, Eric. *Drawn to Trouble: The Forging of an Artist. An Autobiography*. Edinburgh: Mainstream Publishing Projects, 1991.

Hegel, Georg Wilhelm Friedrich. *Vorlesungen über Aesthetik I*, ed. H. G. Hotho. Berlin: Duncker und Humblot, 1835.

Heidegger, Martin "Parmenides." In *Gesamtausgabe*, Bd. 54. Frankfurt: Klostermann, 1982.

Heidenreich, Helmut, ed. *Pikarische Welt. Schriften zum europäischen Schelmenroman*. Darmstadt: Wissenschaftliche Buchgesellschaft, Wege der Forschung, CLXIII, 1969.

Heller, Ágnes, and Ferenc Fehér. *A modernitás ingája* ("The Pendulum of Modernity"). Budapest: T-Twins, 1993.

Henn, Ulrike. "Im Gefängnis bewies Lara sein Fälscher-Genie." *Art* (1987–1988).

Highsmith, Patricia. *Ripley Under Ground*. New York: Vintage Crime/Black Lizard, 1992 [1970].

Hildesheimer, Wolfgang. "Arbeitsprotokolle des Verfahrens 'Marbot.'" In *Das Ende der Fiktionen. Reden aus fünfundzwanzig Jahren*. Frankfurt: Suhrkamp, 1984.

———. *Marbot. Eine Biographie*. Frankfurt: Suhrkamp, 1981.

———. *Paradies der falschen Vögel*. Frankfurt: Suhrkamp, 1975.

Hirsch, E. D., Jr. *Validity in Interpretation*. New Haven, CT: Yale University Press, 1967.

Hitchens, Christopher. *The Elgin Marbles*. London: Chatto & Windus, 1987.

Hoaglund, John. "Originality and Aesthetic Value." *British Journal of Aesthetics* 16, no. 1 (1976).

Hofmann, Werner. *Grundlagen der modernen Kunst. Eine Einführung in ihre symbolischen Formen*. Stuttgart: Alfred Kröner, 1978.

Honan, William H. "Diary Excerpts Said to Be Mussolini." *New York Times*, June 27 1994, 6(A).

Howard, Seymour. "Fakes, Intention, Proofs and Impulsion to Know: The Case for Cavaceppi and Clones." In *Why Fakes Matter*, ed. Mark Jones. London: British Museum Press, 1992.

Huber, Jörg. "Imitative Strategien in der bildenden Kunst." In *Imitationen— Nachahmung und Modell. Von der Lust am Falschen,* ed. Jörg Huber, Martin Heller, and Hans Ulrich Reck. Basel: Stroemfeld/Roter Stern, 1989. Museum für Gestaltung, Zürich. Ausstellungskatalog.

Hume, David. "Of the Standard of Taste." In *Essays.* Oxford, UK: Oxford University Press, 1963.

———. *Letters I–II,* ed. J. Y. T. Greig. Oxford, UK: Clarendon Press, 1969 [1932].

Hutter, Heribert. *Original–Kopie–Replik–Paraphrase.* Ausstellung 8.9.–5.10. 1980. Bildhefte der Akademie der bildenden Künste in Wien. Doppelheft 12/13.

Imdahl, Max. "Überlegungen zur Identität des Bildes." In *Identität (Poetik und Hermeneutik, VIII).* Munich: Fink, 1979.

Ireland, W. H. Vortigern, an Historical Tragedy in Five Acts *Represented at the Theatre Royal, Drury Lane and* Henry the Second, an Historical Drama *Supposed to be Written by the Author of* Vortigern *together with an Authentic Account of the Shaksperian Manuscripst, &c.* New York: Kelley Publishers, 1971 [1799, 1796].

Irving, Clifford. *Fake! The Story of Elmyr de Hory, the Greatest Forger of Our Time.* New York: McGraw-Hill, 1969.

Iser, Wolfgang. "Akte des Fingierens oder Was ist das Fiktive im fiktionalen Text?" In *Funktionen des Fiktiven. Poetik und Hermeneutik X,* ed. Dieter Henrich and Wolfgang Iser. Munich: Fink, 1983, 121–51.

———. *Das Fiktive und das Imaginäre. Perspektiven literarischer Anthropologie.* Frankfurt: Suhrkamp, 1993.

———. *Der Akt des Lesens. Theorie ästhetischer Wirkung.* Munich: Fink, 1976.

Ivins, William M., Jr. *Prints and Visual Communication.* Cambridge, MA: Harvard University Press, 1953.

Jauß, Hans Robert. "Italo Calvino: 'Wenn ein Reisender in einer Winternacht.' Plädoyer für eine postmoderne Ästhetik." In *Studien zum Epochenwandel der ästhetischen Moderne.* Frankfurt: Suhrkamp, 1989.

———. "Spur und Aura: Bemerkungen zu Walter Benjamins 'Passagen-Werk.'" In *Studien zur Epochenwandel der ästhetischen Moderne.* Frankfurt: Suhrkamp, 1989.

———. *Ästhetische Erfahrung und literarische Hermeneutik.* Frankfurt: Suhrkamp, 1982.

———. *Studien zur Epochenwandel der ästhetischen Moderne.* Frankfurt: Suhrkamp, 1989.

Johnson, Samuel. *A Journey to the Western Islands of Scotland* [1775]. New Haven, CT: Yale University Press, 1971.

Jolles, André. "Die literarische Travestien. Ritter–Hirt–Schelm" [1931]. In *Pikarische Welt,* ed. Helmut Heidenreich. Darmstadt: Wissenschaftliche Buchgesellschaft, 1969.

Jones, Mark, ed. *Fake? The Art of Deception.* Berkeley: University of California Press, 1990.

———, ed. *Why Fakes Matter. Essays on Problems of Authenticity.* London: British Museum Press, 1992.

Jung, Carl Gustav. "Zur Psychologie der Schelmenfigur." In Paul Radin, Karl

Kerényi, and C. G. Jung. *Der göttliche Schelm: Ein indianischer Mythenzyklus.* Zürich: Rhein Verlag, 1954.

Justi, Carl. *Winckelmann und seine Zeitgenossen.* Leipzig: F. C. W. Vogel, 1923.

Kant, Immanuel. *Kritik der Urteilskraft. Werkausgabe* Bd X. Frankfurt: Suhrkamp, 1989.

Karpinski, Caroline. "The Print in Thrall to Its Original: A Historiographic Perspective." In *Retaining the Original.* Washington, DC: National Gallery of Art, 1989, 101ff.

Kennick, William. "Art and Inauthenticity." *Journal of Aesthetics and Art Criticism* 44 (1985).

Kerner, Max. "Die Institutio Traiani—spätantike Lehrschrift oder hochmittel alterliche Fiktion?" In *Fälschungen im Mittelalter,* Part 1. Hannover: Hahn, 1988, 715–38.

Kilbracken, Lord [John Raymond] [John Godley]. *Van Meegeren (A Case History).* London: Thomas Nelson & Sons, 1967.

Kocziszky, Éva. "A görögség ideálja a XVIII–XIX. század fordulóján" ("The Ideal of the Greek World at the Turn of the Nineteenth Century"). *Holmi, Budapest* 3 (1994).

Koestler, Arthur. "The Anatomy of Snobbery." *Anchor Review* 1 (1955).

Krauss, Rosalind E. "The Originality of the Avant-Garde." In *The Originality of Avant-Garde and Other Modernist Myths.* Cambridge, MA: MIT Press, 1993 [1985].

Kris, Ernst. *Meister und Meisterwerke der Steinschneidekunst in der italienischen Renaissance.* Vienna: Schroll, 1929.

Kris, Ernst, and Otto Kurz. *Die Legende vom Künstler.* Vienna: Kristall, 1935.

Kristeller, Paul O. "The Modern System of the Arts: A Study in the History of Aesthetics." *Journal of the History of Ideas* XII (1951): 496–527; XIII (1952): 17–47.

Kubler, George. "Towards a Reductive Theory of Visual Style." In *The Concept of Style,* ed. Berel Lang. Philadelphia: University of Pennsylvania Press, 1979.

———. *The Shape of Time: Remarks on the History of Things.* New Haven, CT: Yale University Press, 1962.

Kundera, Milan. *Immortality,* trans. Peter Kussi. New York: HarperPerennial, 1992.

———. *The Art of the Novel.* New York: Grove Press, 1986.

Kunisch, Norbert. "Antikenfälschungen." In *Fälschung und Forschung.* Ausstellung. Museum Folkwang Essen, Oktober 1976–Januar 1977, Skulpturengalerie Staatliche Museen Preußischer Kulturbesitz Berlin, Januar–März 1977.

Kurz, Otto. *Fakes: A Handbook for Collectors and Students.* New York: Dover, 1967.

Ladendorf, Heinz. *Antikenstudium und Antikenkopie. Vorarbeiten zu einer Darstellung ihrer Bedeutung in der mittelalterlichen und neueren Zeit.* Berlin: Akademie, 1953.

Lee, Rensselaer W. *"Ut pictura poesis:* The Humanistic Theory of Painting." *Art Bulletin* 22 (1940): 197–269.

Lehmann, Paul. *Pseudo-antike Literatur des Mittelalters.* Darmstadt: Wissenschaftliche Buchgesellschaft, 1964 [1927].

Leonardo da Vinci. *Treatise on Painting*, trans. A. P. McMahon. Princeton, NJ: Princeton University Press, 1956.

Lessing, Alfred. "What is Wrong with a Forgery?" In *The Forgers Art*, ed. Denis Dutton Berkeley: University of California Press, 1983.

Lewis, Gwyneth. *Eighteenth-Century Literary Forgeries with Special Reference to the Work of Iolo Morganwg*. Unpublished Ph.D. dissertation. Oxford, 1991.

Ligota, C. R. "'This Story is Not True.' Fact and Fiction in Antiquity." *Journal of the Warburg and Courtauld Institutes* 45 (1982): 1–13.

Lippold, Georg. *Kopien und Umbildungen griechischer Statuen*. Munich: Beck, 1923.

Lowenthal, Leo. "The Debate Over Art and Popular Culture: English Eighteenth Century as a Case Study." In *Literature, Popular Culture and Society*. Palo Alto, CA: Pacific Books, 1961.

Luscombe, David. "Denis the Pseudo-Areopagite in the Middle Ages." In *Fälschungen im Mittelalter*, Part 1. Hannover: Hahn, 1988, 133–52.

Mackenzie, Ian. "Gadamer's Hermeneutics and the Uses of Forgery." *Journal of Aesthetics and Art Criticism* 45 (1986).

Maison, K. E. *Themes and Variations*. London: Thames & Hudson, 1960.

Maller, Sándor. *Ossian Magyarországon 1788–1849* ("Ossian in Hungary"). Debrecen: N.p., 1940.

Malraux, André. *The Voices of Silence*. Princeton, NJ: Princeton University Press, 1978.

Mancinelli, Fabrizio. "The Problem of Michelangelo's Assistants." In Michael Hirst [et al.], *The Sistine Chapel: A Glorious Restoration*. New York: Abrams, 1994.

Márkus, György. "Diogenes Laertios *contra* Gadamer: Universal or Historical Hermeneutics?" In *Life After Postmodernism*, ed. John Fekete. New York: St. Martin's Press, 1987.

———. *Walter Benjamin and the Commodity as Phantasmagoria*. Unpublished manuscript.

Marquard, Odo. "Kunst als Antifiktion. Versuch über den Weg der Wirklichkeit in Fiktive." In *Aesthetica und Anaesthetica—Philosophische Überlegungen*. Paderborn: Schöningh, 1989, 82–100.

———. "Kunst als Kompensation ihres Endes." In *Aesthetica und Anaesthetica—Philosophische Überlegungen*. Paderborn: Schöningh, 1989, 121.

———. *Aesthetica und Anaesthetica—Philosophische Überlegungen*. Paderborn: Schöningh, 1989.

Marvin, Miranda. "Copying in Roman Sculpture: The Replica Series." In *Retaining the Original*. Washington, DC: National Gallery of Art, 1989, 29ff.

Meier-Graefe, Julius. "Der Kenner." In *Kunst-Schreiberei*. Leipzig: Gustav Kiepenhauer, 1987.

Meiss, Millard. *The Limbourgs and Their Contemporaries*. New York: Braziller/Pierpont Morgan Library, 1974.

Metz, Peter. "Echt oder falsch? Eine Studie über Grundsätzliches." In *Festschrift Karl Oettinger*, ed. Hans Sedlmayr and Wilhelm Messerer. Erlangen: N.p., 1967.

———. *Bildwerke der christlichen Epochen von der Spätantike bis zum Klassizismus*. Munich: Prestel, 1966.

Mitchell, Charles. "Archaeology and Romance in Renaissance Italy." In *Italian Renaissance Studies. A Tribute to the Late Cecilia M. Ady*, ed. E. F. Jacob. London: Faber & Faber, 1960.

Moos, Peter von. *Mittelalterforschung und Ideologiekritik. Der Gelehrtenstreit um Héloise*. Munich: Fink, 1974.

———. "*Fictio auctoris*. Eine theoriegeschichtliche Miniatur am Rande der Institutio Traiani." In *Fälschungen im Mittelalter*, Part 1. Hannover: Hahn, 1988, 739–80.

———. "Heloise und Abaelard." In *Gefälscht!*, ed. Carl Corino. Nördlingen: Greno, 1988, 150–61.

Moser, Ulli. "Originalitätsdokumente. Die Künstlerin Elaine Sturtevant malt Kopien grossen Zeitgenossen." In "Original Kopie," *Parnass*. Sonderheft 7.

Mossner, Ernest Campbell. *The Life of David Hume*. Oxford, UK: Clarendon Press, 1980.

Mravik, László. "Pulszky Károly müve" ("The Work of Károly Pulszky"). In *Pulszky Károly emlékének* ("In Memory of Károly Pulszky"), ed. László Mravik. Budapest: Szépmüvészeti Múzeum, 1988.

Muller, Jeffrey M. "Measures of Authenticitiy: The Detection of Copies in the Early Literature on Connoisseurship." In *Retaining the Original*. Washington, DC: National Gallery of Art, 1989, 141ff.

Mulot, Sibylle. "Die Fälschung der Fälschung. Wilhelm Hauffs 'Mann im Mond.'" In *Gefälscht!*, ed. Carl Corino. Nördlingen: Greno, 1988, 251–62.

Muschg, Walter. *Tragische Literaturgeschichte*. Bern: Francke Verlag, 1957.

Müller, Carl Werner. "Die neuplatonische Aristoteleskommentatoren über die Ursache der Pseudepigraphie." In *Pseudepigraphie in der heidnischen und jüdisch–christlichen Antike*, ed. Norbert Brox. Darmstadt: Wissenschaftliche Buchgesellschaft, 1977, 264–71.

Neusser, Maria. "Die Ergänzung der Venus von Arles. Ein Beitrag zur Geschichte der nationalen Klassizismus In Frankreich." *Belvedere* 13 (September 1928).

Norton, Paul F. "The Lost *Sleeping Cupid* of Michelangelo." *Art Bulletin* 39, no. 1 (1957).

Ortega y Gasset, José. "Die originelle Schelmerei des Schelmenromans" [1910]. In *Pikarische Welt*, ed. Helmut Heidenreich. Darmstadt: Wissenschaftliche Buchgesellschaft, 1969.

Osterwold, Tillmann. "Die trivialisierte *Mona Lisa*." In *Mona Lisa im XX. Jahrhundert*. Wilhelm Lehmbruck-Museum der Stadt Duisburg, 24. 9.–3. 12. 1978, 119ff.

Pannenberg, Wolfhart. "Das Irreale des Glaubens." In *Funktionen des Fiktiven. Poetik und Hermeneutik X*, ed. Dieter Henrich and Wolfgang Iser. Munich: Fink, 1983, 17–34.

Panofsky, Erwin. "Introductory (Iconography and Iconology: An Introduction to the Study of Renaissance Art)." In *Studies in Iconology*. New York: Icon/Harper & Row, 1974 (1939).

———. "Kopie oder Fälschung. Ein Beitrag zur Kritik einiger Zeichnungen aus der Werkstatt Michelangelos." *Zeitschrift für bildende Kunst* 61 (1927).

————. *Renaissance and Renascences in Western Art.* New York: Icon/Harper & Row, 1975.

Paul, Eberhard. *Gefälschte Antike.* Leipzig: Koehler & Amelang, 1981.

Paz, Octavio. "Apariencia desnuda. La obra de Marcel Duchamp." In *Obras completas VI.* Barcelona: Circuló de Lectores, 1992.

Pelzel, Thomas. "Winckelmann, Mengs and Casanova. A Reappraisal of Famous Eigtheenth-Century Forgery." *Art Bulletin* 54, no. 3 (1972).

Pesty, Frigyes. "Az iteböi prépostság" ("The Provostship of Itebö"). *Századok,* Budapest 1875.

Petersen, Harold L. *How to Tell if It's Fake: Trade Secrets Revealed for Antique Collectors and Dealers.* New York: Scribner's, 1975.

Petsch, Joachim. *Eigeinheim und gute Stube. Zur Geschichte des bürgerlichen Wohnens–Städtebau–Architektur–Einrichtungsstile.* Cologne: DuMont, 1989.

Pias, Claus. "Abschied vom Original? Original, Multiple und kompatible Produktion." In *Das Jahrhundert des Multiple. Von Duchamp bis Gegenwart,* ed. Zdenek Felix. Hamburg: Oktagon, 1994, 74ff.

Pinchbeck, Daniel. "The Second Renaissance." *Wired* (December 1994).

"Plagiarism—A Symposium." *Times Literary Supplement* (9 April 1982).

Pope-Hennessy, John. "Michelangelo's *Cupid*: The End of a Chapter." In *Essays on Italian Sculpture.* London: Phaidon, 1968.

————. *The Study and Criticism of Italian Sculpture.* New York: Metropolitan Museum of Art/Princeton, NJ: Princeton University Press, 1980.

Potts, A[lex] D. "Greek Sculpture and Roman Copies I: Anton Raphael Mengs and the Eighteenth Century." *Journal of the Warburg and Courtauld Institutes* 43 (1980).

Proust, Marcel. *La prisonnière. A la recherche du temps perdu,* V. Paris: Gallimard, 1954.

Radnóti, Sándor. "Mass Culture." In *Reconstructing Aesthetics,* ed. Agnes Heller and Ferenc Fehér. Oxford, UK: Basil Blackwell, 1986, 77–103.

————. "Tisztelt közönség, kulcsot te találj. . ." ("Honored Public, Go On, Find Your Own Ending. . ." [Brecht]). Budapest: Gondolat, 1990.

————. "Vis a tergo. George Kublers Buch 'Die Form der Zeit'—dreißig Jahre später." *Zetischrift für Ästhetik und allgemeine Kunstwissenschaft* 39, no. 2 (1994).

Ralls, Anthony. "The Uniqueness and Reproducibility of a Work of Art: A Critique of Goodman's Theory." *Philosophical Quarterly* 22 (1972).

Retaining the Original. Multiple Originals, Copies and Reproductions. Studies in the History of Art, Vol. 20. Washington, DC: National Gallery of Art, 1989.

Ridgway, Brunilde Sismondo. *Roman Copies of Greek Sculpture: The Problem of the Originals.* Ann Arbor: University of Michigan Press, 1984.

Rollins, Mark, ed. *Danto and His Critics.* Oxford, UK: Blackwell, 1993.

Ronzoni, Luigi A. "Kopien antiken Originale im Wandel der Zeit." In "Original = Kopie." *Parnass* Sonderheft 7.

Rorty, Richard. "Heidegger, Kundera, and Dickens." In *Essays on Heidegger and Others.* Cambridge, UK: Cambridge University Press, 1991.

Röttgen, Steffi. "Storia di un falso: il Ganimede di Mengs." *Arte Illustrata* 54 (1973): 256–70.

Rugási, Gyula. "Az areopagoszi beszéd" ("The Areopagitic Sermon"). In *Majdnem nem lehet másként. Vajda Mihály 60. születésnapjára*, ed. Ferenc Fehér, András Kardos, and Sándor Radnóti. Budapest: Cserépfalvi, 1995.

Sagoff, Mark. "Historical Authenticity." *Erkenntnis. An International Journal of Analitical Philosophy* 12, no. 1 (1978).

———. "On Restoring and Reproducing Art." *Journal of Philosophy* 75 (1978).

———. "The Aesthetic Status of Forgeries." In *The Forgers Art*, ed. Denis Dutton. Berkeley: University of California Press, 1983, 131ff.

Schaller, Hans Martin. "Scherz und Ernst In erfundenen Briefen des Mittelalters." In *Fälschungen im Mittelalter*, Part V. Hannover: Hahn, 1988, 79–94.

Schelling, Friedrich Wilhelm Joseph von. "System des transzendentalen Idealismus." In *Ausgewählte Schriften*, Vol. I (1794–1800). Frankfurt: Suhrkamp, 1985.

Schlegel, Friedrich. "Über das Studium der griechischen Poesie." In *Kritische Schriften und Fragmente (1794–1797)*, Vol. l, ed. Ernst Behler and Hans Eichner. Paderborn: Ferdinand Schöningh, 1988, 62–137.

Schlosser, Julius von. *Die Kunst- und Wunderkammern der Spätrenaissance. Ein Beitrag zur Geschichte des Sammelwesens*. Braunschweig: Klinkhardt & Biermann, 1978.

———. *Die Kunstliteratur*. Vienna: Schroll, 1924.

Schmidt, Jochen. *Die Geschichte des Genie-Gedankens in der deutschen Literatur, Philosophie und Politik 1750–1945*. Darmstadt: Wissenschaftliche Buchgesellschaft, 1988.

Schmidt, Paul Gerhard. "Kritische Philologie und pseudoantike Literatur." In *Die Antike-Rezeption in den Wissenschaften während der Renaissance*, ed. August Buck and Klaus Heitmann. Weinheim: Acta Humaniora, 1983.

Schmitt, Hans-Jürgen. "Der Fall Georg Forestier." In *Gefälscht!*, ed. Carl Corino. Nördlingen: Greno, 1988, 317–29.

Schreiner, Klaus. "'Discrimini veri ac falsi.' Ansätze und Formen der Kritik in der Heiligen- und Reliquienverehrung des Mittelalters." *Archiv für Kulturgeschichte* 48 (1966): 1.

Schüller, Sepp. *Fälscher, Händler und Experten*. Munich: Ehrenwirth, 1959.

Shaftesbury, Anthony, Earl of. "An Essay on the Freedom of Wit and Humour." In *Characteristicks of Men, Manners, Opinions, Times*, Vol. 1. Birmingham: John Baskerville, 1773, 145.

Shearman, John. *Andrea del Sarto*. Oxford, UK: Clarendon Press, 1965.

Shiff, Richard. "Phototropism (Figuring the Proper)." In *Retaining the Original*. Washington, DC: National Gallery of Art, 1989, 161ff.

Silvestre, Hubert. "Die Liebesgeschichte zwischen Abaelard und Heloise: der Anteil des Romans." In *Fälschungen im Mittelalter*, Part V. Hannover: Hahn, 1988, 121–65.

Simmel, Georg. "Philosophie der Landschaft" [1913]. In *Das Individuum und die Freiheit*. Berlin: Wagenbach, 1984, 130ff.

Simpson, Colin, *Artful Partners: Bernhard Berenson and Joseph Duween*. New York: Macmillan, 1986.

Somlyó, György. *Picasso*. Budapest: Magyar Helikon, 1981.

Sox, David. *Unmasking the Forger: The Dossena Deception.* New York: Universe, 1987.

Spear, Richard E. "Notes on Renaissance and Baroque Originals and Originality." In *Retaining the Original.* Washington, DC: National Gallery of Art, 1989, 97ff.

Speyer, Wolfgang. "Religiöse Pseudepigraphie und literarische Fälschung." In *Pseudepigraphie in der heidnischen und jüdisch–christlichen Antike,* ed. Norbert Brox. Darmstadt: Wissenschaftliche Buchgesellschaft, 1977, 264–71.

———. *Die literarische Fälschung im heidnischen und christlichen Altertum.* Munich: Beck, 1971.

St. Clair, William. *Lord Elgin and the Marbles.* Oxford, UK: Oxford University Press, 1983.

Stafford, Fiona J. *The Sublime Savage: A Study of James Macpherson and the Poems of Ossian.* Edinburgh: Edinburgh University Press, 1988.

Steele, Hunter. "Fakes and Forgeries." *British Journal of Aesthetics* 17 (1977).

Stichting Foundation Rembrandt Research Project. *A Corpus of Rembrandt Painting,* Vol. I. The Hague: Martinus Nijhoff, 1982; Vols. II–III. Dordrecht: Martinus Nijhoff, 1986, 1989.

Stratford, Neil. "Gothic Ivory Fakes." In *Fake? The Art of Deception,* ed. Mark Jones. Berkeley: University of California Press, 1990, 180.

Sylvester, David. *Magritte.* London: Thames & Hudson, 1992.

———. *The Brutality of Fact: Interviews with Francis Bacon.* London: Thames & Hudson, 1987.

Syme, Ronald. *Emperors and Biography: Studies in the* Historia Augusta. Oxford, UK: Clarendon Press, 1971.

Szilágyi, János György. "Plautus." In *Paradigmák.* Budapest: Magvetö, 1982.

———. *Legbölcsebb az Idö. Antik vázák hamisítványai* ("Time: The Wisest of Them All. The Forgeries of Antique Vases"). Budapest: Corvina, 1987.

———. "Antikenfälschung und Antikenrezeption." *Acta Antiqua Akademiae Scientiarum Hungaricae* T. XXX, fasc. 1–4 (1988).

Tait, Hugh. "Reinhold Vasters: Goldsmith, Restorer and Prolific Faker." In *Why Fakes Matter,* ed. Mark Jones. London: British Museum Press, 1992, 116ff.

Tatarkiewicz, Wladislaw. *History of Aesthetics I. Ancient Aesthetics.* The Hague: PWN-Polish Scientific Publishers, 1970.

Taylor, Donald S., ed. *The Complete Works of Thomas Chatterton I–II.* Oxford, UK: Clarendon Press, 1971.

———. *Thomas Chatterton's Art: Experiments in Imagined History.* Princeton, NJ: Princeton University Press, 1978.

Tietze, Hans. "Zur Psychologie und Ästhetik der Kunstfälschung." *Zeitschrift für Ästhetik und allgemeine Kunstwissenschaft* 27 (1933).

———. *Genuine and False: Copies, Imitatons, Forgeries.* London: Max Parrish, n.d. [1948].

Tolnay, Charles de. *The Youth of Michelangelo.* Princeton, NJ: Princeton University Press, 1947.

Türr, Karina. *Fälschungen antiker Plastik seit 1800.* Berlin: Mann, 1984.

Tynyanov, Yuriy Nikolaevich. "Literaturniy Fakt" ("The Literary Fact"). In *Poetika.* Moscow: Nauka, 1977.

Varnedoe, Kirk. *A Fine Disregard—What Makes Modern Art Modern.* New York: Abrams, 1990.

Vasari, Giorgio. *The Lives of the Artists.* Oxford, UK: Oxford University Press, 1991.

Vaughan, Gerard. "The Restoration of Classical Sculpture in the Eighteenth Century and the Problem of Authenticity." In *Why Fakes Matter,* ed. Mark Jones. London: British Museum Press, 1992.

Voelkle, William. *The Spanish Forger.* New York: Pierpont Morgan Library, 1978.

Walzel, Oskar. *Friedrich Hebbel und seine Dramen.* Leipzig: Teubner, 1913.

———. *Wechselseitige Erhellung der Künste. Ein Beitrag zur Würdigung kunstgeschichtlicher Begriffe.* Berlin: Kant-Gesellschaft, 1917.

Warburton, Nigel. *Philosophy: The Basics.* London: Routledge, 1992.

Waser, Georges. "Die Angst von dem jungfräulichen Blatt. Ein Besuch beim Kunstfälscher Eric Hebborn." *NZZ Folio. Die Zeitschrift der Neuen Zürcher Zeitung. Fälschungen* (October 1993).

Wellek, René, and Austin Warren. *Theory of Literature.* London: Penguin, 1963.

Weöres, Sándor. *Psyché. Egy hajdani költönö írásai* ("The Writings of a Poetess of Yore"). Budapest: Magvetö, 1972.

Werness, Hope B. "Han van Meegeren fecit." In *The Forgers Art,* ed. Denis Dutton. Berkeley: University of California Press, 1983.

Wethey, Harold E. *The Paintings of Titian,* Vol. II. London: Phaidon, 1971.

Wielands, C. M. *Sämmtliche Werke,* Vol. 33. Leipzig: G. J. Göschen'sche Verlagshandlung, 1857.

Wilde, Johannes. "Eine Studie Michelangelos nach der Antike." *Mitteilungen des kunsthistorischen Institutes in Florenz,* IV, no. 1 (July 1932).

Wilde, Oscar. "The Portrait of Mr. W. H." In *The Works of Oscar Wilde 1856–1900,* ed. G. F. Maine. London: Collins, 1948.

Wimsatt, William K. Jr., and Monroe Beardsley. "The Intentional Fallacy." *Sewanee Review* 54 (1956).

Winckelmann, Johann Joachim. *Geschichte der Kunst des Altertums.* Vienna: Phaidon, 1934.

Wind, Edgar. *Art and Anarchy.* London: Duckworth, 1985.

Winter, Helmut. "Thomas Chatterton—Fälscher oder Originalgenie?" In *Gefälscht!,* ed. Carl Corino. Nördlingen: Greno, 1988, 196–208.

Wittgenstein, Ludwig. *Philosophical Investigations.* Oxford, UK: Blackwell, 1952.

Wittkower, Rudolf, and Margot Wittkower. *Born Under Saturn: The Character and Conduct of Artists. A Documented History from Antiquity to the French Revolution.* New York: Norton, 1969 [1963].

Wollheim, Richard. "Danto's Gallery of Indiscernibles." In *Danto and His Critics,* ed. Marc Rollins. Oxford UK: Blackwell, 1993, 28ff.

———. *Art and Its Objects. With Six Supplementary Essays.* Cambridge, UK: Cambridge University Press/Canto Edition, 1992.

———. *Painting as an Art.* London: Thames & Hudson, 1987.

Wreen, Michael. "Is, Madam? Nay, It Seems!" In *The Forgers Art,* ed. Denis Dutton. Berkeley: University of California Press, 1983.

Wright, Christopher. *The Art of the Forger.* London: Gordon Fraser, 1984.

Würtenberger, Thomas. *Das Kunstfälschertum. Entstehung und Bekämpfung eines Verbrechens vom Anfang des 15. bis zum Ende des 18. Jahrhunderts.* Weimar: Böhlaus Nachf., 1940 (Reprint, Leipzig: Zentralantiquariat der DDR, 1977).

Young, Edward. "Conjectures on Original Composition." In *The Complete Works,* ed. James Nichols. London: William Tegg, 1854 (Reprint, Hildesheim: Georg Olms, 1968), Vol. II.

Xenophon. *Memorabilia,* III. 10.

INDEX

The index doesn't contain the names of editors. For important collections of essays and articles, such as the volumes of Denis Dutton and Mark Jones, see the bibliography.

originality
  autography, of, 38, 51, 117, 118, 148n20, 175
  genius, of, 39, 68, 74, 84, 85, 86, 157
  historicity, as, 4, 5, 38, 41–45, 48, 51, 53, 56, 85, 90, 164
  individuality, as, 4, 5, 6, 37–38, 41, 48–53, 56, 69, 70, 85, 164, 215
  invention, of, 4, 38, 39, 52, 57, 59, 76, 124, 131
  novelty, as, 39, 41, 42, 44, 47, 48, 51, 52, 53, 56, 65, 85
  travesty of, 177
  uniqueness (i.e., material identity), as, 42, 47, 48, 149n27, 215
  uniqueness (i.e., spiritual value), as, 13, 14, 35, 45–46, 65–69, 82, 84–85, 149n27, 150–51n37
  versus beauty, 36–37, 42, 53–56, 62n30
Ortega y Gasset, José, 12, 29n29
Osterwold, Tillmann, 100n51
Ovid (Publius Ovidius Naso), 165

Palmer, Samuel, 23
Pannenberg, Wolfhart, 190, 191, 199n82
Panofsky, Erwin, 4, 15, 27n12, 30n34, 38, 43, 60n10, 61n25, 73, 80, 93, 97n24, 99n39
Paolini, Giulio, 124
Parmeggiani. See Marcy, Louis
Parrhasios, 28n15, 101n58
Pataki, Gábor, 150n30
Pauer, Gyula, 135
Paul, St., Apostle, 168, 195n37, 196n40
Paz, Octavio, 154n86
Pelzel, Thomas, 30n40–41, 30–31n43
Penny, Nicholas, 76, 98n30, 99n36
Percy, Thomas, 196–97n51
Perugino, Pietro (Pietro Vannucci), 50

Pessoa, Fernando António Nogueira de Seabra, 185
Pesty, Frigyes, 192n11
Petersen, Harold L., 61n23
Petöfi, Sándor, 172
Petronius (Gaius Petronius Arbiter), 11, 170
Petsch, Joachim, 101n63
Phaedrus, 101n55
Phidias, 7, 8, 87, 90
Pias, Claus, 148n20
picaresque, 1, 8–33, 44, 53, 128, 177
Picasso, Pablo, 82, 99n45, 128, 129, 130, 131, 140, 141, 142, 145, 151n50, 153n73, 154n86
Piero della Francesca, 59
Pinchbeck, Daniel, 148n20, 215, 216n21
Pindar, 172, 194n32
Pinkerton, John, 180
Piombo, Sebastiano del, 50
Piranesi, Giovanni Battista, 26, 89
Pisano, Nicola and Giovanni, 30n33
Pissarro, Camille, 24
plagiarism, 25, 97n21, 109, 147n8, 181, 182
Platen, August von, Count, 184
Plato, 37, 104, 107, 142, 191, 199n83
Plautus, Titus Maccius 167, 168, 195n39
Pliny the Elder (Gaius Plinius Secundus), 100n55
Plutarch, 155, 165, 194n32
Polónyi, Géza, 50
Pope, Alexander, 68, 104, 182, 194n29
Pope-Hennessy, Sir John, vii, 4, 27n11, 138, 153n79
Porta, Giacomo della, 90
Porta, Tommaso della, 29n24
Potts, Alex D., 31n43, 99n36
Poussin, Nicolas, 81, 82
Praxiteles, 97n20, 101n55
Primaticcio, Francesco, 77, 99n45
Prince, Richard, 124
Proust, Marcel, 151n42